DATE DUE

GAYLORD   PRINTED IN U.S.A.

BLOOM'S

HOW TO WRITE ABOUT

Charles Dickens

AMY S. WATKIN

BLOOM'S
LITERARY CRITICISM
An imprint of Infobase Publishing

Bloom's How to Write about Charles Dickens

Bloom's Literary Criticism
An imprint of Infobase Publishing
132 West 31st Street
New York NY 10001

Library of Congress Cataloging-in-Publication Data
Watkin, Amy S.
   Bloom's how to write about Charles Dickens / Amy S. Watkin; introduction by Harold Bloom.
      p. cm. — (Bloom's how to write about literature)
   Includes bibliographical references and index.
   ISBN 978-0-7910-9850-9 (acid-free paper) 1. Dickens, Charles, 1812–1870—Criticism and interpretation. 2. Criticism—Authorship. 3. Report writing. I. Bloom, Harold. II. Title. III. Title: How to write about Charles Dickens. IV. Title: Charles Dickens. V. Series.
   PR4588.W43 2009
   823'.8—dc22   2008005713

Bloom's Literary Criticism books are available at special discounts when purchased in bulk quantities for businesses, associations, institutions, or sales promotions. Please call our Special Sales Department in New York at (212) 967-8800 or (800) 322-8755.

You can find Bloom's Literary Criticism on the World Wide Web at
http://www.chelseahouse.com

Text design by Annie O'Donnell
Cover design by Ben Peterson

Printed in the United States of America

Bang MSRF 10 9 8 7 6 5 4 3 2 1

This book is printed on acid-free paper.

CONTENTS

Series Introduction   v

Volume Introduction   vii

How to Write a Good Essay   1

How to Write about Charles Dickens   43

   The Pickwick Papers   55

   Oliver Twist   72

   Nicholas Nickleby   92

   A Christmas Carol   110

   David Copperfield   127

   Bleak House   144

   Hard Times   162

   A Tale of Two Cities   186

   Great Expectations   202

   Our Mutual Friend   220

Index   239

SERIES
INTRODUCTION

BLOOM'S How to Write about Literature series is designed to inspire students to write fine essays on great writers and their works. Each volume in the series begins with an introduction by Harold Bloom, meditating on the challenges and rewards of writing about the volume's subject author. The first chapter then provides detailed instructions on how to write a good essay, including how to find a thesis; how to develop an outline; how to write a good introduction, body text, and conclusions; how to cite sources; and more. The second chapter provides a brief overview of the issues involved in writing about the subject author and then a number of suggestions for paper topics, with accompanying strategies for addressing each topic. Succeeding chapters cover the author's major works.

The paper topics suggested within this book are open-ended, and the brief strategies provided are designed to give students a push forward on the writing process rather than a road map to success. The aim of the book is to pose questions, not answer them. Many different kinds of papers could result from each topic. As always, the success of each paper will depend completely on the writer's skill and imagination.

HOW TO WRITE ABOUT CHARLES DICKENS: INTRODUCTION

by Harold Bloom

O NLY SHAKESPEARE surpasses Dickens at peopling an entire world. In regard to the novel, I can think of Balzac as the peer of Dickens. To write about the greatest English novelist at his most vital, you need to explore his gallery of women, men, and children.

As a creator of people, Dickens works more in the mode of Ben Jonson than of Shakespeare, because Dickens mostly portrays grotesques. But they give a new meaning to grotesque: Madame DeFarge, Magwitch, Micawber, Uriah Heep, Gradgrind, Bucket, and the galaxy of so many other exuberant caricatures. Compared to them, Dickens's surrogates Pip and David Copperfield seem to lack color. The greatest of these surrogate protagonists, to me, is Esther Summerson in *Bleak House*.

I suggest, then, that one very fruitful way of writing about Dickens is to contrast his grotesques with his narrators. The autobiographical mode involves Dickens in a kind of self-overhearing that came to him from Shakespeare. Wind your critical path through his narrators and ask yourself what is the effect of their inwardness on your apprehension of the wonderful caricatures that surround them?

My favorite Dickens remains *Pickwick Papers*, where everyone is a loving grotesque. But even there, the narrative voice maintains a framing context of the normative against which the caricatures flare up.

HOW TO WRITE
A GOOD ESSAY

WHILE THERE are many ways to write about literature, most assignments for high school and college English classes call for analytical papers. In these assignments, you are presenting your interpretation of a text to your reader. Your objective is to interpret the text's meaning in order to enhance your reader's understanding and enjoyment of the work. Without exception, strong papers about the meaning of a literary work are built upon a careful, close reading of the text or texts. Careful, analytical reading should always be the first step in your writing process. This volume provides models of such close, analytical reading, and these should help you develop your own skills as a reader and as a writer.

As the examples throughout this book demonstrate, attentive reading entails thinking about and evaluating the formal (textual) aspects of the author's works: theme, character, form, and language. In addition, when writing about a work, many readers choose to move beyond the text itself to consider the work's cultural context. In these instances, writers might explore the historical circumstances of the period in which the work was written. Alternatively, they might examine the philosophies and ideas that a work addresses. Even in cases where writers explore a work's cultural context, though, papers must still address the more formal aspects of the work itself. A good interpretative essay that evaluates Charles Dickens's use of the philosophy of utilitarianism in his novel *Hard Times*, for example, cannot adequately address the author's treatment of the philosophy without firmly grounding this discussion in the book itself. In other words, any analytical paper about a text, even one that seeks to evaluate the work's cultural context, must also have a firm handle on the work's themes, characters, and language. You must look for and evaluate these aspects of a work, then, as you read a text and as you prepare to write about it.

WRITING ABOUT THEMES

Literary themes are more than just topics or subjects treated in a work; they are attitudes or points about these topics that often structure other elements in a work. Writing about theme therefore requires that you not just identify a topic that a literary work addresses but also discuss what that work says about that topic. For example, if you were writing about the culture of the American South in William Faulkner's famous story "A Rose for Emily," you would need to discuss what Faulkner says, argues, or implies about that culture and its passing.

When you prepare to write about thematic concerns in a work of literature, you will probably discover that, as most works of literature do, your text touches upon other themes in addition to its central theme. These secondary themes also provide rich ground for paper topics. A thematic paper on "A Rose for Emily" might consider gender or race in the story. While neither of these could be said to be the central theme of the story, both are clearly related to the passing of the "old South" and could provide plenty of good material for papers.

As you prepare to write about themes in literature, you might find a number of strategies helpful. After you identify a theme or themes in the story, you should begin by evaluating how other elements of the story—such as character, point of view, imagery, and symbolism—help develop the theme. You might ask yourself what your own responses are to the author's treatment of the subject matter. Do not neglect the obvious, either: What expectations does the title set up? How does the title help develop thematic concerns? Clearly, the title "A Rose for Emily" says something about the narrator's attitude toward the title character, Emily Grierson, and all she represents.

WRITING ABOUT CHARACTER

Generally, characters are essential components of fiction and drama. (This is not always the case, though; Ray Bradbury's "August 2026: There

Will Come Soft Rains" is technically a story without characters, at least any human characters.) Often, you can discuss character in poetry, as in T. S. Eliot's "The Love Song of J. Alfred Prufrock" or Robert Browning's "My Last Duchess." Many writers find that analyzing character is one of the most interesting and engaging ways to work with a piece of literature and to shape a paper. After all, characters generally are human, and we all know something about being human and living in the world. While it is always important to remember that these figures are not real people but creations of the writer's imagination, it can be fruitful to begin evaluating them as you might evaluate a real person. Often you can start with your own response to a character. Did you like or dislike the character? Did you sympathize with the character? Why or why not?

Keep in mind, though, that emotional responses like these are just starting places. To explore and evaluate literary characters truly, you need to return to the formal aspects of the text and evaluate how the author has drawn these characters. The 20th-century writer E. M. Forster coined the terms *flat* characters and *round* characters. Flat characters are static, one-dimensional characters who frequently represent a particular concept or idea. In contrast, round characters are fully drawn and much more realistic characters who frequently change and develop over the course of a work. Are the characters you are studying flat or round? What elements of the characters lead you to this conclusion? Why might the author have drawn characters like this? How does their development affect the meaning of the work? Similarly, you should explore the techniques the author uses to develop characters. Do we hear a character's own words, or do we hear only other characters' assessments of him or her? Or, does the author use an omniscient or limited omniscient narrator to allow us access to the workings of the characters' minds? If so, how does that help develop the characterization? Often you can even evaluate the narrator as a character. How trustworthy are the opinions and assessments of the narrator? You should also think about characters' names. Do they mean anything? If you encounter a hero named Sophia or Sophie, you should probably think about her wisdom (or lack thereof), since *sophia* means "wisdom" in Greek. Similarly, since the name *Sylvia* is derived from the word *sylvan,* meaning "of the wood," you might want to evaluate that character's relationship with nature. Once again, you might look to the title of the work. Does Herman Melville's

"Bartleby, the Scrivener" signal anything about Bartleby himself? Is Bartleby adequately defined by his job as scrivener? Is this part of Melville's point? Pursuing questions like these can help you develop thorough papers about characters from psychological, sociological, or more formalistic perspectives.

WRITING ABOUT FORM AND GENRE

Genre, a word derived from French, means "type" or "class." Literary genres are distinctive classes or categories of literary composition. On the most general level, literary works can be divided into the genres of drama, poetry, fiction, and essays, yet within those genres there are classifications that are also referred to as genres. Tragedy and comedy, for example, are genres of drama. Epic, lyric, and pastoral are genres of poetry. *Form,* on the other hand, generally refers to the shape or structure of a work. There are many clearly defined forms of poetry that follow specific patterns of meter, rhyme, and stanza. Sonnets, for example, are poems that follow a fixed form of 14 lines. Sonnets generally follow one of two basic sonnet forms, each with its own distinct rhyme scheme. Haiku is another example of poetic form, traditionally consisting of three unrhymed lines of five, seven, and five syllables.

While you might think that writing about form or genre might leave little room for argument, many of these forms and genres are very fluid. Remember that literature is evolving and ever changing, and so are its forms. As you study poetry, you may find that poets, especially more modern poets, play with traditional poetic forms, bringing about new effects. Similarly, dramatic tragedy was once quite narrowly defined, but over the centuries playwrights have broadened and challenged traditional definitions, changing the shape of tragedy. When Arthur Miller wrote *Death of a Salesman,* many critics challenged the idea that tragic drama could encompass a common man like Willy Loman.

Evaluating how a work of literature fits into or challenges the boundaries of its form or genre can provide you with fruitful avenues of investigation. You might find it helpful to ask why the work does or does not fit into traditional categories. Why might Miller have thought it fitting to write a tragedy of the common man? Similarly, you might compare the content or theme of a work with its form. How well do they work together? Many of Emily Dickinson's poems, for instance, follow the meter of traditional hymns. While some of her poems seem to express traditional religious doctrines, many seem to challenge or strain against traditional conceptions of God and theology. What is the effect, then, of her use of traditional hymn meter?

WRITING ABOUT LANGUAGE, SYMBOLS, AND IMAGERY

No matter what the genre, writers use words as their most basic tool. Language is the most fundamental building block of literature. It is essential that you pay careful attention to the author's language and word choice as you read, reread, and analyze a text. Imagery is language that appeals to the senses. Most commonly, imagery appeals to our sense of vision, creating a mental picture, but authors also use language that appeals to our other senses. Images can be literal or figurative. Literal images use sensory language to describe an actual thing. In the broadest terms, figurative language uses one thing to speak about something else. For example, if I call my boss a snake, I am not saying that he is literally a reptile. Instead, I am using figurative language to communicate my opinions about him. Since we think of snakes as sneaky, slimy, and sinister, I am using the concrete image of a snake to communicate these abstract opinions and impressions.

The two most common figures of speech are similes and metaphors. Both are comparisons between two apparently dissimilar things. Similes are explicit comparisons using the word *like* or *as*; metaphors are implicit comparisons. To return to the previous example, if I say, "My boss, Bob, was waiting for me when I showed up to work five minutes late today—the snake!" I have constructed a metaphor. Writing about his experiences fighting in World War I, Wilfred Owen begins his poem "Dulce et decorum est" with a string of similes: "Bent double, like old beggars under sacks, / Knock-kneed, coughing like hags, we cursed through sludge." Owen's goal was to undercut clichéd notions that war and dying in battle were glorious. Certainly, comparing soldiers to coughing hags and to beggars underscores his point.

"Fog," a short poem by Carl Sandburg, provides a clear example of a metaphor. Sandburg's poem reads:

The fog comes
on little cat feet.

It sits looking
over harbor and city
on silent haunches
and then moves on.

Notice how effectively Sandburg conveys surprising impressions of the fog by comparing two seemingly disparate things—the fog and a cat.

Symbols, by contrast, are things that stand for, or represent, other things. Often they represent something intangible, such as concepts or ideas. In everyday life we use and understand symbols easily. Babies at christenings and brides at weddings wear white to represent purity. Think, too, of a dollar bill. The paper itself has no value in and of itself. Instead, that paper bill is a symbol of something else, the precious metal in a nation's coffers. Symbols in literature work similarly. Authors use symbols to evoke more than a simple, straightforward, literal meaning. Characters, objects, and places can all function as symbols. Famous literary examples of symbols include Moby Dick, the white whale of Herman Melville's novel, and the scarlet *A* of Nathaniel Hawthorne's *The Scarlet Letter.* As both of these symbols suggest, a literary symbol cannot be adequately defined or explained by any one meaning. Hester Prynne's Puritan community clearly intends her scarlet *A* as a symbol of her adultery, but as the novel progresses, even her own community reads the letter as representing not just *adultery,* but *able, angel,* and a host of other meanings.

Writing about imagery and symbols requires close attention to the author's language. To prepare a paper on symbolism or imagery in a work, identify and trace the images and symbols and then try to draw some conclusions about how they function. Ask yourself how any symbols or images help contribute to the themes or meanings of the work. What connotations do they carry? How do they affect your reception of the work? Do they shed light on characters or settings? A strong paper on imagery or symbolism will thoroughly consider the use of figures in the text and will try to reach some conclusions about how or why the author uses them.

WRITING ABOUT HISTORY AND CONTEXT

As noted earlier, it is possible to write an analytical paper that also considers the work's context. After all, the text was not created in a vacuum. The author lived and wrote in a specific period and in a specific cultural context and, as all of us are, was shaped by that environment. Learning more about the historical and cultural circumstances that surround the author and the work can help illuminate a text and provide you with productive material for a paper. Remember, though, that when you write analytical papers, you should use the context to illuminate the text. Do not lose sight of your goal—to interpret the meaning of the literary work. Use historical or philosophical research as a tool to develop your textual evaluation.

Thoughtful readers often consider how history and culture affected the author's choice and treatment of his or her subject matter. Investigations into the history and context of a work could examine the work's relation to specific historical events, such as the Salem witch trials in 17th-century Massachusetts or the restoration of Charles II to the British throne in 1660. Bear in mind that historical context is not limited to politics and world events. While knowing about the Vietnam War is certainly helpful in interpreting much of Tim O'Brien's fiction, and some knowledge of the French Revolution clearly illuminates the dynamics of Charles Dickens's *A Tale of Two Cities,* historical context also entails the fabric of daily life. Examining a text in light of gender roles, race relations, class boundaries, or working conditions can give rise to thoughtful and compelling papers. Exploring the conditions of the working class in 19th-century England, for example, can provide a particularly effective avenue for writing about Dickens's *Hard Times.*

You can begin thinking about these issues by asking broad questions at first. What do you know about the period and about the author? What does the editorial apparatus in your text tell you? These might be starting places. Similarly, when specific historical events or dynamics are particularly important to understanding a work but might be somewhat obscure to modern readers, textbooks usually provide notes to explain historical background. These are a good place to start. With this information, ask yourself how these historical facts and circumstances might have affected the author, the presentation of theme, and the presentation of character. How does knowing more about the work's specific historical context illuminate the work? To take a well-known example, understanding the complex attitudes toward slavery during the time Mark Twain wrote *Adventures of Huckleberry Finn* should help you begin to examine issues of race in the text. Additionally, you might compare these attitudes to those of the time in which the novel was set. How might this comparison affect your interpretation of a work written after the abolition of slavery but set before the Civil War?

WRITING ABOUT PHILOSOPHY AND IDEAS

Philosophical concerns are closely related to both historical context and thematic issues. As historical investigation does, philosophical research can provide a useful tool as you analyze a text. For example, an investigation into the working class in Dickens's England might lead you to a topic on the philosophical doctrine of utilitarianism in *Hard Times.* Many other works explore philosophies and ideas quite explicitly. Mary Shelley's famous novel *Frankenstein,* for example, explores John Locke's tabula rasa theory of human knowledge as she portrays the intellectual and emotional development of Victor Frankenstein's creature. As this example indicates, philosophical issues are somewhat more abstract than investigations of theme or historical context. Some other examples of philosophical issues include human free will, the formation of human identity, the nature of sin, or questions of ethics.

Writing about philosophy and ideas might require some outside research, but usually the notes or other material in your text will provide you with basic information and often footnotes and bibliographies suggest places you can go to read further about the subject. If you have identified a philosophical theme that runs through a text, you might ask yourself how the author develops this theme. Look at character development and the interactions of characters, for example. Similarly, you might examine whether the narrative voice in a work of fiction addresses the philosophical concerns of the text.

WRITING COMPARISON AND CONTRAST ESSAYS

Finally, you might find that comparing and contrasting the works or techniques of an author provides a useful tool for literary analysis. A comparison and contrast essay might compare two characters or themes in a single work, or it might compare the author's treatment of a theme in two works. It might also contrast methods of character development or analyze an author's differing treatment of a philosophical concern in two works. Writing comparison and contrast essays, though, requires some special consideration. While they generally provide you with plenty of material to use, they also come with a built-in trap: the laundry list. These papers often become mere lists of connections between the works. As this chapter will discuss, a strong thesis must make an assertion that you want to prove or validate. A strong comparison/contrast thesis, then, needs to comment on the significance of the similarities and differences you observe. It is not enough merely to assert that the works contain similarities and differences. You might, for example, assert why the similarities and differences are important and explain how they illuminate the works' treatment of theme. Remember, too, that a thesis should not be a statement of the obvious. A comparison/contrast paper that focuses only on very obvious similarities or differences does little to illuminate the connections between the works. Often, an effective method of shaping a strong thesis and argument is to begin your paper by noting the similarities between the works but then to develop a thesis that asserts how these apparently similar elements are different. If, for example, you observe that Emily Dickinson wrote a number of poems about spiders, you might analyze how she uses spider imagery differently in two poems. Similarly, many scholars have noted that Hawthorne created many "mad scientist" characters, men who are so devoted to their science or their art that they lose perspective on all else. A good thesis comparing two of these characters—Aylmer of "The Birth-mark" and Dr. Rappaccini of "Rappaccini's Daughter," for example—might initially identify both characters as examples of Hawthorne's mad scientist type but then argue that their motivations for scientific experimentation differ. If you strive to analyze the similarities or differences, discuss significances, and move beyond the obvious, your paper should bypass the laundry list trap.

PREPARING TO WRITE

Armed with a clear sense of your task—illuminating the text—and with an understanding of theme, character, language, history, and philosophy, you are ready to approach the writing process. Remember that good writing is grounded in good reading and that close reading takes time, attention, and more than one reading of your text. Read for comprehension first. As you go back and review the work, mark the text to chart the details of the work as well as your reactions. Highlight important passages, repeated words, and image patterns. "Converse" with the text through marginal notes. Mark turns in the plot, ask questions, and make observations about characters, themes, and language. If you are reading from a book that does not belong to you, keep a record of your reactions in a journal or notebook. If you have read a work of literature carefully, paying attention to both the text and the context of the work, you have a leg up on the writing process. Admittedly, at this point, your ideas are probably very broad and undefined, but you have taken an important first step toward writing a strong paper.

Your next step is to focus, to take a broad, perhaps fuzzy, topic and define it more clearly. Even a topic provided by your instructor will need to be focused appropriately. Remember that good writers make the topic their own. There are a number of strategies—often called "invention"— that you can use to develop your own focus. In one such strategy, called *freewriting*, you spend 10 minutes or so just writing about your topic without referring to the text or your notes. Write whatever comes to mind; the important thing is that you just keep writing. Often this process allows you to develop fresh ideas or approaches to your subject matter. You could also try *brainstorming*: Write down your topic and then list all the related points or ideas you can think of. Include questions, comments, words, important passages or events, and anything else that comes to mind. Let one idea lead to another. In the related technique of *clustering*, or *mapping*, write your topic on a sheet of paper and write related ideas around it. Then list related subpoints under each of these main ideas. Many people then draw arrows to show connections between points. This technique helps you narrow your topic and can also help you organize your ideas. Similarly, asking journalistic questions—Who? What? Where? When? Why? and How?—can develop ideas for topic development.

Thesis Statements

Once you have developed a focused topic, you can begin to think about your thesis statement, the main point or purpose of your paper. It is imperative that you craft a strong thesis, otherwise, your paper will likely be little more than random, disorganized observations about the text. Think of your thesis statement as a kind of road map for your paper. It tells your reader where you are going and how you are going to get there.

To craft a good thesis, you must keep a number of things in mind. First, as the title of this subsection indicates, your paper's thesis should be a statement, an assertion about the text that you want to prove or validate. Beginning writers often formulate a question that they attempt to use as a thesis. For example, a writer exploring the theme of madness in Dickens's *A Tale of Two Cities* might ask, Why are so many characters so psychologically troubled? While a question like this is a good strategy to use in the invention process to help narrow your topic and find your thesis, it cannot serve as the thesis statement because it does not tell your reader what you want to assert about madness. You might shape this question into a thesis by proposing instead an answer to that question: In *A Tale of Two Cities*, many characters are trying to escape insanity of some kind, but the story presents madness as somewhat inevitable. The novel ultimately argues that complete sanity is nearly impossible during the social, personal, and political upheaval of the French Revolution. Notice that this thesis provides an initial plan or structure for the rest of the paper, and notice, too, that the thesis statement does not necessarily have to fit into one sentence. After discussing madness, you could examine the ways in which madness is presented as inevitable in this novel and then theorize about what Dickens is saying about madness more generally. Perhaps you could discuss how different definitions of madness can make anyone appear insane, particularly in the riotous context of the French Revolution.

Second, remember that a good thesis makes an assertion that you need to support. In other words, a good thesis does not state the obvious. If you tried to formulate a thesis about insanity by simply saying, Madness is important in *A Tale of Two Cities*, you have done nothing but rephrase the obvious. Since Dickens's novel is centered on more than one character battling his or her own definition of madness, there would be no point in spending three to five pages supporting that assertion. You might try to develop a thesis from that point by asking yourself some further questions: What does it mean when any given character says, "It is madness"? Does the novel seem to indicate that to be insane is a natural or unnatural phenomenon for this society? Does it present madness as an advantage in this world of revolution, or is madness presented as a source of vulnerability? Such a line of questioning might lead you to a more viable thesis, such as the one in the preceding paragraph.

As the comparison with the road map also suggests, your thesis should appear near the beginning of the paper. In relatively short papers (three to six pages), the thesis almost always appears in the first paragraph. Some writers fall into the trap of saving their thesis for the end, trying to provide a surprise or a big moment of revelation, as if to say, for example, "Ta-da! I've just proved that in *Hard Times* Dickens uses fire to symbolize the protagonist's frustrations with her life." Placing a thesis at the end of an essay can seriously mar the essay's effectiveness. If you fail to define your essay's point and purpose clearly at the beginning, your reader will find it difficult to assess the clarity of your argument and understand the points you are making. When your argument comes as a surprise at the end, you force your reader to reread your essay in order to assess its logic and effectiveness.

Finally, you should avoid using the first person (*I*) as you present your thesis. Though it is not strictly wrong to write in the first person, it is difficult to do so gracefully. While writing in the first person, beginning writers often fall into the trap of writing self-reflexive prose (writing *about* their paper *in* their paper). Often this leads to the most dreaded of opening lines: "In this paper I am going to discuss . . ." Not only does this self-reflexive voice make for very awkward prose, it frequently allows writers to announce boldly a topic while completely avoiding a thesis statement. An example might be a paper that begins as follows: Hard Times, Dickens's 10th novel, takes place in the factory town of Coketown, where a schoolmaster raises his children to care only about facts. In this paper I am going to discuss how Louisa reacts to him. The author of this paper has done little more than announce a general topic for the paper (the reaction of Louisa to her father, the schoolmaster). While the last sentence might be a thesis, the writer fails to present an opinion about the significance of the reaction. To improve this "thesis," the writer would need to back up a couple of steps. First, the announced topic of the paper is too broad; it largely summarizes the events in the story, without saying anything about the ideas in the story. The writer should highlight what he or she considers the meaning of the story: What is the story about? The writer might conclude that the schoolmaster's tactics create feelings of isolation and frustration in Louisa's life. From here, the author could select the means by which Dickens communicates these ideas and then begin to craft a specific thesis. A writer who chooses to explore the symbols of frustration that are associated with fire might, for example, craft a thesis that reads, Hard Times is a novel that explores the effects of fact-centered education on one woman, Louisa Gradgrind, who yearns for imagination and true feeling in her life. The associations between Louisa and fire symbolize her passionate nature and highlight different layers of Louisa's associations with some of the men in her life.

Outlines

While developing a strong, thoughtful thesis early in your writing process should help focus your paper, outlining provides an essential tool for logically shaping that paper. A good outline helps you see—and develop—the relationships among the points in your argument and assures you that your paper flows logically and coherently. Outlining not only helps place your points in a logical order but also helps you subordinate supporting points, weed out any irrelevant points, and decide if there are any necessary points that are missing from your argument. Most of us are familiar with formal outlines that use numerical and letter designations for each point. However, there are different types of outlines; you may find that an informal outline is a more useful tool for you. What is important, though, is that you spend the time to develop some sort of outline—formal or informal.

Remember that an outline is a tool to help you shape and write a strong paper. If you do not spend sufficient time planning your supporting points and shaping the arrangement of those points, you will most likely construct a vague, unfocused outline that provides little, if any, help with the writing of the paper. Consider the following example.

Thesis: Hard Times is a novel that explores the effects of fact-centered education on one woman, Louisa Gradgrind, who yearns for imagination and true feeling in her life. The associations between Louisa and fire symbolize her passionate nature and highlight different layers of Louisa's associations with some of the men in her life.

    I. Introduction and thesis

   II. James Harthouse
      A. Kindling the flame

  III. Bounderby (husband)
      A. Associations with wind
      B. Blowing out the fire

   IV. Coketown

    V. Louisa Gradgrind
      A. "Never Wonder" chapter
      B. Staring into the fire
      C. Sacrifices
      D. Sissy

   VI. Conclusion
      A. Louisa's associations with fire show readers her warmth, passion, brightness, and vulnerability in various situations with the men in her life

This outline has a number of flaws. First, the major topics labeled with the Roman numerals are not arranged in a logical order. If the paper's focus is on Louisa, the writer should establish the particulars of her character before showing how fire plays a role in her relationships with men. Similarly, the thesis makes no reference to Coketown, but the writer includes it as a major section of this outline. The writer could, however, include the "fires of Coketown" in terms of their place in Louisa's reveries. As the masculine counterpart of Louisa, her brother Tom may well have a place in this paper, but the writer fails to provide details about his place in the argument. Third, the writer includes Sissy's character as one of the lettered items in section V. Letters A, B, and C all refer to specific instances where the symbolism of fire in Louisa's life will be discussed; Sissy does not belong in this list. A fourth problem is the inclusion of a letter A in section II. An outline should not include an A without a B, a 1 without a 2, and so forth. The final problem with this outline is the overall lack of detail. None of the sections provides much information about the content of the argument, and it seems likely that the writer has not given sufficient thought to the content of the paper.

A better start to this outline might be the following:

Thesis: *Hard Times* is a novel that explores the effects of fact-centered education on one woman, Louisa Gradgrind, who yearns for imagination and true feeling in her life. The associations between Louisa and fire symbolize her passionate nature and highlight different layers of Louisa's associations with some of the men in her life.

I. Introduction and thesis

II. Louisa Gradgrind
    A. "Never Wonder" chapter
    B. Staring into the fire
    C. Sacrifices

III. Bounderby (husband)
    A. Associations with wind
    B. Blowing out the fire

IV. James Harthouse
    A. Kindling the flame
    B. Louisa can't end up with him

V. Tom
    A. Can't see into the fires
    B. Louisa is "brighter" than Tom

VI. Conclusion
    A. Louisa's associations with fire show readers her warmth, passion, brightness,

```
and vulnerability in various situations
with these three men in her life
```

This new outline would prove much more helpful when it came time to write the paper.

An outline like this could be shaped into an even more useful tool if the writer fleshed out the argument by providing specific examples from the text to support each point. Once you have listed your main point and your supporting ideas, develop this raw material by listing related supporting ideas and material under each of those main headings. From there, arrange the material in subsections and order the material logically.

For example, you might begin with one of the theses cited above as follows: In *A Tale of Two Cities*, many characters are trying to escape insanity of some kind, but the story presents madness as somewhat inevitable. The novel ultimately argues that complete sanity is nearly impossible during the social, personal, and political upheaval of the French Revolution. As noted above, this thesis already gives you the beginning of an organization. Start by supporting the notion that many characters are trying to escape insanity and then explain how Dickens presents insanity as a natural result of a bloody revolution. You might begin your outline, then, with four topic headings: (1) Manette as an example of precarious sanity and bouts of madness, (2) characters' different definitions of madness, (3) sanity as rare, and (4) sanity as impossible for some characters to sustain during the French Revolution. Under each of those headings you could list ideas that support the particular point. Be sure to include references to parts of the text that help build your case.

An informal outline might look like this:

```
Thesis: In A Tale of Two Cities, many characters are
trying to escape insanity of some kind, but the story
presents madness as somewhat inevitable. Dickens
ultimately argues that complete sanity is nearly
impossible during the social, personal, and political
upheaval of the French Revolution.
```

Introduction and Thesis

1. Dr. Manette fluctuates between sanity and madness
   - Imprisonment led him to question his sanity
   - Shoe-making makes him feel safe and sane
   - Outgrows his need for shoe-making when he is far from the revolution
   - Revolutionary activities and the ironic circularity of his life (first the persecuted and then the persecutor) affect his family, and he goes insane

2. Characters define madness differently
   - Manette
     - In prison, sanity is shoe-making
     - Out of prison, sanity is happiness of his family
     - "For the first time the Doctor felt, now, that his suffering was strength and power"
     - "As he stood staring at them, they asked him no question, for his face told them everything"
   - Charles Darnay
     - "This is madness," as Sydney takes his place in prison
   - Sydney
     - "This is a desperate time, when desperate games are played for desperate stakes. Let the Doctor play the winning game; I will play the losing one"
     - He makes choices rather than following the crowd and/or the frenzy—he is generally solitary
     - His sacrifice at the end is much more poignant because he clearly knows exactly what he is doing

3. Sanity is rare during the French Revolution
   - Of the crowd attacking the Bastille, Dickens writes, "they are headlong, mad, and dangerous"
     - "The characters in A Tale of Two Cities exemplify Dickens's acute understanding of human nature and the workings of the mind under stress" (Glancy, Introduction 2)
     - "It is the effect of the Revolution, its immediate and shocking effect, on individuals that suits Dickens's metamorphosizing imagination best" (Beckwith 11)
   - "The revolutionaries appear to [Dickens] simply as degraded savages—in fact, as lunatics" (Orwell 15)
   - Dickens associates madness with mob mentality—much different from general English individualism of the time
   - Dickens believed in reform but did not think it should be carried out in violent and destructive ways

4. Sanity is impossible for some characters to sustain
   - "a wild infection of the wildly shaken public mind"
     - "Apparently the Citizen-Doctor is not in his right mind? The Revolution-fever will have been too much for him? . . . Many suffer with it"

Conclusion
   - Mob scenes show utter frenzy and lack of deliberation before action
   - Insanity becomes a kind of prison from which no one can escape

- The characters who take the most effective action are clearly sane

You would set about writing a formal outline through a similar process, though in the final stages you would label the headings differently. A formal outline for a paper that argues the thesis about *Hard Times* cited above—that Louisa's association with fire is symbolic of her passionate nature and relationships with men—might look like this:

Thesis: *Hard Times* is a novel that explores the effects of fact-centered education on one woman, Louisa Gradgrind, who yearns for imagination and true feeling in her life. The associations between Louisa and fire symbolize her passionate nature and highlight different layers of Louisa's associations with some of the men in her life.

  I. Introduction and thesis

 II. Louisa Gradgrind's frustrations over her fact-based education and lack of experience
     A. Her childhood
        1. She is told, "Never Wonder," but does it anyway
        2. Staring into the fire allows her to develop her thoughts
     B. Her rebellion
        1. Taking Tom to the circus
        2. Wiping away Bounderby's kiss
     C. Glimpse of another life
        1. Learning details of Sissy's life
        2. Learning details of Stephen Blackpool's life

III. Attempts to adjust to her prescribed life
     A. Marriage to Bounderby
        1. He is wind, blowing out her fire completely

       2. Runs his household, though without
          passion or feeling
    B. Fires of Coketown
       1. Still watching those fires, now at a
          distance
       2. Others cannot see into these fires
    C. Focus on sacrifice
       1. She has done the right thing as long
          as Tom succeeds
       2. Continues to loan money to Tom

IV. Failure to find happiness in her prescribed
    life
    A. James Harthouse kindling the flame within
       her
       1. Wanting to believe in him
       2. Understanding his true nature
    B. Feels the strain of her sacrifice for Tom
       1. Tom's crime and use of Stephen
          Blackpool
       2. Tom cannot achieve what would have
          been easy for Louisa (because she is
          "brighter")
    C. Returning home
       1. Lying at the bottom of the staircase
       2. Can't even allow her father to touch
          her

V. Conclusion
    A. Louisa's associations with fire show
       readers her warmth, passion, brightness,
       and vulnerability in various situations
       with these three men in her life

As in the previous example outline, the thesis provided the seeds of a
structure, and the writer was careful to arrange the supporting points in a
logical manner, showing the relationships among the ideas in the paper.

Body Paragraphs

Once your outline is complete, you can begin drafting your paper. Paragraphs, units of related sentences, are the building blocks of a good paper, and as you draft you should keep in mind both the function and the qualities of good paragraphs. Paragraphs help you chart and control the shape and content of your essay, and they help the reader see your organization and your logic. You should begin a new paragraph whenever you move from one major point to another. In longer, more complex essays you might use a group of related paragraphs to support major points. Remember that in addition to being adequately developed, a good paragraph is both unified and coherent.

Unified Paragraphs

Each paragraph must be centered on one idea or point, and a unified paragraph carefully focuses on and develops this central idea without including extraneous ideas or tangents. For beginning writers, the best way to ensure that you are constructing unified paragraphs is to include a topic sentence in each paragraph. This topic sentence should convey the main point of the paragraph, and every sentence in the paragraph should relate to that topic sentence. Any sentence that strays from the central topic does not belong in the paragraph and needs to be revised or deleted. Consider the following paragraph about Madame Defarge's eerie sanity in *A Tale of Two Cities*. Notice how the paragraph veers away from the main point that friendships are sacrificed for the sake of survival:

> Our introduction to Madame Defarge takes place after the frenzy of the spilled cask of wine and provides a glimpse of her sanity. She remains in the shop, picking her teeth and knitting. She remains staid even while the crowd outside shouts, drinks, dances, attempts to quench their literal and metaphorical thirst, and writes "blood" on the wall. If the isolation of prison causes or fosters insanity, then that would explain Manette. That is, in fact, how Dickens explains Manette's initial problems. He is teetering on the edge of madness, finally saved by the love of his daughter Lucie.

Although the paragraph begins solidly, and the first sentence provides the central idea of the paragraph, the author soon goes on a tangent. If the purpose of the paragraph is to demonstrate that Madame Defarge demonstrates a level of sanity even in the midst of chaotic events, the sentences about the relative insanity of Doctor Manette are tangential here. They may find a place later in the paper, but they should be deleted from this paragraph.

Coherent Paragraphs

In addition to shaping unified paragraphs, you must also craft coherent paragraphs, paragraphs that develop their points logically with sentences that flow smoothly into one another. Coherence depends on the order of your sentences, but it is not strictly the order of the sentences that is important to paragraph coherence. You also need to craft your prose to help the reader see the relationship among the sentences.

Consider the following paragraph about madness in *A Tale of Two Cities*. Notice how the writer uses the same ideas as the paragraph above yet fails to help the reader see the relationships among the points.

Madame Defarge exemplifies sanity throughout the novel.
She is calm and collected even in the most chaotic
times. "There was a character about Madame Defarge, from
which one might have predicted that she did not often
make mistakes against herself in any of the reckonings
over which she presided" (35). She is cold, deliberate,
vengeful, but not particularly excitable and certainly
not insane. The man who writes "blood" on the wall is
perhaps calm but might still be insane. Sydney Carton
may be insane, as well, although he is very solitary
and tells Mr. Lorry, "this is a desperate time, when
desperate games are played for desperate stakes. Let the
Doctor play the winning game; I will play the losing one"
(Dickens 298). If he sees this as a game, we can perhaps
assume that he is quite thoughtful about it, indicating
his sanity as well. Mob mentality was generally frowned
upon in Victorian England, where people preferred to
work on individual terms. Madame Defarge thinks almost

```
completely of herself and getting revenge for actions
perpetrated her family. She is unconcerned with the mob
except in her capacity as their instigator.
```

This paragraph demonstrates that unity alone does not guarantee paragraph effectiveness. The argument is hard to follow because the author fails both to show connections between the sentences and to indicate how they work to support the overall point.

A number of techniques are available to aid paragraph coherence. Careful use of transitional words and phrases is essential. You can use transitional flags to introduce an example or an illustration (*for example, for instance*), to amplify a point or add another phase of the same idea (*additionally, furthermore, next, similarly, finally, then*), to indicate a conclusion or result (*therefore, as a result, thus, in other words*), to signal a contrast or a qualification (*on the other hand, nevertheless, despite this, on the contrary, still, however, conversely*), to signal a comparison (*likewise, in comparison, similarly*), and to indicate a movement in time (*afterward, earlier, eventually, finally, later, subsequently, until*).

In addition to transitional flags, careful use of pronouns aids coherence and flow. If you were writing about *The Wizard of Oz*, you would not want to keep repeating the phrase *the witch* or the name *Dorothy*. Careful substitution of the pronoun *she* in these instances can aid coherence. A word of warning, though: When you substitute pronouns for proper names, always be sure that your pronoun reference is clear. In a paragraph that discusses both Dorothy and the witch, substituting *she* could lead to confusion. Make sure that it is clear to whom the pronoun refers. Generally, the pronoun refers to the last proper noun you have used.

While repeating the same name over and over again can lead to awkward, boring prose, it is possible to use repetition to help your paragraph's coherence. Careful repetition of important words or phrases can lend coherence to your paragraph by reminding readers of your key points. Admittedly, it takes some practice to use this technique effectively. You may find that reading your prose aloud can help you develop an ear for effective use of repetition.

To see how helpful transitional aids are, compare the paragraph below to the preceding paragraph about madness in *A Tale of Two*

Cities. Notice how the author works with the same ideas and quotations but shapes them into a much more coherent paragraph whose point is clearer and easier to follow.

> Madame Defarge exemplifies sanity throughout the novel. She is calm and collected even in the most chaotic times, and Dickens introduces her character by writing, "There was a character about Madame Defarge, from which one might have predicted that she did not often make mistakes against herself in any of the reckonings over which she presided" (35). She is cold, deliberate, vengeful, but not particularly excitable and certainly not insane. A lack of excitability is not in itself the mark of sanity. For instance, the man who writes "blood" on the wall after the cask of wine is spilled is perhaps calm but might still be insane, as he is clearly caught in the frenzy of the crowd. Mob mentality was generally frowned upon in Victorian England, where people preferred to work on individual terms. Sydney Carton worked on individual terms, never becoming part of the mob mentality but working with others enough to sacrifice his lone life for the good of many others. Readers might find Carton insane, too, except that he tells Mr. Lorry, "this is a desperate time, when desperate games are played for desperate stakes. Let the Doctor play the winning game; I will play the losing one" (Dickens 298). If he sees this as a game, we can perhaps assume that he is quite thoughtful about it, indicating his sanity as well. Both Carton and Madame Defarge stand outside mob mentality. Madame Defarge, in particular, thinks almost completely of herself and getting revenge for actions perpetrated upon her family. She is unconcerned with the mob except in her capacity as their instigator.

Similarly, the following paragraph from a paper on Sydney Carton's role in *A Tale of Two Cities* demonstrates both unity and coherence. In it, the author argues that Carton deliberately moves from the most pathetic character in the novel to the position of everyone's hero.

> Sydney Carton is called weak, lost, and miserable, but he is not called mad or associated with frenzy in any way. In the beginning, Carton is the mysterious stranger in Darnay's court case, and remains the mysterious stranger on some level throughout the book, although other characters' and the reader's perceptions of Carton improve as the novel continues, until he finally becomes the undisputed hero at the end, with Dickens using his words to close the novel. Carton doesn't really have a past—not one that matters anyway: "He is a man set apart, with no connection to the French Revolution or to the Manette/Evremonde/Defarge story until he forges a connection himself at the end" (Glancy, *A Tale* 81). He loves, he loses, he schemes, he sacrifices. Exchanging himself with Darnay is not an impulsive act. Carton puts his plan in place little by little, starting with his encounter with Barsad in the street, following Darnay's second arrest. Sydney asks Barsad to speak with him privately, and "Miss Pross recalled soon afterwards, and to the end of her life remembered, that as she pressed her hands on Sydney's arm and looked up in his face, imploring him to do no hurt to Solomon, there was a braced purpose in the arm and a kind of inspiration in the eyes, which not only contradicted his light manner, but changed and raised the man" (Dickens 297). As soon as the plan to save Darnay begins to hatch, Carton is uplifted in others' eyes.

Introductions

Introductions present particular challenges for writers. Generally, your introduction should do two things: capture your reader's attention and explain the main point of your essay. In other words, while your introduction should contain your thesis, it needs to do a bit more work than that. You are likely to find that starting that first paragraph is one of the most difficult parts of the paper. It is hard to face that blank page or screen, and as a result, many beginning writers, in desperation to start somewhere, start with overly broad, general statements. While it is often a good strategy to start with more general subject matter and narrow your focus, do not begin with broad sweeping statements such as Everyone likes to be creative and feel understood. Such sentences are nothing but empty filler. They begin to fill the blank page, but they do nothing to advance your argument. Instead, you should try to gain your reader's interest. Some writers like to begin with a pertinent quotation or with a relevant question. Or, you might begin with an introduction of the topic you will discuss. If you are writing about Dickens's presentation of madness during the French Revolution in *A Tale of Two Cities*, for instance, you might begin by talking about Dickens's definitions of madness. Another common trap to avoid is depending on your title to introduce the author and the text you are writing about. Always include the work's author and title in your opening paragraph.

Compare the effectiveness of the following introductions:

1. Throughout history, revolutions have caused madness. Think how you feel when you really want something: It makes you kind of crazy, doesn't it? In this story, Dickens shows characters' growing insanity caused by revolution by focusing on their thoughts, actions, and beliefs. More important, he shows how and why Madame Defarge remains sane.

2. In *A Tale of Two Cities*, Charles Dickens associates madness (or insanity) largely with frenzy and blindly following others. Dickens makes "The revolutionaries appear . . . simply as degraded savages—in fact, as lunatics" when they are immersed in mob activities such as the broken wine cask and the hunting of Foulon (Orwell 15). Given such a definition, it would be easy to claim that Madame Defarge is insane. But Dickens writes about her in such a way that leads us to believe that she is very much in her right mind.

The first introduction begins with a vague, overly broad sentence; cites unclear, undeveloped examples; and then moves abruptly to the thesis. Notice, too, how a reader deprived of the paper's title does not know the title of the story that the paper will analyze. The second introduction works with the same material and thesis but provides more detail and is consequently much more interesting. It begins by discussing Dickens's definition of madness in the book, briefly mentions one critic's validation of the proposed definition of madness, and then gives specific examples from the book that fit this definition. The paragraph ends with the thesis. This effective introduction also includes the title of the text and full name of the author.

The paragraph below provides another example of an opening strategy. It begins by introducing the author and the text it will analyze, then it moves on by briefly introducing relevant details of the story in order to set up its thesis.

Charles's Dickens 10th novel, *Hard Times*, centers on Gradgrind's school and the stern dissemination of facts and only facts. Perpetuators of this philosophy, namely Mr. Gradgrind and Bounderby, assume that children who grow up only concerned with facts will lead more useful lives than those who are overly concerned with imagination and feeling. Louisa Gradgrind is raised with this utilitarian philosophy and finds refuge in staring at the fire, allowing herself the freedom to wonder—a punishable offense in the Gradgrind household—and comparing herself to the "red sparks dropping out of the fire, and whitening and dying" (Dickens 39). Throughout her sacrifices for her brother, her loveless marriage, and the manipulation of a potential lover, Louisa finds comfort, contemplation, and self-reflection in fireplace fires, the factory fires of Coketown, and the mere idea of fire. *Hard Times* is a novel that explores the effects of fact-centered education on one woman, Louisa Gradgrind, who yearns for imagination and true feeling in her life. The associations between Louisa and fire symbolize her passionate nature and highlight different layers of Louisa's associations with some of the men in her life.

Conclusions

Conclusions present another series of challenges for writers. No doubt you have heard the old adage about writing papers: "Tell us what you are going to say, say it, and then tell us what you've said." While this formula does not necessarily result in bad papers, it does not often result in good ones, either. It will almost certainly result in boring papers (especially boring conclusions). If you have done a good job establishing your points in the body of the paper, the reader already knows and understands your argument. There is no need to merely reiterate. Do not just summarize your main points in your conclusion. Such a boring and mechanical conclusion does nothing to advance your argument or interest your reader. Consider the following conclusion to the paper about Madame Defarge's sanity in *A Tale of Two Cities*.

> In conclusion, Dickens shows revolution as destructive to characters. Madame Defarge is one character who does not suffer adverse mental effects from the revolution. Her death at the end of the story indicates that sanity will not survive in this type of bloody revolution. We should all remember that.

Besides starting with a mechanical transitional device, this conclusion does little more than summarize the main points of the outline (and it does not even touch on all of them). It is incomplete and uninteresting (as well as a little too depressing).

Instead, your conclusion should add something to your paper. A good tactic is to build upon the points you have been arguing. Asking "why?" often helps you draw further conclusions. For example, in the paper on *A Tale of Two Cities*, you might speculate or explain how Madame Defarge's sanity speaks to what Dickens is presenting as madness in the novel in order to convey his beliefs about right and wrong ways to promote reform. Scholars often discuss this novel as a study in character types, rather than precise individuals, and your conclusion could discuss whether the story presents characters as unique people or as representations of historical figures or groups.

Another method for successfully concluding a paper is to speculate on other directions in which to take your topic by tying it into larger issues. You might do this by envisioning your paper as just one section of a larger paper. Having established your points in this paper, how would you build upon this argument? Where would you go next? In the following conclusion to the paper on *A Tale of Two Cities*, the author reiterates some of the main points of the paper but does so in order to amplify the discussion of the novel's central message and to connect it to the historical context of Charles Dickens's work:

> Madame Defarge runs alongside the mob at times, and she certainly inspires and provokes the frenzy more than once, but she remains outside it too. She keeps her single-minded focus and acts according to her individual will rather than the collective desire. In this way, Madame Defarge becomes more English than French, to follow the stereotypes and assumptions of the time, through her desire to act alone rather than blindly following the mob. As much as we may like to believe that her vengeful and bloody activities result from a damaged mind, Madame Defarge is perfectly sane.

Similarly, in the following conclusion to a paper on the symbolism of fire in *Hard Times*, the author draws a conclusion about what the novel is saying about utilitarianism more broadly.

> Ultimately, *Hard Times* is a tale of educational methods that alone cannot help young adults weather the perplexities of society. The fire within Louisa finally does not allow her to settle for the miserable existence prescribed to her. She has been brought, quite literally, to the bottom of the staircase, but her father's understanding and subsequent transformation of ideas help her to reestablish her life as a kind, emotional, fiery woman. It is fitting that the novel ends with Louisa staring into yet another fire, imagining the fates of her friends and family. Some of the future she sees is known, indicating that Louisa is not full of only fancy at this point but lives in the real world

as well. Through Louisa, Dickens demonstrates that some combination of fact and imagination becomes necessary for people to live full, well-rounded lives.

Citations and Formatting

Using Primary Sources

As the examples included in this chapter indicate, strong papers on literary texts incorporate quotations from the text in order to support their points. It is not enough for you to assert your interpretation without providing support or evidence from the text. Without well-chosen quotations to support your argument, you are, in effect, saying to the reader, "Take my word for it." It is important to use quotations thoughtfully and selectively. Remember that the paper presents *your* argument, so choose quotations that support *your* assertions. Do not let the author's voice overwhelm your own. With that caution in mind, there are some guidelines you should follow to ensure that you use quotations clearly and effectively.

Integrate Quotations:

Quotations should always be integrated into your own prose. Do not just drop them into your paper without introduction or comment. Otherwise, it is unlikely that your reader will see their function. You can integrate textual support easily and clearly with identifying tags, short phrases that identify the speaker. For example:

> Sydney Carton demonstrates a "negligent recklessness of manner."

While this tag appears before the quotation, you can also use tags after or in the middle of the quoted text, as the following examples demonstrate:

> "There is nothing more to do . . . until to-morrow. I can't sleep," says Carton.

> "This is a desperate time," Carton tells Mr. Lorry, "when desperate games are played for desperate stakes. Let the Doctor play the winning game; I will play the losing one."

You can also use a colon to formally introduce a quotation:

> Madame Defarge's disdain for Lucie is clear: "Judge you!
> Is it likely that the trouble of one wife and mother
> would be much to us now?"

When you quote brief sections of poems (three lines or fewer), use slash marks to indicate the line breaks in the poem:

> As the poem ends, Dickinson speaks of the power of the
> imagination: "The revery alone will do, / If bees are
> few."

Longer quotations (more than four lines of prose or three lines of poetry) should be set off from the rest of your paper in a block quotation. Double-space before you begin the passage, indent it 10 spaces from your left-hand margin, and double-space the passage itself. Because the indentation signals the inclusion of a quotation, do not use quotation marks around the cited passage. Use a colon to introduce the passage.

> Sydney buys the components (presumably) for ether, and
> says:
>
> > "There is nothing more to do . . . until to-
> > morrow. I can't sleep." It was not a reckless
> > manner, the manner in which he said these words
> > aloud under the fast-sailing clouds, nor was it
> > more expressive of negligence than defiance. It
> > was the settled manner of a tired man, who had
> > wandered and struggled and got lost, but who at
> > length struck into his road and saw its end.
>
> Clearly, Carton demonstrates the antithesis of frenzy
> in the extreme nature of his solitary existence.

> The whole of Dickinson's poem speaks of the imagination:

```
To make a prairie it takes a clover and one bee,
One clover, and a bee,
And revery.
The revery alone will do,
If bees are few.
```

```
Clearly, she argues for the creative power of the mind.
```

It is also important to interpret quotations after you introduce them and explain how they help advance your point. You cannot assume that your reader will interpret the quotations the same way that you do.

Quote Accurately:

Always quote accurately. Anything within quotation marks must be the author's exact words. There are, however, some rules to follow if you need to modify the quotation to fit into your prose.

1. Use brackets to indicate any material that might have been added to the author's exact wording. For example, if you need to add any words to the quotation or alter it grammatically to allow it to fit into your prose, indicate your changes in brackets:

   ```
   The crowd begins Foulon's torture and execution
   and once again it is Madame Defarge who is in
   control: "[She] let him go—as a cat might have
   done to a mouse."
   ```

2. Conversely, if you choose to omit any words from the quotation, use ellipses (three spaced periods) to indicate missing words or phrases:

   ```
   Even during the fall of the Bastille, she
   leads a group of women into the frenzy but
   sets herself outside it somehow: "In the howling
   universe . . . that seemed to encompass this
   grim old officer conspicuous in his grey coat
   and red decoration, there was but one quite
   steady figure, and that was a woman's."
   ```

3. If you delete a sentence or more, use the ellipses after a period:

```
The young boy tells Manette, "We common dogs
are proud too, sometimes. . . . but we have
little pride left, sometimes."
```

4. If you omit a line or more of poetry, or more than one paragraph of prose, use a single line of spaced periods to indicate the omission:

```
To make a prairie it takes a clover and one bee,
. . . . . . . . . . . . . . . . . . .
And revery.
The revery alone will do,
If bees are few.
```

Punctuate Properly:

Punctuation of quotations often causes more trouble than it should. Once again, you just need to keep these simple rules in mind.

1. Periods and commas should be placed inside quotation marks, even if they are not part of the original quotation:

```
The young boy tells Manette, "We common dogs are
proud too, sometimes . . . but we have little
pride left, sometimes."
```

The only exception to this rule is when the quotation is followed by a parenthetical reference. In this case, the period or comma goes after the citation (more on these later in this chapter):

```
The young boy tells Manette, "We common dogs are
proud too, sometimes . . . but we have little
pride left, sometimes" (322).
```

2. Other marks of punctuation—colons, semicolons, question marks, and exclamation points—go outside the quotation marks unless they are part of the original quotation:

> Why does the narrator say that Carton has
> "negligent recklessness of manner"?

> Madame Defarge's disdain for Lucie is clear:
> "Judge you! Is it likely that the trouble of one
> wife and mother would be much to us now?"

Documenting Primary Sources:

Unless you are instructed otherwise, you should provide sufficient information for your reader to locate material you quote. Generally, literature papers follow the rules set forth by the Modern Language Association (MLA). These can be found in the *MLA Handbook for Writers of Research Papers* (sixth edition). You should be able to find this book in the reference section of your library. Additionally, its rules for citing both primary and secondary sources are widely available from reputable online sources. One of these is the Online Writing Lab (OWL) at Purdue University. OWL's guide to MLA style is available at http://owl. english.purdue.edu/owl/resource/557/01/. The Modern Language Association also offers answers to frequently asked questions about MLA style on this helpful Web page: http://www.mla.org/style_faq. Generally, when you are citing from literary works in papers, you should keep a few guidelines in mind.

Parenthetical Citations:

MLA asks for parenthetical references in your text after quotations. When you are working with prose (short stories, novels, or essays) include page numbers in the parentheses:

> The young boy tells Manette, "We common dogs are proud
> too, sometimes. . . . but we have little pride left,
> sometimes" (322).

When you are quoting poetry, include line numbers:

> Dickinson's speaker tells of the arrival of a fly: "There
> interposed a Fly— / With Blue—uncertain stumbling Buzz—
> / Between the light—and Me—" (12-14).

Works Cited Page:
These parenthetical citations are linked to a separate works cited page at the end of the paper. The works cited page lists works alphabetically by the author(s)' last name. An entry for the above reference to Dickens's *A Tale of Two Cities* would read:

```
Dickens, Charles. A Tale of Two Cities. 1859. New York:
    Barnes & Noble, 2004.
```

The *MLA Handbook* includes a full listing of sample entries, as do many of the online explanations of MLA style.

Documenting Secondary Sources:

To ensure that your paper is built entirely upon your own ideas and analysis, instructors often ask that you write interpretative papers without any outside research. If, on the other hand, your paper requires research, you must document any secondary sources you use. You need to document direct quotations, summaries or paraphrases of others' ideas, and factual information that is not common knowledge. Follow the guidelines above for quoting primary sources when you use direct quotations from secondary sources. Keep in mind that MLA style also includes specific guidelines for citing electronic sources. OWL's Web site provides a good summary: http://owl.english.purdue.edu/owl/resource/557/09/.

Parenthetical Citations:
As with the documentation of primary sources, described above, MLA guidelines require in-text parenthetical references to your secondary sources. Unlike the research papers you might write for a history class, literary research papers following MLA style do not use footnotes as a means of documenting sources. Instead, after a quotation, you should cite the author's last name and the page number:

```
Carton has a "negligent recklessness of manner" (Dickens
296).
```

If you include the name of the author in your prose, then you would include only the page number in your citation. For example:

```
According to the narrator in Dickens's novel, Carton
has a "negligent recklessness of manner" (296).
```

If you are including more than one work by the same author, the parenthetical citation should include a shortened yet identifiable version of the title in order to indicate which of the author's works you cite. For example:

```
According to the narrator in Dickens's novel, Carton
has a "negligent recklessness of manner" (A Tale 296).
```

Similarly, and just as important, if you summarize or paraphrase the particular ideas of your source, you must provide documentation:

```
Sydney Carton seems to put his plan in place little by
little, starting with his encounter with Barsad in the
street, following Darnay's second arrest (Dickens 297).
```

Works Cited Page:

Like the primary sources discussed above, the parenthetical references to secondary sources are keyed to a separate works cited page at the end of your paper. Here is an example of a works cited page that uses the examples cited above. Note that when two or more works by the same author are listed, you should use three hypens followed by a period in the subsequent entries. You can find a complete list of sample entries in the *MLA Handbook* or from a reputable online summary of MLA style.

Works Cited

Beckwith, Charles E. "Introduction." *Twentieth Century Interpretations of* A Tale of Two Cities. Ed. Charles E. Beckwith. Englewood Cliffs, NJ: Prentice Hall, 1972. 1–19.

Glancy, Ruth. "Introduction." *Charles Dickens's* A Tale of Two Cities: *A Sourcebook*. Ed. Ruth Glancy. London: Routledge, 2006. 1–4.

———. *A Tale of Two Cities: Dickens's Revolutionary Novel*. Twayne's Masterwork Studies No. 89. Boston: Twayne Publishers, 1991.

Orwell, George. "Charles Dickens." *Dickens, Dali and Others.* New York: Reynal & Hitchcock, 1946. 10–16.

Plagiarism

Failure to document carefully and thoroughly can leave you open to charges of stealing the ideas of others, which is known as plagiarism, and this is a very serious matter. Remember that it is important to include quotation marks when you use language from your source, even if you use just one or two words. For example, if you wrote, Carton has a negligent recklessness of manner, you would be guilty of plagiarism, since you used Dickens's distinct language without acknowledging him as the source. Instead, you should write: Carton has a "negligent recklessness of manner" (Dickens 296). In this case, you have properly credited Dickens.

Similarly, neither summarizing the ideas of an author nor changing or omitting just a few words means that you can omit a citation. Ruth Glancy's book, *A Tale of Two Cities: Dickens's Revolutionary Novel,* contains the following passage:

That Dickens believed in his story, that he had "done and suffered it all" himself, is evident from the intensity of the emotions that we see in the coming storm, in the rising sea of revolutionaries, in the bloodstained stones of the Paris streets and the footsteps echoing in Soho Square.

Below are two examples of plagiarized passages of the above extract from Glancy's book:

Dickens felt that he had lived much of *A Tale of Two Cities,* and this is why some of the imagery in the book, like the oceans of "citizens" fighting for reform or the thunder that foreshadows the revolution's power is so exceptional.

Dickens believed that he had done and suffered all of the events in *A Tale of Two Cities* himself. He wanted to include the imagery of the emotions of the coming storm, the bloody stones on the streets of Paris, and the rising ocean of revolutionaries (Glancy 67).

While the first passage does not use Glancy's exact language, it does list some of the same examples of exceptional imagery in the book. Since this interpretation is Glancy's distinct idea, this constitutes plagiarism. The second passage has shortened her passage, changed some wording, and included a citation, but some of the phrasing is Glancy's. The first passage could be fixed with a parenthetical citation; however, because some of the wording in the second remains the same, it would require the use of quotation marks, in addition to a parenthetical citation. The passage below represents an honestly and adequately documented use of the original passage:

> As Ruth Glancy notes, Dickens felt that he had lived much of *A Tale of Two Cities*. This is why some of the imagery in the novel, such as "the intensity of the emotions that we see in the coming storm, in the rising sea of revolutionaries, in the bloodstained stones of the Paris streets and the footsteps echoing in Soho Square," is so vivid and exceptional (Glancy 67).

This passage acknowledges that the interpretation is derived from Glancy while appropriately using quotations to indicate her precise language.

While it is not necessary to document well-known facts, often referred to as "common knowledge," any ideas or language that you take from someone else must be properly documented. Common knowledge generally includes the birth and death dates of authors or other well-documented facts of their lives. An often-cited guideline is that if you can find the information in three sources, it is common knowledge. Despite this guideline, it is, admittedly, often difficult to know if the facts you uncover are common knowledge or not. When in doubt, document your source.

Sample Essay

Thilda Hanstad
Mr. Thoreson
English II
November 20, 2009

Madame Defarge's Model of Sanity

In *A Tale of Two Cities*, published in 1859, Charles Dickens associates madness (or insanity) largely with frenzy and blindly following others. Dickens makes "The revolutionaries appear . . . simply as degraded savages—in fact, as lunatics" when they are immersed in mob activities such as the broken wine cask and the hunting of Foulon (Orwell 15). Given such a definition, it would be easy to claim that Madame Defarge is insane, but Dickens writes about her in such a way that leads us to believe she is very much in her right mind.

Dickens believed in reform, perhaps more than the average person, and he was "much more in sympathy with the ideas of the Revolution than most Englishmen of his time" (Orwell 16). But while Dickens sympathized with the desires of revolutionaries, he did not condone their means of obtaining them. A good Englishman attached to individualist rather than collective, or mob, mentality, believing that reform comes from within and largely through what he might have called "civilized" means, Dickens seems to find it easy to classify the revolutionaries as insane. John Forster wrote in his biography of Dickens that the book relies "less upon character than upon incident, and . . . actors [are] expressed by the story more than they should express themselves by dialogue" (731). No wonder, then, that we are able to draw parallels between otherwise unlike characters who should have little or nothing in common: They are types, not even that so much as products of the revolution, of the mentality of their age, of the systems in place in France and England, demonstrating the causes and, in the case of madness, the effects of such systems. So, at the same time that Dickens shows the need for reform, he shows that the collective cannot achieve its goals effectively or efficiently. It is the individual will that reigns, that either saves or attempts to destroy others most effectively. The mob remains insane and useless.

Neither useless or insane, the methodical and consistent nature of Madame Defarge's knitting seems to indicate a high level (or at least amount) of thought behind her actions. She never fully becomes part of the mob mentality, either, which is Dickens's symbol for complete madness and chaos. Madame Defarge lives a rather solitary life, holding herself above or at least away from public or mob activities, standing against popular opinion at times, focused on a single goal rather than working wholeheartedly toward the collective goals of the revolutionaries. She is never wholeheartedly part of the mob, which is clearly a model of insanity. Of the crowd attacking the Bastille, Dickens writes, "They are headlong, mad, and dangerous" (218). As a group, certainly they are, though Madame Defarge alone is only headlong and dangerous. She is methodical and deliberate, working through years of repression, resentment, and loss, with fairly good reasons for going insane if that is her path. She is one of the only characters who effectively thinks for herself. Manette tries it, but first it lands him in prison and then it nearly ruins his son-in-law, so he gives up.

Darnay, Lucie, Miss Pross, Lorry, Defarge, the Vengeance, all of them follow the crowds, agree with collective opinion, and act according to what others are doing. Madame Defarge strikes out on her own, so Dickens needs her to remain sane in order to counteract the collective and demonstrate the power of an individual as opposed to the madness of the mob. Madame Defarge can lead and inspire the mob, but she tends to watch the ensuing action rather than participate in it. She only takes action after deliberation and usually only when it concerns (we learn late in the novel) her family's history with the Evrémondes. She plots and she plans. She is diabolical and over-the-top, but she is not mad.

Our introduction to Madame Defarge takes place after the frenzy of the spilled cask of wine and provides a glimpse of her sanity. She stays in the shop, picking her teeth and knitting. She remains staid even while the crowd outside shouts, drinks, dances, attempts to quench their literal and metaphorical thirst, and writes "blood" on the wall. Dickens tells us, "There was a character about Madame Defarge, from which one might have predicted that she did not often make mistakes against herself in any of the reckonings over which she presided" (35). She is cold, deliberate, vengeful, but not particularly excitable and certainly not insane.

Even during the fall of the Bastille, she leads a group of women into the frenzy but sets herself outside it: "In the howling universe of passion and contention that seemed to encompass this grim old officer conspicuous in his grey coat and red decoration, there was but one quite steady figure, and that was a woman's" (Dickens 216). Granted, she is about to cut off his head, but she does so with chilling calm, even a certain disturbing dignity.

When the mob goes after Foulon, Madame Defarge is in its midst but again seems apart from the crowd, calling out orders rather than simply following or allowing herself to be pushed. The crowd begins Foulon's torture and execution, and once again it is Madame Defarge who is in control: "[She] let him go—as a cat might have done to a mouse—and silently and composedly looked at him while they made ready, and while he besought her: the women passionately screeching at him all the time, and the men sternly calling out to have him killed with grass in his mouth" (Dickens 222). She is apart from the crowd, physically and psychologically, and Dickens clearly emphasizes the differences between Madame Defarge and the screeching women. If anything, Madame Defarge is eerily composed.

She runs alongside the mob at times, and she certainly inspires and provokes the frenzy more than once, but Madame Defarge remains outside it. She keeps her single-minded focus and acts according to her individual will rather than the collective desire. As much as we may like to believe that her vengeful and bloody activities result from a damaged mind, Madame Defarge is perfectly sane.

Works Cited

Dickens, Charles. *A Tale of Two Cities*. 1859. New York: Barnes & Noble, 2004.

Forster, John. *Life of Charles Dickens*. 1872–74. London: Uitgeverij Diderot, 2005.

Orwell, George. "Charles Dickens." *Dickens, Dali and Others*. New York: Reynal & Hitchcock, 1946. 10–16.

HOW TO WRITE ABOUT CHARLES DICKENS

HIS LEGACY

IN A life that spanned 58 years, Charles Dickens wrote 15 completed novels leaving one unfinished, five Christmas stories, six short story collections, five nonfiction works, two plays, and a book of poetry. His work was incredibly popular, almost from the printing of the first install-ment of his first serial novel, *The Posthumous Papers of the Pickwick Club,* which nearly singlehandedly established the popularity of the serial novel. Dickens's works have never gone out of print. He changed the way we celebrate Christmas, and he made the middle and lower classes viable subjects for the novel, whereas before they had been largely ignored in print. Dickens put pieces of himself into everything he wrote. Perhaps more important, he put pieces of his world into his writings as well.

Our understanding of Victorian England has been greatly influ-enced by elements and images constructed by Dickens. Few scholars, critics, and readers have ever understood Dickens's works as purely fiction. His contemporaries saw themselves and their worlds reflected back at them through his works. The immense popularity of *The Pick-wick Papers,* which by its final installment was selling 40,000 copies, depended on the realism of its characters. Dickens's second novel, *Nicholas Nickleby,* actually generated anger due to the realistic por-trayal of its notorious schoolmaster, Wackford Squeers. Schoolmas-ters wrote letters of complaint and, strangely, of pride, feeling their lives and activities had been encapsulated in Wackford Squeers.

We can begin to understand a bit about Dickens's legacy when we look at his place in popular culture. The amusement park Dickens World opened recently in England, and there is considerable debate whether this is the highest compliment paid an author or if it is Disneyfication in the extreme, actually ignoring the often dark and bleak issues enveloping much of Dickens's work in favor of frivolity and sentimentality. Surely those who lived in Victorian England would wonder why modern English people and tourists would want to experience the sights, sounds, tastes, and, above all, smells of a society and culture that hurtled through the often awkward and painful developments of the Industrial Revolution as well as the aggressive colonization that marked the times. Certainly, though, Dickens World reflects the extent to which Dickens has endeared himself to a century and a half of readers. Just as eager American fans pulled off pieces of Dickens's fur coat during his first visit to the United States, today's readers desire "pieces" of Dickens to experience and possess.

There can be no doubt that the worlds of film and television have embraced Dickens as well. We can assume that Dickens would be pleased by his theatrical presence in our world, as he participated in and appreciated plenty of dramatic productions and recitations in his day, including his famous talks, in which he boisterously read passages from his novels. Film and television adaptations exist for the vast majority of Dickens's works, and in some cases, such as *A Christmas Carol* and *Oliver Twist*, several widely varying adaptations have taken turns being popular.

The publication and popularity of works such as *Mister Pip, Jack Maggs, Evrémonde,* and "Any Friend of Nicholas Nickleby's Is a Friend of Mine" speaks to the endurance of Dickens's words, characters, and ideas. The first three works are recent publications, all books that either continue a Dickens novel or tell the story from a different perspective. Needless to say, readers and writers alike still find Dickens's novels engaging and relevant.

Another tribute to Dickens's timelessness as well as the depth and breadth of his themes is his contribution in more peripheral aspects of popular culture. The television program *Lost* features a character in possession of a tattered copy of *Our Mutual Friend.* Former Beatle Paul McCartney wrote a song in 2005 titled "Jenny Wren," about the character in *Our Mutual Friend.* Dickens's inclusion in today's pop culture seems fitting, given his use of the popular culture of Victorian England in his writing. Even today we recognize words, phrases, and characters from Dickens as part of our language: *humbug, Scrooge,* "Please sir, I want some more," "It was the best of times, it was the worst of times," *Uriah Heep.* All of these words, phrases, and characters have become nearly cliché, so we almost forget their source, or at least do not need to be steeped in Dickens to understand the terms or sayings as intended. Nevertheless, their presence in our culture underscores the important role Dickens and his work still play in our lives.

HIS INFLUENCES

The list of Dickens's influences is extensive and varied. Born in 1812 in Portsmouth, Dickens read voraciously and was so influenced by earlier writers that he named two of his children Alfred D'Orsay Tennyson Dickens and Henry Fielding Dickens. As is evident at least partly in the reading done by David in the semiautobiographical novel *David Copperfield,* Dickens also enjoyed works by Hans Christian Andersen, Tobias Smollett, Oliver Goldsmith, Thomas Carlyle, William Shakespeare, and Daniel Defoe, to name a few. Dickens particularly loved *The Arabian Nights* and often referred to these tales in novels when he wanted to make a point about the importance of imagination.

It is fair to say, for all of us perhaps but especially for Dickens, that his own life was his greatest influence. This is not especially notable except that Dickens had a way of standing apart from his own life, of being participant and observer all at once, thus giving detailed and not always flattering accounts of what he experienced as well as what he observed. From the ages of five to 10, Dickens lived quite happily in Chatham with his family. Of this time he writes, "When I think of it, the picture always rises in my mind of a summer evening, the boys at play in the churchyard, and I sitting on my bed, reading as if for life." From the list of major influences, it is easy to surmise the kinds of books that young Dickens was devouring.

The things that Dickens particularly lacked or desired in his young life often found their way into his writing. When Dickens was 12 years old, his father was imprisoned at Marshalsea, a debtor's prison, and Charles had to leave school and go to work in a blacking factory to help earn what the family owed. In his unpublished autobiography (pieces of which found their way into *David Copperfield*), Dickens writes of those early days in London: "No words can express the secret agony of my soul, as I sunk into this companionship; compared these everyday associated [coworkers] with those of my happier childhood and felt my early hopes of growing up to be a learned and distinguished man, crushed in my breast." Dickens was miserable, working 12 hours a day at the blacking factory, pawning family goods until there was no more money and the rest of the family (except Dickens, who was then forced to live on his own and keep working) had to move to Marshalsea with Dickens's father.

During this time and long after, probably for the rest of his life to some degree, Dickens resented the lack of education more than anything. His older sister was sent to school, but Dickens stayed behind to earn money for the family. Eventually, he visited libraries and educated himself by reading voraciously, but his books still underscore the importance of education for children. More specifically, his books emphasize the importance of education combined with the stimulation of fancy or imagination in children.

It seems that in many ways Dickens was influenced by his entire world. Rarely has there been an individual who observed, absorbed, and related details and events as well as Dickens:

> As he walks he broods, and his broodings become impressions. He meditates on misery living side-by-side with wanton excess. He wanders. He becomes the people he observes. He cannot describe a scene without also becoming a part of it, and living within it. His genius lay in an imaginative sympathy so strong that the world overpowers him; in a linguistic mastery so great that in turn he can recreate both himself and the world. (Ackroyd 168)

HIS WORK

Dickens's work as a whole clearly shows the influences of his times and his professional and personal experiences. A familiarity with his life, however, is not necessary for doing intriguing analysis of Dickens's work. This volume will guide you through general approaches to his fiction. The remainder of this section will discuss some of the notable elements of Dickens's work: the patterns in his use of themes; his construction of

character; the history and context of his writing; the philosophy under-
lying his literature; the experimental forms some of his stories took; and
his use of symbolism, imagery, and language.

Themes

Partly because his own childhood left such a dramatic imprint on him,
Dickens writes a lot about human rights, children's needs, and reform in
general. Dickens is known for writing the lives of middle- and lower-class
people and throwing the spotlight on this group of otherwise largely
invisible or underrepresented (at least in terms of literature) individuals.
Yet Dickens's works contain representatives of a range of social classes,
and it is fascinating to see how Dickens seems to give many upper-class
characters just enough rope to hang themselves.

Dickens, his narrators, and his lower-class characters do not directly
persecute the upper class (usually). Rather, these upper-class characters
get themselves in trouble. Dickens was known to walk through areas of
London in which many would never set foot, and on these walks he not
only contemplated his own life but observed the lives of others. Often
those he observed lived in squalid conditions. Even as a young boy,
he walked alone through slums that Jack the Ripper would later make
famous. Seeing such conditions firsthand no doubt prompted Dickens to
try to help the less fortunate through his writing. There are those who
argue that Dickens did not care as much about changing societal conditions as about exploiting them to make money and win readers. It is
difficult, however, to argue with the fact that Dickens's books prompted
social change, as in the reform of the Yorkshire schools.

Dickens also writes quite often of family. While *David Copperfield* is
perhaps the most insular of Dickens's novels (meaning it has more concern with family than with larger social or political issues), it is not the
only novel to emphasize family in some way. From the Cratchits in *A
Christmas Carol* to Oliver's makeshift family in *Oliver Twist* and Esther
Summerson's desire to know her family in *Bleak House,* Dickens often
establishes a connection between family and a sense of belonging, or
acceptance.

Likewise, there always seems to be a threat of deception in Dickens's
work, most often in the form of a character pretending to be what he or
she is not. This is most apparent in the murder investigation in *Bleak*

House, perhaps, but it is also the crux of Pip's self-realization in *Great Expectations.* The themes of threats (particularly through appearances differing from reality) and family come together at times, as when Pip's newfound fortune and desire to appear a gentleman threaten to break his ties to Joe. These themes come together, also, when a menacing individual lures another with the promise of familial belonging, as exemplified in Fagin wanting Oliver to become part of his "family" of young pickpockets.

Certainly there are many other themes in Dickens's work, including money and debt (no doubt based on his experiences with his father), prison (literal and metaphorical), morality, imagination or fancy, and love, to name a few. Dickens wrote to entertain, but he also wrote to make a point, or to educate if need be, so his books are filled with difficult and often poignant and timely themes.

Characters

Dickens created more than 2,000 characters in his works, ranging from the morally upright heroes (Charles Darnay, David Copperfield, Oliver Twist, Esther Summerson, Nicholas Nickleby, and Sam Weller) to degenerates who end up either punished or transformed (Gaffer Hexam, Jo, Fagin, Bill Sikes, Alfred Jingle, Madame Defarge, Scrooge). Sometimes Dickens's characters become nearly mythical, like Jenny Wren or even Bill Sikes, or frighteningly real, such as Wackford Squeers, Madame Defarge, Mr. Gradgrind, and Wilkins Micawber. A few characters, such as David Copperfield and Sydney Carton, even closely resemble Dickens as he envisioned and remembered himself.

Characters are the heart of Dickens's work, often tied so closely with setting that one would hardly survive (or at least be nearly as compelling) without the other. This perhaps explains why Dickens's works are rarely updated or adapted into modern settings. Although the messages and often the characters in Dickens's works are still recognizable and even applicable to us today, Dickens's characters seem to derive an energy from their historical context, and one is loath to drag them into another time or place. Imagine what Mrs. Jellyby's philanthropy would look like without the context of 19th-century missionary zeal. Certainly Mrs. Jellybys exist in the world today, but the precise level of humor that infuses her character does not survive outside the context of the British Empire and the Angel in the House ideology, which posited a romanticized vision of the perfect Victorian wife and mother.

One argument about Dickens's characters that is becoming more and more popular concerns the ways in which he treats (or more accurately, does not treat) female characters. Some argue that Dickens ignores them and lets men steal the limelight, while others believe that women are often the driving forces without being given credit (at least by other characters). The debate perhaps stems from the many contrasting female characters in Dickens's works. A female character like Lucie Manette Darnay in *A Tale of Two Cities* seems decorative, while Miss Pross and Madame Defarge burst with life. Perhaps the dichotomy of Dickens's portrayals of women is best displayed in *David Copperfield*. Dora is (like Lucie) decorative, flimsy, and weak (even Dora recognizes this about herself), while Agnes is wise and substantive and Aunt Betsey is entirely her own vigorous person.

Surely Dickens's treatment of female characters demonstrates Victorian ideologies that he could not escape entirely. There are practicalities to the matter, as well. David Copperfield, Nicholas Nickleby, and Oliver Twist are male rather than female title characters because women could not move as freely in the world and were generally more confined and thus less likely to encounter interesting characters like Vincent Crummles. The restrictions placed on Victorian women's lives and freedom would limit Dickens's scope in significant ways. And yet, *Bleak House* centers largely on women—Esther, Ada, and Lady Dedlock. Even Miss Flite is no small part of the storyline, so there are examples of strong, major female characters carrying large portions of a Dickens book.

Other examples of integral female characters abound. In *A Tale of Two Cities*, women (Lucie—mother and daughter—and Madame Defarge's sister) provide the impetus for many actions and also carry out some important actions themselves (Madame Defarge and Miss Pross). In *Hard Times*, it is Louisa who shows true potential and Sissy who turns things around, both contrasting greatly with the languor and helplessness of Mrs. Gradgrind.

The Pickwick Papers, on the other hand, has been read as nearly misogynist. Certainly Dickens's first novel is critical of women (or at least a certain type of woman), but the book almost seems to be striving to avoid women entirely. If the adage "Write what you know" is true, then it makes sense that Dickens would focus (especially early in his career) on male characters.

Throughout his career, Dickens created characters that covered the spectrum of good and evil, whether male or female. As a testament to his skill, Dickens's novel with arguably the least memorable or lesser-known characters would be *A Tale of Two Cities*, which is also one of his most widely read. Scholars and critics who contend that *A Tale of Two Cities* stands out from Dickens's other work do so because this is his least character-driven book. Characters act because the actions and settings force them to, not because they are psychologically developed.

Even those who have not read Dickens are likely familiar with Tiny Tim, Scrooge, Fagin, Oliver, Miss Havisham, Pip, and David Copperfield. Their characterizations have become iconic—standing for something larger and more meaningful than just one person. They have endured myriad adaptations, and even in the most modernized of these, their essential characters remain similar and faithful to Dickens's original vision of them.

History and Context

Dickens both reflected and helped create what we now conceptualize as Victorian England. His stories and characters do not seem to work as well out of context, not because the story and message are not timeless or universal, but partly because the world around the characters is vivid and alive in ways that seem simply magical.

Certainly Dickens wrote to entertain, but he also wrote to instruct and, perhaps more important, to provoke readers' emotions and inspire reform. It is impossible to read Dickens and not detect his views on many of the issues of his day: child labor, workhouses, factory workers, class structures and divisions, missionary zeal, education, revolution, imagination, virtue, disability, health and sanitation, prison systems, court and legal systems, charity, unions, marriage, orphans, and crime.

One of the most jarring and wonderful things about a Dickens novel is its realistic root. The specific jobs or circumstances of the characters really did exist in Victorian England: There were Gaffer Hexams making their living dredging dead bodies from the river; there were Oliver Twists left at the mercy of an unforgiving social welfare system; there were Mrs. Jellybys, more concerned with misguided efforts to civilize Africa than the well-being of their own families; there were Wackford Squeerses, proven by the response to *Nicholas Nickleby* by schoolmasters who felt that Dickens was surely writing about them; there were Mr. Gradgrinds, as this character was modeled on Jeremy Bentham, one of the leaders of the utilitarians; there were Magwitches and Pips, Pickwicks and Wellers.

Philosophy and Ideas

Dickens is perhaps most notable for his arguments against particular philosophies of his time: utilitarianism or some revolutionary ideologies, for example. Dickens believed in reform, though in a systematic, regulated sort of way. His work focuses on the individual and a person's power to change and/or to create and influence change, or sometimes simply to tolerate and endure change.

Dickens was diligent and imaginative, and he looked for these qualities in others, too. The vehemence with which he defended and promoted the play of imagination and childhood in such works as *Hard Times* and *Oliver Twist* suggests that the author himself never completely grew up, an assessment that he most likely would have been happy to hear.

Dickens also wrote often about self-knowledge. Characters such as Pip and Esther and David ultimately come to an understanding about who they truly are, and not until then is the novel able to conclude. *David Copperfield* is the obvious manifestation of Dickens's own search for self-knowledge, but close readers will see that there is a piece of Dickens in everything he wrote, suggesting that his search for self-knowledge never quite ended.

Form and Genre

Form and genre play enormous roles in shaping Dickens's writing and his reputation. Writers employed the serial novel form both before and after Dickens, but not as captivatingly. Whether written as a monthly or weekly serial, a Dickens work reads like a novel rather than a series of installments. The exception to this is *The Pickwick Papers*, which represents Dickens's first attempt at the form, and even then in the end he is able to deliver a cohesive story.

To study genre properly in Dickens's writing, the reader needs to pull each book apart to find the sections or bits and pieces that might fall into particular categories. *Nicholas Nickleby,* for example, is in itself a bildungsroman, a novel about the growth and development of its protagonist, but it also contains farce and melodrama. Yet these genres do not even address the episodic stories featured in the novel. Each Dickens novel is a conglomeration in some way of several genres, making it hard to classify Dickens's oeuvre as anything but genuinely great writing. Other lesser writers would potentially tangle themselves up in the numerous plot threads, but Dickens appears to manage them as well as the perils of serialization (Dickens tried to stay about six weeks ahead of each installment's appearance in print) and use of various genres to tell, ultimately, one story. Dickens makes it look effortless and purposeful.

Language, Symbols, and Imagery

Any discussion of language, symbols, and imagery in Dickens must begin with the fog of *Bleak House,* which somehow naturally leads to the marshes of *Great Expectations* and the mist on the river of *Our Mutual Friend.* Dickens was a master of characterization, but readers forget that setting in Dickens plays a large role, too. Nineteenth-century writer and critic George Gissing demonstrates Dickens's influence best when he writes about his own perceptions of London:

> London of that time differed a good deal from the London of today; it was still more unlike the town in which Dickens lived when writing his earlier books; but the localities which he made familiar to his readers were, on the whole, those which had undergone least change. . . . I had but to lean, at night, over one of the City bridges, and the broad flood spoke to me in the very tones of the master. . . . To this day, they would bear for me something of that old association; but four and twenty years ago, when I had no London memories of my own, they were simply the scenes of Dickens's novels. . . . The very atmosphere declared him; if I gasped in a fog, was it not Mr. Guppy's "London particular"?—if the wind pierced me under a black sky, did I not see Scrooge's clerk trotting off to his Christmas Eve in Somers Town? . . . In time I came to see London with my own eyes, but how much better when I saw it with those of Dickens. (9)

It becomes hard to tell which images of England—and particularly London—stem from historical fact and which have been drawn from Dickens's novels. One expression of the talent that Dickens possessed is that separating fact from artifice does not really matter. History and fiction combine in his work to give us what perhaps becomes an even more nuanced and complex picture of his world.

The world that Dickens creates surrounds characters and envelops readers. His mastery of language is equally apparent in the symbolism of want and ignorance in *A Christmas Carol*, of fire in *Hard Times*, and of knitting in *A Tale of Two Cities*. He captured dialects to convey characters such as Sam Weller in all their colloquial glory and left readers with startling and unshakable images such as Oliver asking for more.

Compare and Contrast

Dickens created more than 2,000 characters in his works, making it relatively easy to find points of comparison and contrast among them. Characters from the same book, for example Fagin and Sikes from *Oliver Twist*, are often viewed in terms of one another. Perhaps the best known comparison/contrast study of Dickens's characters is about Sydney Carton and Charles Darnay from *A Tale of Two Cities*. Are they, ultimately and essentially, the same person? Are they both representative of Dickens as he viewed himself? These are fascinating questions to answer as you develop theories.

Of course it is also possible to compare Dickens's characters from different books. Is Louisa Gradgrind from *Hard Times* another manifestation of Estella from *Great Expectations*? What connections can be found between Esther Summerson of *Bleak House* and Lizzie Hexam of *Our Mutual Friend*? Clearly, there is a wealth of information, in terms of number of characters and their various quirks, traits, and developments from which to choose.

Naturally, critics like to compare Dickens's books as a whole, as well. Why are *Bleak House, Hard Times,* and *Our Mutual Friend* examples of what scholars call his darker works? How do they compare with *Nicholas Nickleby, The Pickwick Papers,* and *David Copperfield*? While a complete stack of Dickens's works might look intimidating, these novels offer nearly infinite opportunities for students and scholars to weave together and pull apart characters or other elements found in one book or several.

FINAL WORDS

A little girl, upon learning of Dickens's death, is rumored to have asked, "Does this mean Father Christmas is dead?" [Callow 13]. Sentiments like this help us to begin to see the depth and breadth of Dickens's influence on his time as well as our own. Dickens was buried in Westminster Abbey, appropriately near the busts of Shakespeare and John Milton. He had wished to be buried quietly near Gad's Hill, his final home, but the English wanted to send off this iconic writer with a flourish and lay him to rest in a place of appropriate honor. A quiet ceremony preceded his burial in Westminster Abbey, followed by a two-day procession of people paying their respects. Several visitors left ragged bundles of wildflowers, a sure and delicate symbol of the reverence held for Dickens by those with little or no means.

Works Cited

Ackroyd, Peter. *Dickens.* New York: Harper Collins, 1990.

"Charles Dickens." The Victorian Web. Available online. URL: http://www.vic torianweb.org/authors/dickens.index.html. Retrieved November 28, 2007.

Callow, Simon. *Dickens' Christmas: A Victorian Celebration.* New York: Harry N. Abrams, 2003.

Forster, John. *Life of Charles Dickens.* 1872–74. London: Uitgeverij Diderot, 2005.

Gissing, George. *The Immortal Dickens.* 1925. New York: Kraus Reprint, 1969.

Smiley, Jane. *Charles Dickens.* New York: Viking, 2002.

THE PICKWICK PAPERS

READING TO WRITE

WHAT IS the proper title of this work? Is it *The Pickwick Papers*? Is it *The Posthumous Papers of the Pickwick Club*? Why are scholars so concerned about its "correct" title? This alone makes an interesting subject for study. Investigate the history of each title, and note the significance of each. How does each title lead to a particular understanding of what is contained within the novel? Why and how was the title changed?

The Pickwick Papers is unique for many reasons, not the least of which is the fluctuation of its title. Published in 1836–37, this is Dickens's first novel, his first attempt at serialization on this scale. Many critics would say that the disjointed nature of the beginning parts of *The Pickwick Papers* reveals that Dickens is clearly inexperienced in this particular form of writing. According to Dickens's contemporary G. K. Chesterton, Dickens would not have minded such criticism: "He was more concerned to prove that he could write well than to prove that he could write this particular book well" (17). Critics seem to agree, however, that by the end of the novel he has tied up the loose ends and created a rather fluid reading experience that would only improve through the course of writing his subsequent novels in the same serialized manner.

Without a doubt, critics and scholars agree that it is the characters in *The Pickwick Papers* that remain in readers' thoughts and seem to dwell even in their lives somehow. In Dickens's time, people regarded the characters as if they were in fact real, and, indeed, in some ways they were in that they had been borrowed from Dickens's actual experiences and observations. Dickens aided this interpretation by referring to

Mr. Pickwick as "our excellent old friend" (558) late in the book, as if to include readers in the Pickwick Club and acknowledge that Pickwick actually exists.

It seems that Dickens wrote himself into every one of his novels in some way. If that is true here, then it is generally understood that together the characters of Mr. Pickwick and Sam Weller make up Dickens's self-portrait. What might these characterizations reveal about Dickens? Conduct some research into Dickens's life, philosophies, behavior, and ideas to determine whether his characterizations of Pickwick and Sam also apply to himself to any degree. It might be important to note here that Dickens is known for his exaggeration.

Characters in *The Pickwick Papers* also help to create the colloquial nature of the story. At the time of the publication of *The Pickwick Papers*, it was relatively rare to find an author writing about lower classes, but Dickens wrote about nearly all classes of people in one way or another. This made him very popular with average people, who finally found themselves reflected in print.

The party at Bath in chapter 35 is a pivotal scene for several reasons. We first get a clear characterization of Angelo Cyrus Bantam, Esquire, M.C., through his description of the party to come: "The ball-nights in Ba–ath are moments snatched from Paradise; rendered bewitching by music, beauty, elegance, fashion, etiquette, and—and—above all, by the absence of tradespeople, who are quite inconsistent with Paradise; and who have an amalgamation of themselves at the Guildhall every fort-night, which is, to say the least, remarkable" (Dickens 465). How would Dickens's first readers have interpreted this description? Who were the tradespeople in Dickens's time, and what would readers' relationships with them have been? Would upper-class readers have understood that they are being made fun of in this section?

Once the party at Bath begins, Dickens treats us to a description of the various groups in attendance:

> In the tea-room, and hovering round the card-tables, were a vast number of queer old ladies and decrepid old gentlemen, discussing all the small talk and scandal of the day, with a relish and gusto which sufficiently bespoke the intensity of the pleasure they derived from the occupation. Mingled with these groups, were three or four matchmaking mammas,

appearing to be wholly absorbed by the conversation in which they were taking part, but failing not from time to time to cast an anxious sidelong glance upon their daughters, who, remembering the maternal injunction to make the best use of their youth, had already commenced incipient flirtations in the mislaying of scarves, putting on gloves, setting down cups, and so forth; slight matters apparently, but which may be turned to surprisingly good account by expert practitioners.

Lounging near the doors, and in remote corners, were various knots of silly young men, displaying various varieties of puppyism and stupidity; amusing all sensible people near them with their folly and conceit; and happily thinking themselves the objects of general admiration. A wise and merciful dispensation which no good man will quarrel with.

And lastly, seated on some of the back benches, where they had already taken up their positions for the evening, were divers unmarried ladies past their grand climacteric, who, not dancing because there were no partners for them, and not playing cards lest they should be set down as irretrievably single, were in the favourable situation of being able to abuse everybody without reflecting on themselves. In short, they could abuse everybody, because everybody was there. (468)

A number of questions come to mind after reading this passage. Answering these questions can lead to very interesting paper topics. What is *puppyism*? How does the context alone explain to us what this word means? What kind of connotation does the word convey? Note the final words "everybody was there." We know that everybody, in the literal sense, was certainly not there, partly because of Bantam's explanation for the exclusion of tradespeople. Why is this group still widely considered to be "everybody"? How does this one line, in connection with Dickens's descriptions and the continuation of the scene, demonstrate class differences in the 19th century? What tone does Dickens convey in this passage? How does he feel about the people attending such a party? Is he impressed by them? Why or why not? Which words indicate his feelings? How does the passage relate gender differences to us? Why are there no men "seated on some of the back benches," waiting to find partners and desperate not to appear "irretrievably single"?

Whatever readers think of *The Pickwick Papers*, it is not a novel one can easily forget. Many scholars feel that it represents the essence of

Dickens, and that elements in his subsequent novels can all be found in *The Pickwick Papers*. Chesterton perhaps sums it up best: "Before he wrote a single real story, he had a kind of vision. It was a vision of the Dickens world—a maze of white roads, a map full of fantastic towns, thundering coaches, clamorous market-places, uproarious inns, strange and swaggering figures. That vision was *Pickwick*" (16).

TOPICS AND STRATEGIES

This section addresses various possible topics for writing about *The Pickwick Papers* as well as general methods for approaching these topics. These lists are in no way exhaustive and are meant to provide a jumping-off point rather than an answer key. Use these suggestions to find your own ideas and form your own analyses. All topics discussed in this chapter could turn into very good papers.

Themes

Themes are prevalent in *The Pickwick Papers*, likely because it was Dickens's first attempt at a serial novel, and therefore each installment tends to dwell on a particular topic or convey a particular message (at least in the beginning of the novel). At the same time, there is no pervasive theme throughout the entire novel. *The Pickwick Papers* stands out among Dickens's other novels because people perceive it as much more of a series of incidents involving the same people than as a cohesive novel such as *Bleak House* or *Great Expectations*. Near the middle of *The Pickwick Papers* it appears that Dickens figured out how to tell one big story rather than several small ones, but the book is nonetheless an obvious first attempt at a serial novel and simply does not read as seamlessly as his later work. Taken for what it is, however, *The Pickwick Papers* is a glowing demonstration of many of Dickens's talents: realistic characters (in fact, readers continue to refer to Pickwick and his friends as if they are actual people and not fictional characters!), social commentary (Dickens's views of marriage and prison are particularly evident), and, perhaps most important, theme.

In the case of *The Pickwick Papers*, serialization lent itself well to the establishment of several important themes. Each chapter, scene, vignette, or incident in the book seems to carry with it a particular comment. Just a few of the themes identified in *The Pickwick Papers* include

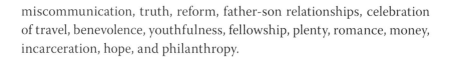

miscommunication, truth, reform, father-son relationships, celebration of travel, benevolence, youthfulness, fellowship, plenty, romance, money, incarceration, hope, and philanthropy.

Sample Topics:

1. **Miscommunication/misunderstanding:** Why does the plot of *The Pickwick Papers* need to depend so heavily on miscommunication and/or misunderstanding?

   So many events and plot points in *The Pickwick Papers* center on or stem from miscommunications or misunderstandings that you may start to wonder how readers are able to make any sense of it. The fact is that readers are generally expected to know better than the characters, either because readers have additional information or because readers are presumably smarter than the characters. What effect do the miscommunications and misunderstandings have on the book in general? Readers' perceptions of the characters? How is it that a fairly oblivious man like Mr. Pickwick, whose life is full of misunderstandings and miscommunications, ends up being so realistic and likable?

2. **Truth:** How important is truth in this book? Do characters want truth, or do they just want to have a good time?

   Mr. Winkle is supposedly a good sportsman. Alfred Jingle manipulates and lies. Characters put up with such deceptions because they are often too ashamed to tell the truth. Nearly all of the characters operate on falsehoods to some degree, either accidentally or with intentions to deceive.

3. **Reform:** Are the characters in *The Pickwick Papers* set in their ways, or is Dickens able to demonstrate that people really can change for the better?

   Many readers find it hard to believe that such characters as Alfred Jingle and Job Trotter have sincerely reformed by the end of the book. If reform rings false to readers, is it because Dickens is trying to convey an idea that people like these men can never really change? Part of Dickens clearly believed in reform on some level, because most of his books advocate some sort of societal, legal, or social reform.

Characters

Characters in *The Pickwick Papers* are usually not what or who they claim to be, making them particularly interesting subjects for study. How well do any of these characters know themselves? You might look at the methods Dickens uses for distinguishing one character from another, particularly those who might otherwise be very similar. How does Dickens develop the differences and similarities between the men of the Pickwick Club? Do these differences and similarities bode well for any character in particular? Why or why not?

You can also study the ways in which a character changes throughout the book. Pickwick is perhaps the clearest example, but you may decide to look at a character whose changes are much more subtle—Sam, for instance. You will need not only to make note of any changes in character that you find significant; you will also need to provide your interpretation of these changes. Dickens's writing techniques are another compelling aspect of character. Which words, phrases, or settings are typically associated with a particular character?

The characters are without question the driving force behind *The Pickwick Papers*. Readers' responses to the work as the first installments came out were sluggish but rose dramatically with the introduction of Sam Weller. Many characters in the novel provide various forms of comic relief, but readers then and now seem to latch onto Sam as the voice of reason and much-needed perspective. At the same time, it is impossible to forget Mr. Pickwick, Alfred Jingle, Bob Sawyer, Mr. Tupman, Mr. Winkle, and Mr. Snodgrass, and readers responded (eventually) so enthusiastically to the book surely because they found themselves and their acquaintances reflected somewhere within it.

Nineteenth-century writer and critic George Gissing claims that:

> Among the various endowments essential to a novelist of the first rank, the most important is that which at once declares itself to critical and

uncritical reader alike; the power of creating persons. Force or charm of style, adroitness in story-telling, the gift of observation and of acumen, these are all subservient to that imaginative vigour which through language fashions a human being, and indues [sic] him with identity as unmistakable as that of our living acquaintances. Were it only by the figures of Sam and Tony Weller, Dickens would in this book have proved himself a born master in the art of fiction. (47)

Sample Topics:

1. **Mr. Pickwick:** Is Pickwick innocent, ignorant, or simply naive?

Scholars have several opinions about Mr. Pickwick's character. G. K. Chesterton claims that Pickwick "changes from a silly buffoon to . . . a solid merchant" throughout the novel (19). Poet and critic W. H. Auden discusses ways in which the plot centers on the figure of Pickwick:

> It is the story of a man who is innocent[;] who has not eaten of the Tree of the Knowledge of Good and Evil and is, therefore, living in Eden. He then eats of the Tree, [and] he becomes conscious of the reality of Evil but, instead of falling from innocence into sin—this is what makes him a mythical character—he changes from an innocent child into an innocent adult who no longer lives in an imaginary Eden of his own but in the real and fallen world. (408)

Is Mr. Pickwick actually mythical? What are his realistic and unrealistic qualities? Remember to ground your perceptions of his character in the framework of the early 19th century.

2. **Alfred Jingle:** Is he a bad guy or just a clever person dealing with a particularly naive group?

Alfred Jingle does not obey the rules of friendship that are such a prevalent part of this novel. His jerky, stream-of-consciousness speech indicates random associations and is perhaps a metaphor for Jingle's random associations with people. In what ways does the plot of *The Pickwick Papers* center on Jingle, and/ or in what ways is he a secondary character? Do you believe in his power to reform himself? Does Dickens want you to? Why or why not?

3. **Sam Weller:** Is Sam the only truly and consistently honest character in the novel? If so, why would Dickens choose him to stand out from this crowd of characters?

The Pickwick Papers did not sell well until Sam's character appeared in chapter 10, or the fourth installment. Sam provides a fresh perspective and seems to see things more clearly than the other men do. He uses lots of expanded clichés, which were very popular and became known as "Wellerisms." Examples of Wellerisms include "Business first, pleasure arterwards, as King Richard the Third said wen he stabbed the t'other king in the Tower, afore he smothered the babbies" (Dickens 317), or "out with it, as the father said to the shild, wen he swallowed a farden" (Dickens 148).

These Wellerisms elaborate on regular speech in a way that rang true to the actual wit of the English poor: "Sam Weller is the great symbol in English literature of the populace peculiar to England" (Chesterton 21). Why is Sam such a popular character? What would happen to the other characters without Sam around? Why?

History and Context

The Pickwick Papers is, in some ways, a story (or series of stories) out of time; in other words, the book showcases human follies in ways that still may apply and are not only relatable in their 19th-century context. Yet, of course, there are elements in the book that benefit from knowledge of their history and context. Dickens scholar Peter Ackroyd writes: "The impact of topical and journalistic events on *The Pickwick Papers* has never been properly studied (perhaps with good reason, since it would take a lifetime to pick out all the obliquities and passing references) but there is no doubt that this monthly series was very much 'up to the minute' in its details and references" (192). For the purposes of writing a paper, it is worth taking a cue from Ackroyd and choosing one or two "topical and journalistic events" from the novel to study in detail in terms of its relation to English life in the 19th century. Dickens is famous for writing books containing messages about the needs of his own time. Can we find such messages in his very first novel?

As *The Pickwick Papers* was Dickens's first book, he had yet to master the technique for which he would eventually become known—blending historical reality and fiction so as to make them nearly indistinguishable from each other. *The Pickwick Papers* does not contain the rather large-scale references to history and context that *A Tale of Two Cities* or even *Our Mutual Friend* do. Perhaps, then, one of the most interesting aspects of history and context for *The Pickwick Papers* is the author's background. How was *The Pickwick Papers* conceived? What was happening (or had happened) in Dickens's life that might parallel some of the events in the book? What circumstances in England in the early 1830s may have helped *The Pickwick Papers* become so wildly popular? What precedent does this book set for Dickens's novel writing and/or writing in general?

Sample Topics:

1. **Fleet Prison:** In what ways do the sections in or about the prison become less about the characters and more about criticizing the system?

   It was possible, at this time, to buy your way out of punishments. "Witness . . . Dickens's hatred of social injustice, as evidenced by a judicial system that treated debtors worse than felons" (Russo xiii).

2. **Writing context:** How might the circumstances under which Dickens wrote *The Pickwick Papers* have affected the work, particularly at the beginning?

   Dickens wrote *The Pickwick Papers* during a time of great upheaval. The initial understanding was that the illustrator's work would lead the way, and Dickens's writing would focus on those drawings. Dickens very quickly took over production and made sure that his writing came before Robert Seymour's illustrations. Seymour killed himself shortly thereafter, but the work continued. Public reception of the work was moderate until Dickens added Sam Weller, after which sales soared. All this time Dickens was only 24 years old.

3. **Bardell-Pickwick case:** Which parts of this case are taken from reality? Why?

The court case in which Mr. Pickwick and Mrs. Bardell become embroiled is modeled after a real court case on which Dickens had been writing. For some of the details of the actual case, see Philip Hobsbaum's *A Reader's Guide to Charles Dickens*. Which facts of the case does Dickens change? Why? Why would this case have caught the attention of both Dickens and the reading public? Would most of Dickens's readers have recognized this case as real? If so, what is the significance of that fact?

Philosophy and Ideas

Investigating the philosophy and ideas of any novel requires us to consider broad implications of ideas contained in the novel and then to investigate how and why the author comments on these ideas and/or philosophies. A book such as *The Pickwick Papers* can be misleading because of its apparent simplicity, but even these scenes in the lives of bumbling men contain any number of universal ideas.

Just a few possibilities for further investigation here include benevolence, youthfulness, fellowship, plenty, romance, money, fatherhood, incarceration, philanthropy, hope, providence, masculinity, fraternity, and poetic justice. Fraternity, for example, contains the idea of an ideal brotherhood, a particular bond among men. Certainly we can find several examples of fraternity between Pickwick, Sam Weller, Tupman, Winkle, and Snodgrass. The word *fraternity* may have also held historical associations for Dickens's readers, both then and now. During the French Revolution of the late 18th century, "Liberty, Equality, Fraternity" was the anthem of revolutionaries, declaring their strongest desires and rationale for overthrowing the French monarchy and government. What associations would Dickens's first readers have had with the word *fraternity*? Would they have understood it as something to be desired or as a threat to national security? What understanding did (or do) women have with such a word/concept? In what ways does the philosophy behind fraternity exclude women, and in what ways can the word become gender neutral, standing for something more than simply a group of men?

Sample Topics:

1. **Masculinity:** What does it mean (or take) to be a man?

Some of the women characters seem harsher than the Pickwick Club members, yet the book clearly relishes in masculine enjoyments or male bonding. What did it mean to be masculine in 1836? How would Dickens's readers have regarded the masculinity of these characters? Is Dickens poking fun at the manliness of these characters, or do they possess admirably male qualities?

2. **Boyishness/fraternity:** What point is Dickens trying to make by emphasizing the activities and associations of groups of men?

Certainly women in the novel appear as peripheral characters, important only in the ways that they impact the lives of the men. The concept of fraternity had historical implications by Dickens's time, tied to the late 18th-century French Revolution. Does Dickens seem to be promoting this sense of boyishness and fraternity, or is he advocating something else?

3. **Poetic justice:** Do characters in *The Pickwick Papers* always get what is coming to them?

Mrs. Bardell ends up in prison and is then dependent on Pickwick, which seems just retribution for her behavior and accusations. Does this kind of poetic justice happen again anywhere else in the novel? Which types of characters seem to suffer the consequences of their actions?

Form and Genre

Some of the longest-standing scholarly debates about *The Pickwick Papers* concern its form and/or genre. It is often referred to as a novel, yet for many, *The Pickwick Papers* does not comfortably fit that description. At the same time, *The Pickwick Papers* is slightly more than a series of scenes or a book of short stories, since eventually the events in the book do begin to fold and flow together into a more coherent whole. Dickens's biographer Peter Ackroyd notes that "in a sense [*The Pickwick Papers*] became a work of journalism as well as of fiction, and the audience increased immeasurably when it was realised that such a work did not have the conventional inhibitions of ordinary fiction" (190). More than anything, *The Pickwick Papers* seems to be an evolving text. Reading it reveals Dickens's series of decisions concerning form and genre, and these decisions revolved largely around conceptions of serial writing.

Dickens was hired by publisher Chapman and Hall to write a series of stories based on Robert Seymour's drawings. The negotiation process led to the opposite situation: Seymour (eventually replaced by Hablot Knight Browne) would create a series of drawings based on Dickens's writing. It seems as if Dickens began writing vignettes that happened always to center on the same characters but then in the fourth installment had a better idea. The introduction of Sam Weller led to enormous reader appeal and, perhaps more interestingly, a more developed, cohesive story. Dickens clearly saw the benefits of this change once sales increased from 400 copies to the eventual 40,000 at last printing, and he would go on to become the master of the serialized novel (Ackroyd 196).

Sample Topics:

　　1. **Interpolated tales:** What do the interpolated tales—"The True Legend of Prince Bladud" or "The Convict's Return," for example—add to or take away from the novel as a whole?

　　Tales told by various characters are often dark compared to the action of the novel. Do they become "absurd and grotesque stories intent on diverting, misappropriating, and misdirecting the characters, the story, and the good reader with their violence, melodrama and ghosts" (Bowen 48), or do these tales have other functions in the novel?

2. **Comedy:** How does Dickens help readers distinguish between comedy and serious social criticism in *The Pickwick Papers*?

Some scholars claim that this is the funniest of Dickens's novels. Perhaps that is due to the farce in the book, consisting often of "men trapped, hiding and finally exposed, in sexually compromising circumstances" (Parker 108). Yet, there are serious elements to the book as well, particularly regarding issues of class and money. What techniques does Dickens use to cue readers to laugh? Is humor in the serialized novel more popular than drama? Are there occasions where the humor in *The Pickwick Papers* does not translate to 21st-century sensibilities?

3. **Serial form:** Are there indications in the novel that this was Dickens's testing ground for the serialized novel?

This is a form of writing that Dickens would go on to perfect. In what ways does *The Pickwick Papers* read like a series of stories, and in what ways does it read like a cohesive whole? What, in your estimation, is the element that brings the story together as a novel? Why has *The Pickwick Papers* never been sold as a series of stories rather than a novel?

4. **Bildungsroman:** What do the characters in this novel learn through their experiences? What, if anything, does Dickens expect readers to learn?

A bildungsroman is a novel about a young person's journey through struggles to reach maturity. Mr. Pickwick is not necessarily young, yet he probably learns more than any other character. Does he ever reach maturity as his society defines the term? Does he ever reach maturity as readers today define the term? Why or why not? *The Pickwick Papers* is certainly a novel about learning. Readers follow Mr. Pickwick's journey to knowledge, although where he ends up on the spectrum of knowledgeable, worldly men is still open for debate.

Language, Symbols, and Imagery

The Pickwick Papers is a fascinating novel to study in terms of style. It is often, for example, studied for its utilization of language. The novel in some ways centers on language itself, or the act of writing. Pickwick is threatened by the driver after writing down their conversation about the driver's horse. Sam writes a touching letter to his father after Sam's stepmother dies. Many problems are created and solved through language, particularly writing. The use of language and writing in this book also reveals much about the characters. Pickwick records nearly everything onto paper, yet he is so literal minded that he does not understand much of it. Sam, on the other hand, seems to be Pickwick's opposite on these terms. He does not write very often, but he understands the world around him quite well. Sam also uses more elaborate speech, incorporating more metaphors and similes, than other characters.

Studying any text in terms of language, symbols, and imagery requires you to avoid summarizing the text unnecessarily and focus instead on the ways in which the work is written. It no longer concerns what the novel is about but rather how it is written. Studying the language of a text allows you to look carefully at syntax, word choice, and general diction. You might, for example, study the various accents and colloquialisms expressed by characters in *The Pickwick Papers* to help you delve more deeply into Dickens's characterizations. What does a character's use of language reveal about him or her? Language might also mean a search into the words most commonly used to describe a character, a setting, or an activity. Look at the tone (or mood) surrounding the Pickwick Club, for example, and pinpoint elements of language that help create that tone. Then take it a step further by discussing why it is significant that such a mood is connected with these particular characters. Remember that in this book the readers are often in on the joke before or instead of the characters, so a character's response may be heartfelt, whereas if the character knew what the readers know, the same response might be sarcastic or more cynical.

Sample Topics:

1. **Time:** What is the significance of Dickens's use (or misuse) of time in the novel?

Time in *The Pickwick Papers* should not be taken too seriously. The action is chronologically inaccurate; often, more or less time has passed than we have been told, or events are brought up anachronistically. This feeling of time folding over and back upon itself helps to give the world of the Pickwick Club a fantastical aura and seems to establish it firmly within the bounds of fiction. Yet, the characters and action were and are regularly mistaken for actual people and events. Does this irony indicate that the novel's use of realism in regard of time is irrelevant?

2. **Irony:** Are characters in *The Pickwick Papers* ever aware of the irony of their situations?

A number of instances of irony occur in this novel. For example, in chapter 34, Pickwick lectures others about causing romantic problems, even while Mrs. Bardell is suing him because he misled her into believing that he was proposing marriage. Is Pickwick aware of the irony of his lecture? Why is a character's awareness of irony important to readers' perceptions of the character and action? Why would Dickens want to make certain characters appear rather ignorant, even of their own words and actions?

Compare and Contrast Essays

The Pickwick Papers offers no shortage of characters, scenes, and various literary elements to be compared and contrasted with one another. Of course, you will find similarities and differences between two characters in a novel just as you would find similarities and differences between any two people you know. So what? You must draw conclusions from those similarities and/or differences.

Often, the most interesting comparison or contrast papers stem from the least likely or obvious pairings. In this case, you might compare Pickwick with Sam Weller, or even Sam and Tony Weller with each other. An advantage to using *The Pickwick Papers* for this type of paper is Dickens's use of distinct scenes or vignettes, which offer opportunities for comparison in themselves. How, for example, is the "dueling" scene comparable to Mr. Pickwick's "proposal" to Mrs. Bardell?

It is important to remember that comparison and contrast papers involve more than simply making lists of similarities and differences.

You need to explore theories and interpretations (yours and/or others') regarding reasons behind similarities and differences as well as their overall effect on the novel.

Sample Topics:

1. **Women and men:** Who is in charge here?

The issues that Mr. Pickwick faces thanks to Mrs. Bardell are the most obvious example of troubles between men and women, but conflicts between the genders run rampant through this book. Are the men always at the mercy of women, who often have hidden motives and/or tendencies for revenge? Are the men afraid of women? Afraid they will lose power to them or around them? With which gender does Dickens seem to expect readers to sympathize? Why and how can you tell?

2. **Marriage and courtship:** Does *The Pickwick Papers* seem to suggest a series of courtships rather than eventual marriage?

It seems that in this book marriage is negative, but courtship is lovely and desirable. Incidents addressing marriage in some fashion are usually problematic, and marriage does not seem inevitable for these characters the way it does for characters in other Dickens novels or other 19th-century novels. What relationship status does Dickens seem to be advocating here?

3. **Freedom versus prison:** How creatively does Dickens address both freedom and imprisonment?

Richard Russo calls *The Pickwick Papers* "nothing less than a jailbreak of the writer's imagination" (xvi). Certainly the book also contains characters who are literally imprisoned. How are prison and freedom addressed in ways other than the literal? For example, the alternative to imprisonment (or feelings of imprisonment) seems to be travel. Who gets to travel the most? Why? Which characters seem to be imprisoned by their own thoughts, limitations, or prejudices? Why?

Bibliography and Online Resource for *The Pickwick Papers*

Ackroyd, Peter. *Dickens.* New York: Harper Collins, 1990.

Auden, W. H. "Dingley Dell and the Fleet." *The Dyer's Hand.* New York: Random House, 1962. 407–428.

Bowen, John. "Adjestin' the Differences: *Pickwick Papers.*" *Other Dickens: Pickwick to Chuzzlewit.* Oxford: Oxford UP, 2000. 44–81.

Chesterton, G. K. "Pickwick Papers." *Appreciations and Criticisms of the Works of Charles Dickens.* 1911. New York: Haskell House, 1970. 13–25.

Dickens, Charles. *The Pickwick Papers. The Posthumous Papers of the Pickwick Club.* 1836. New York: Modern Library, 2003.

Gissing, George. "The Pickwick Papers." *The Immortal Dickens.* London: Cecil Palmer, 1925. 41–62.

Hobsbaum, Philip. "*Pickwick Papers* (1836–37)." *A Reader's Guide to Charles Dickens.* London: Thames & Hudson, 1972. 28–36.

Parker, David. "*Pickwick Papers*: Horses and Ignominy." *The Doughty Street Novels: Pickwick Papers, Oliver Twist, Nicholas Nickleby, Barnaby Rudge.* New York: AMS, 2002. 82–120.

"The Pickwick Papers." David Perdue's Charles Dickens Page. Available online. URL: http://www.charlesdickenspage.com/pickwick.html. Retrieved November 14, 2007.

"The Pickwick Papers." Victorian Web. Available online. URL: http://www.victorianweb.org/authors/dickens/pickwick/pickwickov.html. Retrieved November 28, 2007.

Russo, Richard. "Introduction." *The Pickwick Papers.* New York: Modern Library, 2003. xi–xx.

OLIVER TWIST

READING TO WRITE

*O*LIVER *TWIST* is a clear example of what Charles Dickens is known for. In this, his second novel, again published in serial form from 1837 to 1839, he writes about the lower classes and the activities in the underbelly of London society. We see some characters doing illegal, nasty, and sometimes horrifying things, yet Dickens is careful to give at least some of these lower-class characters a code of ethics, adding realism and respectability. The character that perhaps best embodies such a code of ethics is Nancy, and looking closely at her scenes can lend great insight into our reading of *Oliver Twist*:

> The Jew inflicted a smart blow on Oliver's shoulders, with the club; and was raising it for a second, when the girl, rushing forward, wrested it from his hand. She flung it into the fire, with a force that brought some of the glowing coals whirling out into the room.
>
> "I won't stand by and see it done, Fagin," cried the girl. "You've got the boy, and what more would you have?—Let him be—let him be—or I shall put that mark on some of you, that will bring me to the gallows before my time."
>
> . . . The girl laughed again: even less composedly than before; and, darting a hasty look at Sikes, turned her face aside, and bit her lip until the blood came.
>
> "You're a nice one," added Sikes, as he surveyed her with a contemptuous air, "to take up the humane and gen-teel side! A pretty subject for the child, as you call him, to make a friend of!"

"God Almighty help me, I am!" cried the girl passionately; "and wish I had been struck dead in the street, or had changed places with them we passed so near to-night, before I had lent a hand in bringing him here. He's a thief, a liar, a devil, all that's bad, from this night forth. Isn't that enough for the old wretch, without blows?" (149–150)

This passage reveals much about Sikes, Fagin, and Nancy in particular. A good way to get started when you are looking for a paper topic is to ask questions about a passage or scene from the book. This scene is completely understandable in its context. We know that Nancy and Sikes have just recaptured Oliver as he ran an errand for Mr. Brownlow. Nancy is obviously regretting her part in Oliver's captivity, so we can start by asking questions about her. Fagin and Sikes can be pretty frightening men, so where does Nancy get the nerve to stand up to them, both physically and mentally/emotionally? Why are her sympathies for Oliver suddenly so strong? Does this scene demonstrate that Nancy is one of very few characters in the novel (certainly the only member of Fagin's gang) who is willing to take action to help others, even when there is no benefit (and may in fact be harmful) to herself? Why does she stand up to Sikes and Fagin on Oliver's behalf yet later in the book refuses to run away from them for her own sake? Maybe it is tempting to claim that Nancy suffers through bouts of insanity, demonstrated here by her laughing "less composedly" all the time. Are there other passages that support this claim? Why does Nancy feel so incredibly guilty about her role in Oliver's life, although, we assume, she can steal from people without remorse? (Keep in mind, however, that we never actually see Nancy stealing, nor do we hear her discussing it. We cannot give her thoughts and feelings that are not supported by Dickens's words.)

This passage reveals a bit about Sikes, too. The look that he gives to the woman he supposedly loves is "contemptuous," and he makes fun of (and eventually threatens) her rather than taking her side or even trying to understand her point of view.

Why does Nancy draw the line at this point? She does not argue that they should let Oliver go or bring him back to Mr. Brownlow's, and she does not say that Oliver should not be forced to pick pockets. She seems resigned to these circumstances as foregone conclusions, but she will not tolerate Fagin hitting Oliver. Why?

TOPICS AND STRATEGIES

This section addresses various possible topics for writing about *Oliver Twist* as well as general methods for approaching these topics. These lists are in no way exhaustive and are meant to provide a jumping-off point rather than an answer key. Use these suggestions to find your own ideas and form your own analyses. All topics discussed in this chapter could potentially turn into very good papers.

Themes

A theme in a literary work is an idea, an action, an occurrence, or a system that in some way threads itself throughout the book. Themes are often identifiable through a close reading of words, phrases, ideas, and even chapter titles, and they are recognizable as something about which the character(s) and/or author appear to have much to say. In other words, if a book's action and/or characters continually return to a similar idea, you have probably identified a theme of the book.

A novel can have any number of themes, so when you are writing your paper, it is usually important to focus on only one. Just a few of the possible themes worth writing about from *Oliver Twist* include family, child labor, corruption, crime, class system, punishment, justice, and love. Begin your brainstorming process by asking lots of questions. If the theme you choose to write about is love, for example, you can start by asking how various characters might define and/or show love. Which character's definition and/or demonstration of love does Dickens seem to be endorsing? Why? How can you tell? What are various characters willing to sacrifice in the name of love? Fagin, for example, loves money and power (though he appears to have no large amount of either), and in pursuit of these things, he sacrifices an upstanding life, good reputation in society, and the lives and time of many young boys and girls. Often these characters sacrifice things they could or might have had, rather than things they already have. Oliver, for example, would presumably sacrifice anything for parental love, but he has nothing to begin with. Do you think that Oliver would eventually have found an opportunity to turn Fagin in and return to Brownlow? Oliver's soft spot for Fagin reveals an interesting love situation. Certainly Oliver does not love or respect Fagin the way he eventually loves and respects Brownlow, yet Oliver makes no immediate threats to leave Fagin or expose his practices to the authorities. What is Dickens trying to convey through Oliver's affection for Fagin? Is Nancy's love (for Sikes, for Oliver, for Fagin) greater than everyone else's because she does the most dangerous deeds and risks death as a consequence? Does Nancy go back to Sikes because of her love for him, or are there other reasons?

These are just a few questions to help you see where brainstorming can take you.

Sample Topics:

1. **Child labor:** Why was it so common to employ children in the 19th century? What does Dickens say about this practice in *Oliver Twist*?

Children in the novel are employed not only legally, in factories and workhouses, but also illegally, as pickpockets. Does Dickens place significant blame or responsibility on the children, or are adults the ones to blame? It is easy to believe that Oliver does not deserve to have to work hard and suffer punishment, but the Artful Dodger and Master Bates seem to be enjoying themselves. Do they have other options and simply refuse to stop working for Fagin? What, if anything, does Dickens offer as a possible solution to the issues of child labor?

2. **Corruption:** Is it better to try to be an upstanding citizen, or is there more merit in just admitting that you are corrupt?

Clearly Fagin's "business" operates under an umbrella of corruption. No one denies it, which seems, for Dickens, to be more upstanding than the establishments and people who claim to be Christian, caring, and helpful yet operate in corrupt and self-serving manners:

> [Mrs. Mann] appropriated the greater part of her weekly stipend to her own use, and consigned the rising parochial generation to even a shorter allowance than was originally provided for them. Thereby finding in the lowest depth a deeper still; and proving herself a very great experimental philosopher. (30)

Mrs. Mann is a hypocrite, whereas Fagin is upfront (as least as far as he can be without getting arrested) about his immoral and illegal practices. Is Dickens trying to expose a certain level of humanity present in the underworld of crime? How do we define corruption? Are there degrees of corruption, one kind being worse than another? How would Dickens address these questions?

3. **Class system:** Does Dickens punish characters who do not appear to deserve their wealth? Why and how so?

It is clear that Mr. Brownlow is of a much higher class than Fagin, Sikes, and Nancy. Perhaps it is more interesting to note the class system that lies within a group of people. Charity boys like Noah Claypole scorn workhouse orphans like Oliver, making readers wonder if class is as much about money as it is about stereotypes and the perverse joy of being better off than someone else. One of the points about class that Dickens seems to be making in *Oliver Twist* is that class is about happenstance and luck, and those in higher classes are not necessarily better or worthier people than those less fortunate.

Oliver and Nancy run with criminals and, in Nancy's case, have broken laws and run wild for a while. However, both surface as inherently good people who deserve better lives but are unable to achieve them without help from others. What qualities does Dickens convey as redeeming, no matter what class an individual is in? Are characters such as the Artful Dodger redeemable? It is also interesting to note how Oliver seems to fit into whichever class he is currently a part of, whether it is the higher class of Brownlow's society or the criminal class of Fagin. Is this how Dickens demonstrates that one's class is simply a matter of chance?

Characters

Writing about a character allows you to choose one person from the novel to study in great detail. You can investigate how Dickens differentiates between characters. How, for example, does he help readers form immediate distinctions between Sikes and Fagin? These two characters could easily have turned out to be very similar to each other, but Dickens instead makes readers see and feel different things about each man. What effects do these differences have on readers? Are we more sympathetic to Sikes or to Fagin? What is it about these characters that creates such impressions and emotions? The characters in *Oliver Twist* are some of the best-known characters in all of literature. Why do you suppose that these particular characters are so memorable?

You might also study characters in terms of how they change (or remain the same) throughout the novel. If a character such as Sikes or Fagin or the Artful Dodger starts out very heartless and corrupt, is there any indication that he has become less (or more) so by the end of the book? What do the apparent changes that Nancy undergoes reveal about her character? Are there characters who seem to remain the same throughout the novel? If so, does this static quality make them less interesting and/or important than the changing characters?

Sample Topics:

1. **Sikes:** Do we feel just a little bit sorry for him?

> Although he is big and menacing, Sikes also carries an air of desperation that makes some readers sympathize with him. Look at descriptions of and dialogue about Sikes early in the novel to find indications that he might be a redeemable character. Clearly, we know that there is a turning point after which Sikes is definitely a villain and readers might be glad to see him die. How interesting, though, that he hangs himself rather than being killed by someone else. Is this Dickens's brand of poetic justice? What is the turning point at which Sikes becomes the villain? For the Artful Dodger, it is Sikes's murder of Nancy that makes the Dodger willing to risk his own life to punish Sikes. Are there moments or situations earlier in the book that identify Sikes as the main villain?

2. **Nancy:** Why does she consistently return to Sikes? Why is she compelled to help Oliver?

Nancy is a fascinating character because there seems to be a clear line between right and wrong in her life, yet her choices do not lead her to a better or the "right" life. Nancy gets a couple of chances to take money, to escape life with Sikes and Fagin, and even to leave London if necessary. She does not have any fantasies that her life will turn around on its own or that Sikes will turn into a kind and respectful person. Why, then, does she return to him? Does her subsequent murder make her a martyr? Why does she risk herself for Oliver? Is Nancy possibly the kindest character in the book? Dickens tells readers a number of times that it is unlikely that a person in Nancy's situation would do anything that does not benefit him- or herself somehow. Why might it be important to Dickens that someone as destitute as Nancy saves Oliver?

3. **Oliver:** How is it that Oliver does not seem to play a key role in his own story?

In some ways, he becomes part of the background, while everything that occurs ends up concerning him. Is Oliver a believable character? Most orphans in Dickens's time were abandoned and largely forgotten, making the intense focus on Oliver in this book quite unrealistic. It seems that the story Dickens wants to tell is bigger than Oliver, perhaps bigger than any individual character. Does Dickens have a social purpose for giving Oliver such an unlikely life? If Oliver does not seem to be a proactive character, should the book have a different title?

4. **Fagin:** How does Dickens seem to want us to feel about Fagin?

Fagin is often interpreted as a sympathetic character, even though he masterminds the crime ring and is nearly the only one reaping its benefits. What role does his Jewish religion play in his appearance, demeanor, lifestyle, and reputation? Dickens repeats "Fagin the Jew" enough times to lead us to believe it is an important aspect of Fagin's character, personality, and life. In what ways is Fagin both a comic character and a villain? How does Dickens's writing style allow readers to know when to laugh and when to sneer? Is Sikes the real boss, or does Fagin have more control than anyone realizes? What should have happened to Fagin? What would have happened if Sikes had not killed Nancy?

History and Context

The realities in which Dickens's books are set offer compelling settings and storylines for further investigation. In many ways, the worlds that Dickens created and reflected have become the dominant conceptions of the Victorian world as we remember it today. How is Dickens able to blend fiction and reality so seamlessly?

One reason for the realism in Dickens's works is his focus on the overarching issues of his day. In *Oliver Twist*, he writes about orphans, workhouses, and charity, three overwhelming issues of the mid-19th century. The laws and philosophies of 19th-century England had a distinct "live and let die" aspect that left little room for altruism or attempts to solve problems created largely by poverty. Dickens was an advocate who used his writing to send messages about the lower classes. One way to investigate the history and context of *Oliver Twist* is to research and evaluate how Dickens's messages were received. Did any reform occur as a result (whether direct or indirect) of Dickens's novels? Did orphans, for example, receive more attention and better care after *Oliver Twist* was published?

Certainly the most controversial aspect of this novel is Dickens's characterization of Fagin as a Jew. This is clearly not meaningless or accidental, as readers are continually reminded of Fagin's background when he is referred to as "the Jew." A woman wrote to Dickens complaining about the negative stereotyping of Jewish people in the book, and Dickens replied: "Fagin is a Jew because it is unfortunately true, of the time to which the story refers, that that class of criminal almost invariably was Jewish" (Howe xix). In later editions of the book, Dickens removed many (but not all) references to Fagin as a Jew, and in later works such as *Our Mutual Friend*, he includes favorably characterized Jewish people. Even today, most film and stage versions of *Oliver Twist* do not focus on Fagin's religious background, if they mention it at all. Was Dickens correct in claiming that most criminals like Fagin were

Jewish? How would this idea (whether it is true or just a societal perception) affect people's understanding and treatment of Jewish people?

Another aspect of history and context to study is the author's background. Was there anything in particular about Dickens's life that led him to write *Oliver Twist*? If so, what bearing does Dickens's life have on the novel? Is this one of those novels that could only have been written (and well received) at a particular time by a particular person? Did Dickens have personal reasons for writing about orphans or the lower classes or crime rings? If so, how do those reasons surface, and what influence do they have on the book and/or its readers? If not, does this mean that Dickens was purely a do-gooder, out to correct the evils of the world through his writing? Or, was he simply capitalizing on topics he knew would interest readers and make him a wealthy man and popular writer?

Writing about the history and context of a novel always involves outside research. It is important to allow your paper topic to remain somewhat flexible, as the information you find through research might require a topic change later. It is also important that you remain selective when writing. Do not include all of the history you find about the 19th century and/or Charles Dickens. Choose only the most relevant details from your research to include in your paper, and support them with your ideas and evidence from Dickens's novel.

Sample Topics:

1. **Jews in England:** Were criminals of Fagin's ilk really largely Jewish as Dickens indicates? If so, why?

Dickens received a lot of attention for his characterization of Fagin the Jew. He claimed that he was not using Fagin to represent Jews in general or to convey that Jewish people are always criminals. Rather, he said, it was well known that certain crime rings were run and populated by Jewish people, making Fagin's religion simply an element of realism. Be careful to look at this issue through a 19th-century lens so that you don't confuse English issues regarding Jews with today's knowledge and history of Jewish people. It must be clear why people could have been offended by Dickens's characterization of Fagin the Jew, but are there any reasons why Jewish people might feel flattered or redeemed by this representation? What was the true situation of Jewish people in England?

2. **Charity:** What were the predominant 19th-century attitudes toward charity?

Many felt that only certain people deserved charity or that help was something that needed to be earned. "God helps those who help themselves" was a popular saying to rationalize workhouses and charity in general. The Industrial Revolution caused a large number of poor people to move to cities in search of work in factories. Factory conditions were life threatening, and the compensation was meager. What were lawmakers doing to help the working poor? Many different "factory acts" were passed in the 19th century, because as England became the Workshop of the World, its cities degenerated and slum areas expanded. Were the factory acts written to protect and help the poor? Was there any legal action taken to help the poor people who were unable to work? Many upper-class women were involved in charity organizations. What was considered helpful? How did various ways of helping the poor fall in and out of fashion in upper-class circles?

3. **Attitudes toward workhouses:** How does the workhouse in *Oliver Twist* use God as justification or motivation for the children?

Philosophies and plans behind workhouses often cited God as support for ideas that now strike us as quite unchristian or even antireligious. What kind of people actually believed that the poor enjoyed workhouses? Did they need to believe this to soothe their conscience?

4. **Orphans:** Several Dickens books show us orphans who are somehow blamed or punished for the actions (or inactions) of their parents and/or relatives. Was this the prevailing attitude toward orphans in 19th-century England? How common was it for orphans to be adopted?

Many families already had several children of their own, leading us to wonder why they might choose to adopt another child. Were orphans generally only adopted by wealthy people such as Mr. Brownlow? Were they often taken in by friends or extended family members? It might also be interesting to look at the reasons behind the large number of orphans in 19th-century England. Was it due to war? Poverty? Lack of available birth control? Religious practices? Studying orphans could also give you the opportunity to study 19th-century beliefs about nature versus nurture. Were people inherently good or bad? Were orphans commonly given chances to redeem themselves, if need be?

Philosophy and Ideas

Philosophy and ideas in a novel are similar to theme, but they are more general or more universal. Writing about the philosophy and ideas in a book means that you identify broad philosophical ideas and investigate the ways in which the book comments on them. Some examples of philosophy and ideas in *Oliver Twist* include necessity, religion, nature versus nurture, and individualism. Studying these concepts might necessitate research into the history of the philosophy and/or history of the time to show how ideas are linked to their context. Outside research can be important, but a close reading of Dickens's novel should be your focus. Do not make claims that cannot be supported by the words of the novel itself.

Individualism is a key philosophy in *Oliver Twist,* and it certainly does seem as if everyone is living for his or her own gain with no regard for others. But are there any characters in the novel who do not live by the "look out for number one" philosophy? Look at which characters are most closely associated with individualism. What do they have in common? How does Dickens treat them? What does Dickens want readers to think or believe about individualism? How can you tell?

Sample Topics:

1. **Necessity:** Is there ever a circumstance that makes crime necessary and/or permissible/forgivable?

Would readers have forgiven Nancy if she had killed Sikes or Fagin? If Fagin's kids were stealing simply to put food in their mouths, would their activities seem more acceptable? It is not farfetched to speculate whether Dickens felt it was society's own fault for structuring itself in ways that allow and even necessitate people to fall through the cracks and resort to crime in their destitution. Are there always moral, ethical, and religious implications for a crime, or is it ever just enough to say that it was necessary for life? We tend to look at murder in self-defense quite differently from all other murders, to the point where sometimes the perpetrator is not punished. Does this justification work for other crimes? Where should the line be drawn? Where does Dickens draw that line?

2. **Religion:** How does religion play varied roles in different classes?

Bumbles, as an ex-beadle, does many things for what he considers "parochial" reasons. Fagin's religion is certainly prominent. The last lines of the book indicate that Agnes has somehow been rejected by religion in some way. Oliver gives thanks to God at the end of the book, and says, "Oh! God forgive this wretched man!" (461) when he sees Fagin in prison for the last time. Taken alone or together, these and other scenes in the book address the role of religion for people of various classes. Dickens seems to believe that those who make mistakes belong to and deserve the church more than those who use the church for status and shun others. Does Dickens appear to invoke a Christian philosophy? How is such a philosophy defined and understood in his time and in ours? Why is it that most of the people in the book who claim to be religious are in many ways the worst offenders to society and humanity?

3. **Individualism:** Fagin says that in the gang they all look out for number one, but that type of society falls apart. Does Dickens propose an alternative philosophy?

We see individualism backfire in Oliver's first pickpocketing exercise. The other boys pickpocket Mr. Brownlow and then leave Oliver to take the blame, but they end up inadvertently reuniting Oliver with family and friends and beginning the sequence of events that will eventually get him off the streets and into upper-class society. Presumably Fagin's boys would not want this for Oliver, since looking out only for oneself would never involve helping someone else without reward. Is Nancy also practicing individualism? She helps Oliver but accepts no reward and is adamant about returning to her horrid life. Which character is the most self-serving? Which character shows the most helpful (altruistic) nature? A popular precept in Dickens's time was "God helps those who help themselves." How does Dickens comment on that idea in *Oliver Twist*?

4. **Nature versus nurture:** Are there hereditary traits that prevail over social circumstances, or vice versa?

Dickens writes that "Nature or inheritance had implanted a good sturdy spirit in Oliver's breast" (31). What happens when a child is orphaned and then repeatedly told he is foolish and worthless? What would Oliver have been like if Mr. Brownlow had not rescued him? There is widespread debate about the respective influences of nature and nurture. How does Dickens address the issue? Does he appear to favor one over the other?

Form and Genre

The way in which a book is written and presented can have an enormous impact on readers' reception and interpretations. The form that a work takes involves its shape and stucture: chapter length, format, etc. A work's genre is its classification.

Oliver Twist fits well into the 19th-century novel's expectations, partly because it is in part a sensation novel. The sensation novel was disdained by literary critics but remained a very popular genre throughout the 19th century. The parts of *Oliver Twist* that come closest to the sensation novel's prescriptions are those in which the most shocking and gruesome things happen. The death of Sikes and his dog are quite graphic for the time and would have scandalized some readers (thought the vast majority would have read on, delighted).

Oliver Twist is also a fairy tale of sorts. Like many fairy tales, the main character does little or nothing to change his situation, yet the world around him revolves in such mysterious and coincidental ways that everything turns out well in the end.

It is clear that form and genre are both inseparable from content. Why would Dickens choose these particular forms and genres? Where in the text do you find the clearest examples of these forms and genres? How do these forms or genres help make *Oliver Twist* similar to and/or different from Dickens's other works and other works of Dickens's time?

Sample Topics:

1. **Sensation novel:** What would 19th-century readers have considered "sensational" about *Oliver Twist*?

   The sensation novel was wildly popular in 19th-century England and generally contained a murder or crime and some type of scandal. Wilkie Collins and Mary Elizabeth Braddon are two well-known sensation novelists of the 19th century. Why would Dickens use elements of the sensation novel when certain people would have turned up their noses and regarded it as "lesser" literature? In terms of book sales as well as the book's reception by the literary elite, was it worthwhile to write sensation novels?

2. **Fairy tale:** In what ways does the fairy-tale nature of *Oliver Twist* make it appropriate for both children and adults?

   Oliver Twist is in some ways less involved and more like a fable or parable than Dickens's other works. Oliver is so pure and good that Dickens spends most of his time with other (perhaps more believable) characters. Oliver requires a lot of rescuing, and there are a few love entanglements as well. In the end, things come full circle, and for better or worse, all characters seem to get what they deserve. Are there ways in which *Oliver Twist* does not fit into the fairy-tale mold? It is important to consider Dickens's knowledge and interpretations of fairy tales, which in their original forms were much more gruesome and dirty than the stories we know today. Why might Dickens have chosen to use fairy-tale elements in this novel? Is this book directed toward children?

Language, Symbols, and Imagery

To effectively study language, symbols, and imagery, you must move beyond unnecessary summary to investigate how the book is written and then make speculations about how these methods of writing and literary elements affect the content of the novel. Closely studying language in *Oliver Twist* can alert you to instances when Dickens uses sarcasm to convey a particular message. It is quite difficult to write sarcastically, as readers can easily mistake sarcasm for heartfelt statements. What kinds of signals or indications does Dickens provide so that readers correctly interpret his sarcasm? For example, are there particular characters who use sarcasm? If so, what kinds of personalities do these characters seem to have? Are there characters who seem to inspire or provoke others into using sarcasm? Does Dickens use sarcasm to help readers sympathize with a particular character, or does the use of sarcasm demonstrate a character's intelligence or perceptiveness? Start answering some of these questions (or questions of your own), and then elaborate on your answers by looking at the significance of those answers and/or related issues. What bearing, for example, does sarcasm have on the overall tone of a scene or the novel in general?

If you are interested in considering symbols, look at some of the significant objects in the novel and investigate whether they stand for something else. Do the handkerchiefs stolen by Fagin's kids come to represent something more? We know that the books that Oliver is returning for Mr. Brownlow when he is recaptured by Sikes and Nancy come to represent Brownlow's trust and Oliver's disgrace (until, of course, the facts are brought to light). What other symbols are at work in this novel? What is their significance to not only the plot but the themes, philosophies, or ideas as well?

Certainly *Oliver Twist* gives readers frighteningly clear images of workhouses and life on the streets in 19th-century London. Dickens is particularly good at imagery because he uses all five of readers' senses: smell, touch, taste, sight, and sound. Some of the characters' names even contribute to our perceptions of their demeanor and thus the imagery that surrounds them. Names like Bumbles and Crackit enhance our images of those characters considerably, giving us an immediate understanding of the nature of these characters.

Oliver Twist is one of Dickens's best-known and most widely read novels and has been adapted for stage and screen a number of times, indicating that the imagery in the book lends itself well to actual visual adaptation. How is it that Dickens is able to help readers conjure up such clear images of scenes and settings? Is the imagery he provides historically accurate? Why, when we're reading about workhouses and criminal gangs, is it so important for readers to be able to perceive these people and places with their five senses? How does Dickens's imagery embed itself within his philosophies, ideas, and themes?

Sample Topics:

1. **Revealing narrative structure:** Why does Dickens interrupt the story and take so much time to explain what he's doing, in terms of writing?

One of the instances in which Dickens reveals his own narrative structure occurs at the beginning of chapter 17. After a couple of paragraphs describing common tactics of narration, Dickens asks readers simply to follow his story without being too jarred by a rather sudden setting change:

> Let it be considered a delicate intimation on the part of the historian that he is going back to the town in which Oliver Twist was born: the reader taking it for granted that there are good and substantial reasons for making the journey, or he would not be invited to proceed upon such an expedition. (153–154)

Does this strategy undermine Dickens's narration? Many readers feel that this glimpse into the "bones" of the book makes Dickens more trustworthy. They feel that he will not lead them astray without sufficient preparation or explanation.

2. **Comedy and tragedy:** How do comedy and tragedy work together in this novel?

When Oliver is in the workhouse, Dickens writes,

> one boy . . . hinted darkly to his companions, that unless he had another basin of gruel *per diem*, he was afraid he might some night happen to eat the boy who slept next to him, who happened to be a weakly youth of a tender age. He had a wild, hungry, eye; and they implicitly believed him. (38)

This scene is comic in that readers know that none of the boys in the workhouse will become cannibals. Readers also know that a room full of starving, lonely young boys would be very likely to believe the boy's threats, lending sympathy to their plight and reminding us of their tragic innocence. Of course, this scene leads directly to Oliver asking for more gruel, thus changing his destiny forever. Is one type of character typically involved more often in either comedy or tragedy? Does one genre overpower the other?

3. **Character names:** How does a character's name reveal something about that character before the reader is fully introduced to him or her?

The name *Scrooge* has developed its own meaning to the extent that we now use it as a noun, verb, and adjective out of the context of the book to describe a miser or miserly activities. Dickens often gives characters names that already have a meaning. What are the "twists" in Oliver and/or his life? How does the former beadle "bumble" his way through life? Remember to put words in their 19th-century context—they might mean something different now. Have any names from *Oliver Twist* acquired a life of their own and come into common usage? Has the meaning of any character's name changed over time, making the word either more or less significant to readers' understanding of the character?

4. **Sarcasm:** When are there instances of characters speaking sarcastically? When do you know that it is Dickens who is being sarcastic, even if the character is speaking seriously?

Sarcasm occurs when what is intended is in fact the opposite of what is said or written. Oliver arrives at the workhouse and stands in front of the board, "whereupon a gentleman in a white waistcoat said he was a fool. Which was a capital way of raising his spirits, and putting him quite at ease" (36). Dickens seems most sarcastic about those in power who either remain ignorant, choose to do nothing, or do precisely the wrong thing. Of the board in charge of the workhouse, for example, he writes, "What a noble illustration of the tender laws of England! They let the paupers go to sleep!" (37). It can be difficult to detect sarcasm in Dickens, partly because it is hard to write and even harder to find when reading, and partly because Dickens's use of language and of course the context in which he writes are very different from ours. It might be helpful to research Dickens's beliefs and attitudes when searching for his sarcasm. Knowing how he felt can provide clues to his writing methods. In general, reading the text closely is always the best way to find something such as sarcasm.

Compare and Contrast Essays

We can often get a clearer idea of what something is by understanding what it is not, and vice versa. Papers that use comparison and contrast methods include not just lists of similarities and differences, but theories and interpretations about why such similarities and differences exist and what effect they have on the novel as a whole.

Several characters in *Oliver Twist* seem to have a counterpart somewhere in the story. Oliver and the Artful Dodger, for example, may be more similar than their obvious differences would indicate. The word *artful* has several different definitions, some of which clearly apply to the Dodger (Jack Dawkins). Do any definitions of "artful" apply to Oliver? If the two characters really are similar, then is Dickens making a point about fate or circumstance or luck of the draw? If you determine that the Dodger and Oliver are essentially quite different, perhaps Dickens is making a point about the nature of people who tend toward crime as opposed to the types of people who live upstanding lives.

Sample Topics:
  1. **Oliver and the Artful Dodger:** Are there any ways in which Oliver might be considered "artful" as well?

  Oliver and the Artful Dodger are alike in many ways. Why does Oliver end up on a more "virtuous," upstanding path? Do the two make different choices, or do their situations (and the choices of others) force them into particular circumstances? The Artful Dodger seems to take genuine delight in stealing, yet he also seems at times simply friendly and helpful. He is actually a quite complicated character, though we likely do not get enough of his story or perspective to be able to tell just how complicated. Is Dickens using these characters to show the story from various angles? In other words, could Oliver's fate have befallen Jack Dawkins, and vice versa?

  2. **Nancy and Rose:** How do both Nancy and Rose become the true heroes of the story?

  At times in the novel, Nancy and Rose seem to be interchangeable. Both feel deeply for the people they care about, both do their best to help others (namely Oliver), and both feel a sense of shame over some aspect of their life. What is it, then, that differentiates these women? Perhaps Dickens purposely made them very similar in order to illustrate the happenstance or dumb luck that can put people either in dire straits or in the upper classes. If Rose and Nancy had been in the same economic class (either upper or lower), how would they have been similar and/or different?

  3. **Country versus city:** Can people get away with more mischief in the city, where they are a face in the crowd, or in the country, where there is no one to bear witness?

  Readers often want to stereotype settings just as they stereotype characters. Often we assume that the country is a purer, better place than the city. In *Oliver Twist*, however, one could argue that some of the things happening in the country are as bad or worse than things happening in the city. Mrs. Mann steals the money that is supposed to feed the children. How is this similar to or different from Fagin's operation with the pickpockets? How does the setting influence people's activities? Look closely at words and phrases that Dickens uses to describe the city as well as the country. What tone does he give to each? How does this affect our reading?

Bibliography for *Oliver Twist*

Chesterton, G. K. "Oliver Twist." *Appreciations and Criticisms of the Works of Charles Dickens.* 1911. New York: Haskell House, 1970. 38–49.

Dickens, Charles. *Oliver Twist.* 1837. New York: Barnes & Noble Classics, 2003.

Dunn, Richard J. *Oliver Twist: Whole Heart and Soul.* Twayne's Masterwork Studies No. 118. New York: Twayne Publishers, 1993.

Howe, Irving. Introduction. *Oliver Twist.* New York: Bantam Dell, 1982. xi–xxii.

NICHOLAS NICKLEBY

READING TO WRITE

OFTEN IN Dickens's novels (particularly those whose title comes from the character's name) the action revolves around the main (title) character, rather than actually involving him to a large degree. Nicholas Nickleby, however, is not simply a character connecting a network of other characters. He is knee deep in the story and does not always act in fully redeemable ways. He fights (literally as well as figuratively) and spends a lot of his time as quite an angry young man. Dickens writes about Nicholas in his preface to the novel: "If Nicholas be not always found to be blameless or agreeable, he is not always intended to appear so. He is a young man of an impetuous temper and of little or no experience; and I saw no reason why such a hero should be lifted out of nature." (7). Unlike Oliver Twist and David Copperfield, Nicholas seems to be an agent of action in his own life rather than a victim or coincidental bystander.

In some ways, Nicholas is the least interesting character in the novel, as fascinating and compelling things happen to other characters, too. Late Victorian novelist George Gissing defends Nicholas as the central character:

> Dickens thought himself, and was thought, to have done a bold thing in taking for his hero this penniless youth of the everyday world. . . . He was opening in truth a new era of English fiction, and the critic of our day who loses sight of this, who compares Dickens to his disadvantage with novelists of a later school, perpetrates the worst kind of injustice! (94)

At the same time, there are as many colorful characters in *Nicholas Nickleby*, published serially in 1838–39, as in any typical Dickens novel. Readers are as interested in what happens to Kate Nickleby, Wackford Squeers, Ralph Nickleby, Smike, and Madeline Bray as they are in what happens to Nicholas.

One of the most compelling aspects of *Nicholas Nickleby* is its treatment of the class system in 19th-century England. Since this is a novel that came early in Dickens's career, we can look for the beginnings of his social and political activism here: "*Nickleby* taught him his power as a social reformer, and it is not the least wonderful feature of his career that again and again he repeated this success, combining, with much felicity, the moral and the artistic purpose, generally incompatible" (Gissing 99). The problems for Nicholas, Kate, and their mother begin only after Mr. Nickleby dies, leaving them dependent on Ralph Nickleby. Ralph turns up his nose at this family who does not run in the same social circles as he. In what becomes a near obsession, Ralph introduces his relatives to all the people and situations that nearly become their downfall. In the meantime, Kate and Nicholas (and to some extent, Mrs. Nickleby) learn many things about class difference.

It is certainly not unusual for Dickens to use a character's prison experiences to exemplify class differences and the need for legal and social reform. *Nicholas Nickleby* is no exception, and the following description gives readers some of Dickens's eloquent opinions:

The place to which Mr. Cheeryble had directed [Nicholas] was a row of mean and not over-cleanly houses, situated within "the Rules" of the King's Bench Prison, and not many hundred paces distant from the obelisk in Saint George's Fields. The Rules are a certain liberty adjoining the prison, and comprising some dozen streets in which debtors who can raise money to pay large fees, from which their creditors do *not* derive any benefit, are permitted to reside by the wise provisions of the same enlightened laws which leave the debtor who can raise no money to starve in jail, without the food, the clothing, lodging, or warmth, which are provided for felons convicted of the most atrocious crimes that can disgrace humanity. There are many pleasant fictions of the law in constant operation, but there is not one so pleasant or practically humorous as that which supposes every man to be of equal value in its impartial

eye, and the benefits of all laws to be equally attainable by all men, without the smallest reference to the furniture of their pockets. (583–584)

This of course describes Nicholas's journey to meet Madeline Bray's
father. The description of Mr. Bray's "cell" marvels at the hominess of the
place and its utter lack of recognizable prison features. Certainly readers
see the ridiculous nature of the situation: Inmates pay exorbitant fees
simply to live in comfort, even though such fees do nothing to repay the
debts that led to their imprisonment in the first place. We are left to
ponder the priorities of those who pay for comfort rather than release, as
well as the ethics of those who charge such fees and imprison people for
debt in the first place. The final sentence of this passage is perhaps the
most telling and most important, in terms of Dickens's opinions. Who
does Dickens feel is being cheated by the legal system? Why? Does Dickens feel pity for Mr. Bray, or does he consider Bray part of the problem?
Where does Madeline fit into all of this, and why is she in prison with her
father? Answers to these questions can lead to intriguing investigations
of the text, Dickens, and the historical context.

TOPICS AND STRATEGIES

This section of the chapter addresses various possible topics for writing
about *Nicholas Nickleby* as well as general methods for approaching these
topics. These lists are in no way exhaustive and are meant to provide a
jumping-off point rather than an answer key. Use these suggestions to
find your own ideas and form your own analyses. All topics discussed in
this chapter could potentially turn into very good papers.

Themes

Discovering and working with a novel's themes involves careful consideration of words, phrases, ideas, and even chapter titles. You will
recognize a theme when you hit upon something about which the
character(s) and/or author have much to say. A novel such as *Nicholas
Nickleby* can contain many themes, so it is usually important to focus
your argument on only one. It is equally (if not more) important to find
something to say about a theme, rather than merely pointing out that
it exists in the text.

A few of the themes present in *Nicholas Nickleby* include love, family, betrayal, fighting, money, and theater. Begin brainstorming by asking a lot of questions. If you choose to write about the theme of theater, for example, you can start by asking where in the book does the theater or the theatrical play a role? Obviously Vincent Crummles's acting company is a large part of this theme's expression, but are not the scenes at Dotheboys at times equally theatrical? Fanny Squeers in particular is clearly playing a role in acting out her imagined courtship with Nicholas. Again, after Nicholas and Smike leave Dotheboys, the Squeers family stages a melodrama in which Nicholas supposedly "dashed [Mrs. Squeers] to the earth, and drove her back comb several inches into her head" (184). The fantasy that the Squeers family creates pervades the atmosphere at Dotheboys and follows Mr. Squeers into town, where he explains to Ralph Nickleby that Mrs. Squeers treats the boys with every kindness.

In many ways, it seems that most characters in *Nicholas Nickleby* act on some sort of imagined stage rather than out of genuine feeling or profound understanding. In what ways is the theater theme less pronounced on Vincent Crummles's stage than anywhere else in the book? Which characters' actual lives seem to be more of a fabrication than any fictional drama? How does the theme of theater find its way into Dickens's writing style? Are there scenes that could be readily translated into scripts for a stage production? Does Dickens find any place in the novel to regard theater or theatricalities ironically?

Such questions followed by (or stemming from) close reading of the text will help you develop ideas and arguments about theme in *Nicholas Nickleby*.

Sample Topics:

1. **Family:** Is family important in the novel for its own sake, or are there certain qualities a family or family member must have in order to be valued?

   Nicholas Nickleby shows us that family can at times be more of a burden than a comfort. Kate, Nicholas, and Mrs. Nickleby definitely care for one another, but their family is completely disrupted by their connection to Ralph Nickleby. In what ways is Ralph a part of the Nickleby family, and in what ways is he completely outside of it? Why do Nicholas, Kate, and Mrs. Nickleby depend on Ralph so heavily, even after he has revealed himself as an unethical man? Are there opportunities in the novel for family to save people? Who takes advantage of such opportunities, and what does this seem to say about him or her?

2. **Fighting:** Are there times when it is absolutely necessary to fight?

Nicholas spends a lot of time fighting, both figuratively and literally, in the book. Does "the bad guy" always throw the first punch? Nicholas seems often to come out swinging, and he does cause serious injuries, yet we root for him. What does the physical fight reveal about the personalities of those involved? What does Dickens appear to be saying about fighting (physical or figurative) in general?

3. **Class system:** Are there any situations or characters in the book for which the class system is not a crucial factor?

Most of the characters' actions are motivated in some way by money—trying to survive without it, trying to connect oneself to someone who has it, trying to keep it, trying to get more of it. Dickens shows people in the lower classes who are at the mercy of those with money. Does money always equal power in this book? Who suffers because of the class system, and who benefits? Why? What does Dickens's portrayal of these characters reveal about his opinions of the class system?

Characters

One of the more fascinating results of Dickens's writing is the consistency with which readers seem to find themselves—their own lives and personalities—in the novels. Certainly we all hope to be as morally upstanding (if not quite as naive) as Nicholas or as sweet and kind as Smike. It is all the more remarkable then that the character about which Dickens acknowledges receiving the most "fan mail" about is Wackford

Squeers: "More than one Yorkshire schoolmaster lays claim to being the original of Mr. Squeers" (5).

Dickens goes on to relate briefly humorous anecdotes regarding these schoolmasters' plots to receive credit for being the model for the character. Then Dickens adds:

> While the Author cannot but feel the full force of the compliment thus conveyed to him, he ventures to suggest that these contentions may arise from the fact, that Mr. Squeers is the representative of a class, and not of an individual. Where imposture, ignorance, and brutal cupidity, are the stock in trade of a small body of men, and one is described by these characteristics, all his fellows will recognize something belonging to themselves, and each will have a misgiving that the portrait is his own. (5)

In this brief passage, Dickens tells us two important things: First, he writes from life, borrowing characteristics and traits from real people in order to round out his characters; and second, Mr. Squeers (and, presumably, other characters as well) is not the reflection of an individual but a mirror turned on society, revealing the ugly realities in the lives of any number of people, in this case, those who think and act similarly to Mr. Squeers and those who are so negatively and profoundly affected by such thoughts and actions.

Scholars and critics often regard characters representing "types" as less worthy than characters representing individuals. For Dickens, however, it is most complimentary and beneficial for some of his characters to be recognized as types, rather than individuals. If readers find glimpses of reality in the novel and recognize a character such as Squeers as part of that reality, it is better they understand that England contains any number of Squeers-esque people in order to grasp fully the scope of the problem at Yorkshire schools. Grasp they did, and reform quickly followed *Nicholas Nickleby*'s publication.

Sample Topics:

1. **Kate:** Is she a strong woman making her own decisions, or is she at the mercy of the men around her?

   Nicholas is not the only one with a fiery temper. Why is Kate's encounter with Hawk so very scandalous? Is it better that she and Nicholas sacrifice their happiness, or should Kate go after what she wants? Her scenes with Mrs. Nickleby perhaps best demonstrate Kate's wisdom and calm demeanor. She is not ridiculous, as several other female characters of the novel are:

> "In the mean time," interrupted Kate, with becoming pride and indignation, "I am to be the scorn of my own sex, and the toy of the other; justly condemned by all women of right feeling, and despised by all honest and honourable men; sunken in my own esteem, and degraded in every eye that looks upon me. No, not if I work my fingers to the bone, not if I am driven to the roughest and hardest labour. Do not mistake me. I will not disgrace your recommendation. I will remain in the house in which it placed me, until I am entitled to leave it by the terms of my engagement; though, mind, I see these men no more! When I quit it, I will hide myself from them and you, and, striving to support my mother by hard service, I will live, at least, in peace, and trust in God to help me." (366)

What does this passage reveal about Kate, particularly because she speaks these words to Ralph? Does Kate depend on Nicholas, or would it be more accurate to say that Nicholas depends on Kate? Remember, Kate is widely regarded as a passive character.

2. **Smike:** Why do we care so much about him? Why does he have to die? What would have happened to him if he had lived?

Who is most responsible for Smike's miserable life as well as his death? Everyone loves Smike—characters and readers alike. Think about the people who Smike represents: poor children, helpless people, the uneducated. Why would it be important to Dickens that readers sympathize with Smike, who Gissing describes as a "shadow, never either boy or man" (99)? It is interesting to note that Smike was often played by a woman in stage productions. What does this indicate about the character and readers' perceptions of him?

3. **Ralph Nickleby:** Is there ever a time when readers feel sorry for him?

At times, it seems as if Ralph might come around. He shows he cares about Kate, although he is unable (or unwilling) to express it. The climax of the book for Ralph is learning that Smike is his son. Why is his reaction so extreme? Does Ralph feel remorseful about his treatment of Smike, or is he merely humiliated by the connections to the lower class? What would have happened if Ralph (or Smike, for that matter) had lived longer?

4. **Mrs. Nickleby:** How does Dickens convey the humor that generally surrounds her?

She is maybe a bit too ridiculous for readers to want to actually know someone like her, but she is a fascinating and entertaining character. She is so often wrong, and yet rarely does anyone correct her. Mrs. Nickleby is "a representative woman of the decent English household [around 1848], and who may still be met with more frequently than is desirable in the middle-class home" (Gissing 101). Women of a certain class were expected to be fools, and perhaps Dickens uses examples like this to further the cause for education for women.

5. **Newman Nogs:** What is his role in this book?

Newman Nogs appears to be on Ralph's side (or works for him, anyway) but does what he can to help those less fortunate. He used to be a gentleman, and while he resents Ralph and others of the upper classes, he helps to keep others from being ruined in the way that he was. How are readers expected to feel about Newman Nogs? Why?

History and Context

Some scholars argue that *Nicholas Nickleby* falls a bit flat because Dickens tried too hard to engage with issues of his time and not hard enough to write a great story. Whether you believe this is true, it is clear that the history and context of *Nicholas Nickleby* are important factors for understanding the novel.

There are three broad categories into which a study of history and context can be placed. The first is an investigation into how a work was received. How well did *Nicholas Nickleby* sell in its original serial form? What factors may have influenced sales? What did Dickens's contemporary readers and reviewers have to say about *Nicholas Nickleby*? What might help to explain such responses? It can be enlightening to learn about a book's initial reception.

The second category includes the author's background. This investigation can go beyond notations about which elements of Dickens's life surface in the novel. Such a discussion addresses factors in Dickens's life that might have led him to create the characters, issues, and situations of *Nicholas Nickleby*.

Finally, the third category for studying history and context covers material in the novel that has some basis in reality. The critics (mentioned above) who believe that *Nicholas Nickleby* fails as a novel feel that Dickens wrote it simply to frame his rants about Yorkshire schools. Whether you believe the novel fails, clearly Dickens does have points to make regarding schools represented by Dotheboys Hall. What were the Yorkshire schools? Did Dickens hold any particular affiliation with them? Was any social or legal action taken with regard to Yorkshire schools around the time (immediately before or after) of *Nicholas Nickleby*'s publication?

Writing about the history and context of a novel always involves outside research. It is important to allow your paper topic to remain somewhat flexible, as the information you find through research might require a topic change. It is also important that you remain selective when writing. Do not include all of the history you find about the 19th century and/or Charles Dickens. Choose only the most relevant details from your research to include in your paper, and support them with your ideas and evidence from Dickens's novel.

Sample Topics:

1. **Schools for boys:** How does the name *Dotheboys* reveal Dickens's opinions of Victorian education (or at least particular schools)?

The Yorkshire schools, or "cheap schools," had been active for nearly 100 years by the time Dickens visited some in 1838:

> It is in Dotheboys Hall that the interest of this book really centres; to attack the "Yorkshire schools" was his one defined purpose when he sat down to write, and it seems probable that much more space would have been given to Dotheboys had not the subject proved rather refractory." (Gissing 97)

Yorkshire schools were places where orphaned and unwanted children were dropped off and then forgotten. Dickens's preface to *Nicholas Nickleby* outlines the necessity he felt in exposing such places and shutting them down. He was quite happy when, about five years after the publication of *Nicholas Nickleby*, theses types of schools had all but vanished:

> Mr. Squeers and his school are faint and feeble pictures of an existing reality, purposely subdued and kept down lest they should be deemed impossible. . . . [I have] received, from private quarters far beyond the reach of suspicion or distrust, accounts of atrocities, in the perpetration of which upon neglected or repudiated children, these schools have been the main instruments, very far exceeding any that appear in these pages. (5–6)

He makes clear (more than once) that the harm done to Smike and others at Dotheboys is an understatement of the real activities and horrors at these schools.

2. **Class system in 19th-century England:** What were the various classes in England during the Victorian period, and how are they represented in the novel?

Much of the status attached to particular characters (Ralph Nickleby, Mr. and Mrs. Mantalini) seems ridiculous and fairly arbitrary to us now. Did Dickens intend it this way? If so, what point might he be making about class systems in 19th-century England?

3. **Prison:** Does Dickens seem to consider prison necessary or ridiculous?

There were more than 30,000 people in debtors' prisons in 1837, "a typical year" (Paterson 223). Dickens's own father, John Dickens, was imprisoned for debt when Dickens was a boy. Families often moved to prison, too, though only the actual debtors were imprisoned (family members and servants came and went freely). Nineteenth-century prisons were sometimes "like small self-contained towns" where people had much in common (Paterson 225). If Dickens could have reformed prisons into whatever system he liked, what do you think he would have done?

Philosophy and Ideas

Philosophy and ideas in a novel are similar to theme, but they are more general or more universal. Writing about the philosophy and ideas in a book means that you identify broad philosophical ideas and investigate the ways in which the book comments on them. Some examples of philosophy and ideas from *Nicholas Nickleby* include necessity, individualism, and usefulness. Studying these concepts might necessitate research into the history of the philosophy and/or history of the time to show how these ideas are linked with history and context. Outside research can be important, but a close reading of Dickens's novel should be your focus. Do not make claims that cannot be supported by the words of the novel itself.

Individualism becomes an integral part of the philosophy and ideas in *Nicholas Nickleby.* In some ways, the idea contrasts the novel's theme of family quite nicely, yet individualism pervades the novel in ways that family does not. Ask questions about the philosophy and ideas in order to find and/or narrow your thesis. Which characters in *Nicholas Nickleby* appear to think only (or at least primarily) of themselves? How does Dickens portray such characters, and how does this portrayal help establish Dickens's own sentiments about the character(s)? Does he seem to want readers to like such characters? Why or why not? How can you tell? Are there characters who practice individualism against their will or better judgment? Kate Nickleby, for example, in some instances looks out only for herself. Are these instances examples of true individualism, or are they brief detours into individualism on the way to a different ideal? How would Dickens have understood and reacted to individualism? Where in *Nicholas Nickleby* can such understanding and reaction be found?

Sample Topics:

1. **Individualism:** Is looking out for oneself always a selfish act in this novel?

In Dickens's time, England favored a sense of individualism over what they regarded as "mob mentality" in countries such as France. Yet, in *Nicholas Nickleby,* characters like Ralph, who only look out for themselves, are villainized. Why? Kate and Nicholas take care of each other, yet each of them is required to protect him- or herself as well. Is the life of Crummles's theater another example of individualism? Certainly an actor wants his or her time alone in the spotlight, yet the atmosphere that Dickens conveys is convivial and cooperative, exemplifying a form of society that, if not so elaborately ridiculous, just might function better than Ralph Nickleby's every-man-for-himself world.

2. **Usefulness:** Who are the most useful characters in the novel? How can we tell? Why is this such an important part of their character?

Nicholas needs to be useful in order to earn money for his family. He tries teaching, acting, writing, and ends up a clerk. The Cheeryble brothers seem to be the happiest characters, perhaps because they help others and give away so much money. Are characters such as Ralph and Smike useful? To whom? How does their usefulness (or lack thereof) affect readers' interpretations of their characters? What is Dickens's overall message about usefulness in the novel?

Form and Genre

Nicholas Nickleby does not demonstrate the sophistication of Dickens's later works in terms of its seamlessness of form. Many scholars have noted that *Nicholas Nickleby* reads a bit like a series of essays in which the same characters appear as if by coincidence rather than design. Since *Nicholas Nickleby* was Dickens's third novel, written shortly after *The Pickwick Papers,* which clearly is (or at least begins as) a series of loosely related tales, it is not surprising that Dickens had not perfected the serial novel by the time he penned *Nicholas Nickleby.*

Two things that Dickens does remarkably well in *Nicholas Nickleby* are the use of farce to create a comic tone and the interspersing of episodic stories to add layers to the novel. Critics will note that Dickens consistently exaggerates. This technique, used to generate humor, was not uncommon in the early to mid-19th century. It seems to work particularly well in *Nicholas Nickleby,* however, perhaps because several variations exist in this novel. Characters (particularly those at Vincent Crummles's theater) often unwittingly present themselves in a farcical manner, even while other characters recognize the exaggerated humor (and often pretend they do not). On top of that, it is possible to perceive Dickens himself making fun of his characters so that it becomes difficult at times to tell when you have noted a particularly funny scene on your own or Dickens has manipulated the presentation in a way that makes the humor more apparent. Individual farces inevitably hold together to create a novel dominated by farce.

The episodic tales within the book, such as "The Baron of Grogzwig," are reminiscent of Dickens's form in *The Pickwick Papers.* It is a form that Dickens appears to outgrow, using it in later novels. Writing about these episodic tales will lead you to investigate them largely in terms of metaphor. Does the tale represent a character, plotline, or other element of the larger story? Is it significant that a particular character is the one to relay the story? Is it significant that a particular character is the one to hear the story?

Sample Topics:

1. **Farce:** How does Dickens use farce in *Nicholas Nickleby*?

Exaggerated humor was a well-established literary element by Dickens's time. Which characters are in on the joke, and which are being made fun of, either by other characters or by Dickens? Mr. Mantalini is just one of several examples of farce in the novel:

With this affecting speech Mr. Mantalini fell down again very flat, and lay to all appearance without sense or motion, until all the females had left the room, when he came cautiously into a sitting posture, and confronted Ralph with a very blank face, and the little bottle still in one hand and the tea-spoon in the other.

"You may put away those fooleries now, and live by your wits again," said Ralph. (561)

Mr. Mantalini's entire character seems to be constructed by farce, although sometimes the exaggeration may produce frustration in the reader instead of humor. Is the rift in the Mantalini marriage due to Mrs. Mantalini's recognition of Mr. Mantalini's ridiculousness? Does Mr. Mantalini come to a similar realization? Why or why not? It is interesting to note that Douglas McGrath, director-writer of the 2002 film adaptation of *Nicholas Nickleby*, took the farce even further and played up the rather masculine description of Mrs. Crummles by casting a man in the role.

2. **Episodic stories:** Do these tales read as part of the *Nicholas Nickleby* story, or do they appear to be interruptions?

Nicholas Nickleby was the last novel in which Dickens used episodic stories such as "The Baron of Grogzwig" and "Five Sisters of York." Did Dickens intend these episodes as interruptions? If so, why? Are there parallels that can be drawn between either of these stories and the stories with which *Nicholas Nickleby* is more directly concerned? Why might Dickens have chosen these particular two stories for inclusion? Why would Dickens have stopped using this technique (most prevalent in *The Pickwick Papers*) after *Nicholas Nickleby*?

3. **Serialization:** What was gained and/or lost by serializing this particular story? (Remember the installments came first and were then compiled into novel form.)

Nicholas Nickleby does not seem to hold together as well as some of Dickens's other novels: "It is difficult not to feel that Dickens hit upon Yorkshire schools as a good subject, played it out, thought of a traveling theater company, played that out too, and finally introduced a quite different set of characters to restore the fortunes of Nicholas and his family" (Parker 148). Can you guess where the breaks might have been for the original serialized version? What are the indications? Verify your guesses with information about actual breaks. What does this tell you?

Language, Symbols, and Imagery

In general, there seems to be a wealth of literary device in any Dickens novel. Readers can rarely take a character or a prop at face value and must instead remain ready to understand and interpret these things as devices used toward a larger whole. In *Nicholas Nickleby*, for example, Dickens's use of personification is prevalent. Characters work on their own, but they become even more interesting when we begin to see what they represent or personify. On several occasions, one character's personification depends on another's, pulling the threads of the novel together so that we come to find overarching themes and ideas instead of disparate episodes.

Dickens's use of language is widely regarded as masterful in all of his writing. He was clearly an observer and careful listener with a gift for setting down on paper various accents, dialects, and idiosyncrasies. Think how different our recognition of the Squeers family would be if they were not differentiated by their dialect and language use. This element of language plays a crucial role in characterization and helps readers understand Dickens's perceptions of and attitudes toward his bevy of characters.

Sample Topics:

1. **Personification:** Which characters or inanimate objects seem to represent larger things or ideas? What is the significance of this technique?

Nicholas Nickleby is interesting and, one might argue, unusual in that Dickens not only uses traditional personification in the novel; he also uses most characters as personifications.

Whereas in his later works such as *Bleak House* and *Great Expectations* the characters are generally well-rounded individuals, even the main characters in *Nicholas Nickleby* seem to be representing larger ideas. In this way, readers get the impression that the characters survive only in relation to one another. For example, if Ralph Nickleby personifies evil, and Smike personifies purity and innocence, we need to see them in contrast to one another in order to appreciate these attributes. How, in other words, can we know just how evil Ralph is until we discover what he did to Smike?

A paper on this topic might begin by identifying what it is that various characters personify. From there, you can ask whether a character's personification of a concept or quality would be as evident without prompting from or contrast with other characters. Such an exercise might lead you to larger philosophical questions as well. In the case of Ralph (evil) and Smike (innocence), you might ask whether innocence can even exist (at least recognizably) without the presence of evil and experience.

2. **Dialect:** Is it fair of Dickens to use slang and poor grammar to classify characters and situations into a particular social class?

A certain misuse of language can make characters seem more evil or ignorant or laughable, as in Fanny Squeers's letter to Ralph Nickleby:

> When your nevew that you recommended for a teacher had done this to my pa and jumped upon his body with his feet and also langwedge which I will not pollewt my pen describing, he assaulted my ma with dreadful violence, dashed her to the earth, drove her back comb several inches into her head. A very little more and it must have entered her skull. We have a medical certifiket that if it had, the tortershell would have affected the brain. (183–184)

In this case, the content and style of Fanny's letter reflect each other. Her attempt at deceit (charging Nicholas with events that never occurred) seems to be mirrored by her attempt at scholarly, or higher-class, language. Both the deceit and the language seem arbitrarily thrown together. Why does she know how to spell *recommended* but not *nephew*? Why is the dialect of John Browdie no obstacle for readers in seeing his good character? Note, also, that Smike speaks quite well, at times almost eloquently when he has had little or no education and spent a number of years surrounded by the Squeers family. Why did he not pick up any of their habits?

Compare and Contrast Essays

We can often get a clearer idea of what something is by understanding what it is not, and vice versa. Papers that use comparison and contrast methods include not just lists of similarities and differences, but theories and interpretations about why such similarities and differences exist and what effect they have on the novel as a whole.

As fascinating as it can be to compare and contrast one character with another, it is equally interesting at times to compare a character with him- or herself. How, for example, is Nicholas at the beginning of the novel comparable to Nicholas at the end? What about Smike? Perhaps in this book, the best character for this kind of study is Ralph Nickleby. Are there significant changes that occur in this character between the beginning and the end of the novel? If so, what are they, and what causes them? If not, why not? Do the revelations at the end of the book explain or even justify Ralph's behavior earlier in the story?

Sample Topics:

1. **Kate and Mrs. Nickleby:** Do they influence each other in any noticeable ways?

   Do Kate and Mrs. Nickleby represent a strong woman versus a dependent, subservient woman, or are they both strong or both dependent and subservient? Does their behavior and strength depend on the situation, or are they both consistent in their ways of dealing with the world?

2. **Literary Kates:** Do you think there are Kates in literature written before or after *Nicholas Nickleby* that can be compared with Kate Nickleby?

There are many literary characters named Kate, and it seems that several of them are strong, feisty women who refuse to be victimized by their lives or other people. Are there Kates in later literature modeled on Kate Nickleby, or from before Dickens's time on whom Kate Nickleby might be modeled? We know, for example, that Dickens was very familiar with the works of William Shakespeare. What is the significance of similarities and differences between Kate Nickleby and Kate from Shakespeare's *The Taming of the Shrew*? Do you think Dickens intended to make such connections?

Bibliography for *Nicholas Nickleby*

Bradbury, Ray. "Any Friend of Nicholas Nickleby Is a Friend of Mine." *I Sing the Body Electric.* New York: Alfred A. Knopf, 1972. 200–229.

Chesterton, G. K. *"Nicholas Nickleby." Appreciations and Criticisms of the Works of Charles Dickens.* 1911. New York: Haskell House, 1970. 26–37.

Collins, Philip Arthur William. *Dickens and Education.* London: Macmillan, 1963.

Dickens, Charles. *Nicholas Nickleby.* 1838. New York: Barnes & Noble, 2005.

Gissing, George. *"Nicholas Nickleby." The Immortal Dickens.* 1925. London: Kraus Reprint, 1969. 88–111.

Parker, David. *"Nicholas Nickleby*: Love and Money." *The Doughty Street Novels: Pickwick Papers, Oliver Twist, Nicholas Nickleby, Barnaby Rudge.* New York: AMS, 2002. 147–180.

Paterson, Michael. *Voices from Dickens' London.* Cincinnati, OH: David & Charles, 2006.

A CHRISTMAS CAROL

READING TO WRITE

A CHRISTMAS CAROL (1843) is a deceptively simple story. The only truly "bad" character in the novella is not even that bad, and he spends the entire end of the tale making up for his wrongs so that all is well. The paradox of *A Christmas Carol* is that it has been widely regarded as the least well-written of Dickens's works and yet is probably the best known of his many works. But those who call this the least literary or least psychologically complex or least developed of Dickens's works perhaps have not read it closely enough.

The complexity of the story begins with its title. Dickens associates his story with holiday music, going so far as to call each section or chapter a "stave," elongating the musical metaphor. This is one of many elements in this story that make its historical context so fascinating. Why would Dickens want to tie his story to the Christmas carolers, traveling from house to house, looking for alms or a refill of the wassail bowl? Historical context also draws us into Dickens's position as a social activist. His writing always has a larger point to make about the world in which he lived and, strangely, usually ends up making a point about the world in which the readers live, regardless of century.

In stave 3 of the story, we find a scene that lends itself to greater study for several reasons:

Then up rose Mrs. Cratchit, Cratchit's wife, dressed out but poorly in a twice-turned gown, but brave in ribbons, which are cheap and make a goodly show for sixpence; and she laid the cloth, assisted by Belinda Cratchit, second of her daughters, also brave in ribbons; while Master

110

Peter Cratchit plunged a fork into the saucepan of potatoes, and getting the corners of his monstrous shirt collar (Bob's private property, conferred upon his son and heir in honour of the day) into his mouth, rejoiced to find himself so gallantly attired, and yearned to show his linen in the fashionable Parks. And now two smaller Cratchits, boy and girl, came tearing in, screaming that outside the baker's they had smelt the goose, and known it for their own; and basking in luxurious thoughts of sage and onion, these young Cratchits danced about the table, and exalted Master Peter Cratchit to the skies, while he (not proud, although his collar near choked him) blew the fire, until the slow potatoes bubbling up, knocked loudly at the saucepan to be let out and peeled. (52)

This paragraph is an excellent example of Dickens's work in many ways. You might notice that it is only two sentences long, and studying the use of punctuation can reveal something about the excitement of the scene and the idea that several things are happening all at once in the Cratchit house. We also get an idea of the number of children the Cratchits have, which is important in terms of their class and the emphasis on family in the tale.

The ribbons in this paragraph are also indicators of class and the level of dignity that the Cratchits attempt to maintain. These details, along with others, such as the foods the Cratchits are eating, might lead you to research the value of money in Victorian England. What is today's equivalent to sixpence, and what can we learn about the Cratchits knowing that sixpence was all that could be spared for vanity? Two young Cratchits come running from the baker's, making it important to note that poor people's homes at the time did not contain ovens, so bakeries would leave their ovens hot so that on Sundays and special occasions they could be used by the less fortunate. An astute reader and researcher would use this opportunity to ask larger questions about the text: What makes the Cratchit family an important part of the story? In other words, what message is Dickens trying to convey through his portrayal of the Cratchit family? Dickens clearly feels that the entire Cratchit family, not just Tiny Tim, is important to the story. Think about issues surrounding their economic class, their general attitudes toward life, the holiday spirit, treating others as one would like to be treated, or dealing with adversity to help you find more specific paper topics about the Cratchits and their role in the tale.

Questions about style also make good starting points for paper topics. How does Dickens employ writing techniques and vivid description to convey both a sense of realism and particular emotions that become associated with characters?

A careful reading of the text will allow you to look for elements that interest you and might be drawn into larger questions, issues, patterns, and ideas. Familiarizing yourself with the text itself becomes very helpful when finding necessary evidence in the story to support the claims in your paper.

TOPICS AND STRATEGIES

This section of the chapter discusses various possible topics for essays on *A Christmas Carol* and general approaches to these topics. Be aware that the material below is only a starting point, not some kind of master key to the perfect essay. Use this material to prompt your own thinking. Every topic discussed here could encompass a wide variety of good papers.

Themes

There are a number of possible themes worth writing about in *A Christmas Carol*. Writing about the theme of a particular work requires you to search the text for clues to that theme: words, phrases, chapter titles, and ideas that occur throughout the work. If the theme you have chosen to write about is family, for example, you might start by identifying the various families in the story: Scrooge and his nephew, the Fezziwigs, and the Cratchits. What do they have in common, and how are they different? What commentary does the narrator and/or Dickens make about the families? What kinds of words are used to describe particular families and families in general? (When is Scrooge described as a "father," for instance?) Using this textual evidence, you can determine what you think the story portrays about the theme of family. You can also look at the question of why a particular theme is so strong in the story. This line of questioning involves additional research into Dickens's time period and possibly his intentions for writing. Other themes can be written about in similar ways. The theme of holiday spirit, for example, might prompt you to ask what it means to "keep Christmas well" (88) in the story.

Sample Topics:

1. **Family:** How does the story represent and/or undermine the importance of family? What are the qualities that a good family possesses?

To write an essay on the theme of family, begin by identifying the families represented in the story, and then look at the words Dickens uses to describe and judge these families, as well as the nature of what happens to them. What changes occur in families or because of families? This information will help you develop an argument about families in the story.

2. **Holiday spirit:** Of course, Dickens uses literal spirits in the story, but this theme refers to the nature of the holidays. What kind of meaning or ambience does the story create surrounding Christmas?

One angle to take when studying this theme is the role of religion. Study the parts of the story in which religion is specifically mentioned or referred to, and from there you can infer the role of religion in the holiday spirit of *A Christmas Carol.* You might also look at the various Christmas scenes portrayed here to determine what is emphasized and what kinds of feelings and behavior seem to reap rewards. What kind of feelings does Dickens seem to want the reader to have when finished with the story?

3. **Death:** Death plays a large role in this story, in terms of the already dead Christmas spirits, the ideas of what might happen when a person dies, and the threat of death overhanging various characters because of their financial circumstances. Can death be considered a character in the tale? Why does death play such a prominent role in a story about Christmas?

This topic might require some historical research to determine why death was such a prevalent theme in the story. You will want to study the text carefully to evaluate how various characters think about and react to death in general or the deaths of specific people. Why does each character have his or her respective reaction? What kind of mood is created by the theme of death?

4. **Human rights:** If Dickens is trying to convey a particular message with this work, how might that message concern human rights?

A Christmas Carol provides several widely varying images of people, both the ones suffering and those who are in a position to help them. You might focus on one example, and look at the message that this portrayal conveys (then and now): Which actions, thoughts, and/or feelings are rewarded? Which are punished? Why? How does Dickens both draw groups of people together, demonstrating similarities, and pull them apart, emphasizing differences? How and why do various ideas and interpretations of people's lives and actions (or inaction) populate the story? For which type or group of people does Dickens seem to be advocating?

Characters

Characters can be written about in several different ways, including character development (such as how Scrooge changes or remains the same throughout the work, or how Dickens distinguishes between Scrooge and Bob Cratchit); methods of characterization (such as what we learn about Scrooge through his own revelations versus what we learn about him through others' comments, behavior, and observations); and even how we determine who is a character and who is not (in this case, we can ask whether the narrator should be considered a character and why or why not). Many of the categories in this book overlap, allowing one observation to lead to deeper meaning. For example, noting the prevalence of children as characters in *A Christmas Carol* might lead you to discover a particular theme in the work.

When you write about characters, you need to determine how we as readers get to know the characters in the story. The ways in which an author leaks information about a character can be as important as the characterization itself. Do we learn the most about Scrooge through his own words? Through his actions? Through the other characters' reactions to him or conversations about him? How do the spirits serve as windows into Scrooge's characterization? Dickens gives us a number of characters for such a short piece of fiction, and writing about character might mean determining how one character is distinguished from another. The Fezziwigs might in some ways be similar to Scrooge's nephew and his household. How does Dickens differentiate his characters, and how does he make them seem so real to us? It is important to look at characters in terms of broad strokes, such as the specific actions certain characters take, but it is equally important to study the methods of characterization that are easy to overlook: a character's manner of speaking, the images or setting connected with a character, repetition of words and phrases associated with a character, other characters' reactions to and discussions about a character, and the narrator's (and/or author's) commentary about a character.

Sample Topics:

1. **Scrooge's character development:** How does Scrooge change (or not) throughout the story? Why?

A *Christmas Carol* hinges on Scrooge's transformation, so it is important to look for the ways in which Scrooge changes. You might also look at readers' feelings toward Scrooge and Dickens's writing style. Is there anything in the first descriptions of Scrooge that leads readers to feel sorry for him? Does he seem to be purely evil? Provide evidence from Scrooge's words and actions as well as the words and actions of other characters.

2. **Narrator as character:** Can the narrator in this story be considered a character? Why or why not?

Look carefully for the places in the story that provide a distinct voice for the narrator (the first couple of paragraphs are a good example). Then decide whether you feel that the narrator tells the story in an objective (not personally biased) or subjective (introspective) style. Whatever you decide, using evidence from the text, you can then determine how the narrator's style affects (or does not affect) the outcome or portrayal of the story. Would the story end differently if told in a different way or by a different type of narrator? Would the story leave readers with a different tone or mood if told by a different type of narrator? Another angle on this topic is to look at whether we can assume that the narrator is actually Charles Dickens.

3. **Children:** How and why are the characters of children significant? Could the story be told as effectively without them?

Many people who have not even read *A Christmas Carol* have heard of Tiny Tim. Why? What is his significance to the story? What message is conveyed through Dickens's use of children (Tiny Tim, Want and Ignorance, Ebenezer as a child, etc.)? Look at what these children have in common, and how they differ. Do these characterizations seem realistic? Why or why not? Why does Dickens include so many children?

History and Context

Another fascinating approach to literature involves looking at the effects that a particular place and time period have on a work. Dickens wrote *A Christmas Carol* in England in 1843, and it can be very enlightening to investigate who was the original audience for the work, what might have inspired Dickens to write it, what readers' reactions were to the story, and how many incarnations the story had in Dickens's time.

Dickens wrote during the Victorian period, defined by Queen Victoria's 1837–1901 reign. Studying the class system in England can provide important background information for the story. Dickens was one of the first novelists to include and sometimes focus on poor and lower-class characters, giving readers then and now portraits of lives that might have previously been ignored or glossed over. Dickens's reasons for doing this revolve around his sense of social activism, or, in other words, his sense that the divide between the haves and the have-nots should not be so large. Much of his inspiration came from legal decisions and documents (such as the 1842 Parliamentary Report) as well as his many lengthy walks, observing people from all classes.

Choosing to write about history and context might involve drawing connections between the 1842 Parliamentary Report on the employment and condition of children in mines and manufactories and *A Christmas Carol*, in terms of how such a document could or would have affected Dickens's characters. No one in the story works in a mine or factory, but under different circumstances, the Cratchits, for example, might have. How does Dickens create sympathy for those characters, thus indirectly influencing readers' opinions on the Parliamentary Report and what it might mean for those characters?

There are many options for writing about this story in terms of history and context. You could look specifically at food, for example, in terms of its position as a status symbol and/or a tradition of the time. This ties in somewhat with Christmas celebrations, which seem to have blossomed after *A Christmas Carol* was published. Dickens might be said to have both created and followed several holiday traditions in the story, making the work so iconic that a little girl learning of Dickens's death reportedly asked if Father Christmas was dead, too.

Sample Topics:

1. **Class system in England:** The characters in the story represent several different classes in Victorian England. How does Dickens represent these classes of people? What is the purpose of drawing such distinctions between them?

   A paper on this topic would need to research the class system in Victorian England, reading various perspectives (from then and now) on the economic and political reasons for the class divisions. Start with encyclopedia entries to gain basic information, and then look at books such as William B. Thesing's *A Companion to the Victorian Novel* for more information and background. Next, you would want to study how Dickens illustrates the various classes of people, and try to determine why he includes this facet of society as such as important part of his story.

2. **Christmas celebrations:** In what ways does *A Christmas Carol* accurately portray Christmas in Victorian England? In what ways does the story change the way Christmas is celebrated in England (and perhaps elsewhere)?

Various groups of people in the story celebrate Christmas in different ways, but they have much in common (the importance of specific foods, for example). How are the Christmas celebrations in the story similar to (and different from) actual celebrations in England at this time? Did Christmas celebrations change after the story was published? If so, how and why? If not, why not?

3. **1842 Parliamentary Report:** In what ways can you see Dickens using this document on the employment and condition of children in mines and manufactories as a source for his story?

The story does not contain direct references to this report, nor does it focus on child labor, yet Dickens points out that Martha Cratchit works long hours as a milliner's apprentice and that Peter Cratchit is soon to begin work as well. Studying the parliamentary report in terms of its influence on Dickens and its place in *A Christmas Carol* can lead to insights about Dickens's intentions for the work as well as his opinions on child labor.

Philosophy and Ideas

Philosophy and ideas in a literary work are similar to theme, although they are usually much less specific. Studying philosophy and ideas in a work of literature means that you generally agree that literature influences life and inspires a deeper level of thinking about particular topics. Scholars look at Dickens to tell us about life in 19th-century England—not just in terms of what people did, but how and what they thought, and the insights those thoughts can offer.

This line of thinking allows you to look at *A Christmas Carol* in a broad context. For example, is there such a thing as a philosophy of Christmas, and how does this story examine that? Some believe that this work is blasphemous in its lack of attention to Christianity and what they feel is a misguided attention to money, food, and material goods. How is it possible to write *A Christmas Carol*, a work whose very name ties it to religion, without significant focus on Christ? This leads to the larger idea about Christmas—that the holiday is in fact larger, or somehow more important, than any given religion, and that the goodwill on which Dickens focuses transcends religious boundaries and conveys a more insightful message.

Sample Topics:

1. **Religion:** Scholars disagree about the place of religion in *A Christmas Carol*. Some say that Dickens managed to write a Christmas story with little or no religious content, while others argue that the story contains characters representing biblical figures of the Old and New Testaments. Is *A Christmas Carol* a religious work?

   This kind of essay requires you to form an argument regarding the religious content (or lack thereof) in the story and support it with evidence from the text. *A Christmas Carol* is not full of direct references to religion, but look for allegories, characters as representations, and subtle references to what Dickens would have known as Christian tenets. You might start by researching whether someone from a non-Christian background gleans the same themes and messages from the story as someone from a Christian background.

2. **Ethics and responsibility:** Dickens certainly wrote to entertain, but he also wrote about social, political, and economic matters that weighed on his mind. To what degree do Dickens's themes, characters, and ideas affect readers' consciences?

   As with any writing about literature, you will want to work closely with the text. In this case, you might start by looking at the ethics and responsibility practiced by various characters in *A Christmas Carol*. For what kinds of actions and thoughts are characters either rewarded or punished? Scrooge, for example, says "It's enough for a man to understand his own business, and not to interfere with other people's" (Dickens 15) at the beginning of the story. After his visits from the spirits, Scrooge finds himself greatly concerned by the "business" of others and does what he can to help. How does this part of Scrooge's transformation demonstrate Dickens's points about ethics and responsibility?

3. **Self-knowledge:** It is easy for readers to determine what they know about characters in a story but more challenging to look for what the characters know about themselves. Which characters seem to know themselves best?

The idea of self-knowledge becomes important when it is understood that someone who knows him- or herself well is better equipped to know (and conceivably help) others. You might say that Scrooge's journey in this book takes him from ignorance to self-knowledge. What does it take for characters in this story to develop self-knowledge, and how are they rewarded once they obtain it? It is clear that Scrooge has to be literally shown his own life in order to learn about himself, but how does Dickens let us know that such characters as Tiny Tim and the Fezziwigs already know and accept themselves?

Form and Genre

The form of *A Christmas Carol* is a short novel, or novella, and the genre is seasonal, meaning that it is specifically connected with a time of year or a holiday. However, the complexity of Dickens's work reveals more: The story's title along with the section break titles (stanzas) reveal its underpinnings as a song or carol. Sections of the story utilize poetic elements, making the work at times more of an extended poem. Shortly after publication, the story was adapted for the stage, where it is still widely seen today, compelling us to look at the story as a play. And the fact that Dickens essentially created the seasonal story genre with this work gives us even more to study.

Sample Topics:

1. *A Christmas Carol* **as a poem:** Dickens uses a number of poetic elements such as alliteration, simile, assonance, internal rhyme, and apostrophe. What effects do these poetic elements have on the story?

Two examples of poetic lines in the story include "dead as a doornail" (9) and "How it bared its breadth of breast" (58). Search the story carefully for other examples of poetic elements. Are certain poetic elements associated with particular scenes or characters? What can these associations tell us about the scene or characters that we would not understand through the average prose style?

2. *A Christmas Carol* **as a play:** Though Dickens dabbled in acting and loved the theater, the story is not written as a play. Immediately following its publication, however, it was adapted for the stage, and versions of it have been acted on stage ever since. What is it about the style and structure of this story that lends itself well to the play form?

Dickens was reportedly disappointed in the stage versions of *A Christmas Carol* that he saw, leaving us to wonder about his penchant for the stage and how he might have envisioned the story on it. What characteristics does the story share with a play? For example, does the story rely mainly on dialogue, as plays do? Does Dickens's narration provide stage directions (telling the characters how to move about the stage, etc.)? How does this affect the telling of the tale?

3. *A Christmas Carol* **as a song:** Dickens connects his novella with music when he titles it *A Christmas Carol* and divides it into staves. What role does music play in both the content and structure of the story?

Dickens seems to place his short novel firmly in the tradition of Christmas singing through its title, compelling readers to find other musical elements within the story and perhaps to combine the structural analysis with content as well as historical context. If in your detailed study of the text you conclude that it can in some way be classified as a song, your next step might be to look at context to determine the place of the Christmas carol and/or the practice of Christmas caroling in Dickens's time. How does Dickens's tale fit into or break such traditions? What does the piece's categorization (in part) as a song say about its overall message?

Language, Symbols, and Imagery

Any work containing as many poetic elements as this one deserves to be studied for its language, symbols, and imagery. Studying these elements requires you to avoid summarizing the content of the piece, concentrating instead on how the content is conveyed and how these style choices add to or detract from the theme, philosophy, and ideas presented.

Studying language means that you are looking at word choice, syntax, and general diction. For example, you might try to determine why Dickens at times chooses old-fashioned, almost biblical language in places: "Spirit of Tiny Tim, thy childish essence was from God!" (78).

Symbols are things in a literary work that stand for something else. Some scholars believe that the spirits in *A Christmas Carol* are actually symbols of Scrooge's conscience. Symbols can embody universal meaning, as a journey usually symbolizes life, but they might also have specific or changing meanings, depending on how they are used in the work. Tiny Tim, for example, might symbolize hope to his family but uselessness to someone like Scrooge.

Imagery is an element of the text that invokes at least one of the five senses.

Sample Topics:

1. **Want and Ignorance:** These two characters are children (a boy and a girl), which is very important to Dickens's message. They are described as "Yellow, meagre, ragged, scowling, wolfish; but prostrate, too, in their humility" (66). These are "Man's children" (66), as the spirit describes, and the symbolism they embody is deep. What do these two children symbolize? (Think about not only what Dickens tells us about them, but what we are left to determine on our own.)

   We know that Want and Ignorance are symbols, but a close investigation of the short scene in which they appear tells us much more than that. As you read this scene again, ask yourself questions: What do these children symbolize exactly? Why are they children? Why in such awful condition? What message, other than what is literally mentioned in the story, is Dickens trying to send to readers through these symbols?

2. **Fog/weather:** Scholars have argued that the heavy fog in *A Christmas Carol* is meteorologically inaccurate for the time of year. Why then, is it there?

Fog is an integral element of Dickens's work, appearing at times as almost a character. We know that London was often foggy, not only with clouds but with the soot and grime from factories, in the 19th century. What does fog, or weather in general, seem to represent in *A Christmas Carol*? Do certain kinds of weather coincide with certain kinds of activity in the story? Searching for such clues can lead you to draw conclusions about Dickens's intentions in his use of fog and weather in general.

3. **Darkness and light:** Light and darkness are often literal in *A Christmas Carol,* such as the "darkest night" (58) in which Scrooge is led by a spirit. Darkness and light are also symbolic in the story: What kinds of events happen in the darkness? In the light?

To write a paper on darkness and light as symbolic, you will want to pay particular attention, of course, to literal darkness and light and which characters are associated with each. But you will also want to look at the use of words associated with the concepts, such as *bright*, which is often used to describe people's faces. You might look particularly at the Ghost of Christmas Past, whose strange hat Scrooge presses down "with all his force, [but] he could not hide the light" (44). What might such a light symbolize?

Compare and Contrast Essay

Comparison and contrast papers search for similarities and differences between characters or elements in the story, but the work does not end there. It is crucial that you comment on those similarities and/or differences. There is no purpose to just pointing out similarities between Scrooge and Cratchit, for instance, if you cannot reach some sort of conclusion or argument about them. Avoiding this last part of comparison and contrast papers turns your work into a list rather than a cohesive paper that invites readers' interest.

The most obvious and sometimes most complicated comparison and contrast papers usually compare one character to another, and they are often more interesting when you use two characters who are at first glance quite different, such as Scrooge and Bob Cratchit. You might compare characters from different works: How is Scrooge similar to and different from Mr. Skimpole in *Bleak House,* for example? Or, you could look at what Dickens does with *A Christmas Carol* versus one of his other seasonal stories.

Once you decide on your elements for comparison and delineate what the similarities and differences are, you will need to determine what is important about such similarities and differences. What do they reveal about each character, or about the work as a whole, or about the work's message, etc.? What do the various attitudes toward death in *A Christmas Carol* say about 19th-century attitudes toward death in general? Or, what do they say about the effect a person's economic class might have on his or her attitude toward death? It is crucial that the similarities and differences you notice lead to some sort of point or purpose.

Sample Topics:

1. **Scrooge and Cratchit:** At first glance, it seems there could hardly be two characters more different than Scrooge and Bob Cratchit, but in what ways are they actually similar to each other? Studying their differences and any possible similarities might lead to larger revelations about class, family, and self-knowledge.

   At the beginning of the story, it seems that Scrooge and Cratchit are polar opposites, though as the narrative progresses we learn some of their reasons for behaving the way they do. Scrooge in particular undergoes a transformation in the story, making him both more similar to and different from Cratchit. What do these two characters together reveal about holiday spirit, the class system in Victorian England, the importance of self-knowledge, or attitudes toward family?

2. **The spirits—visions or dreams?** Scholars continue to argue whether Scrooge's visits from the spirits were actual visits or simply dreams. If the spirits' visits take place in Scrooge's imagination, does that devalue the story? Or, is it somehow less valuable if the spirits are real and Scrooge did not reach these conclusions on his own? Comparing and contrasting the two readings will allow you to speculate about the forces at work in *A Christmas Carol.*

This topic requires you to read carefully through the story twice—once as if the spirits are actually visiting Scrooge and once as if Scrooge is only dreaming about the spirits. How are the two readings similar and dissimilar? What impact does each reading have on the outcome of the story? You may end up making an argument about whether outside forces are at work in the story, or if it is simply Scrooge's conscience guiding him to change.

3. **Attitudes toward death:** Perhaps the most striking examples of attitudes toward death occur when Scrooge and the spirit look upon the scenes surrounding Scrooge's own death. These reactions are clearly a result of Scrooge's surliness toward these people. What is Scrooge's reaction to his own death? Why is this such a turning point in the story? Broaden the scope a bit, and look at other characters' attitudes toward death as well.

Death surrounds the Cratchits to the point where many readers come away believing that Tiny Tim dies at the end of the story. He does not, but it is certainly a very real possibility. How do the Cratchits deal with this shadow in their lives? How is this similar to and different from the ways in which the servants and people on the street react to Scrooge's death? How has Jacob Marley dealt with his own death? Does it appear that some characters are more prepared for the likelihood of death because of their lifestyle or their class? What message might Dickens be trying to send through the various attitudes in the story?

Bibliography and Online Resources for *A Christmas Carol*

Callow, Simon. *Dickens's Christmas: A Victorian Celebration*. New York: Harry N. Abrams, 2003.

"Charles Dickens." Victorian Web. Retrieved 10 May 2007. <http://www.victorian web.org/authors/dickens/dickensov.html>.

Davis, Paul. *The Lives and Times of Ebenezer Scrooge*. New Haven, CT: Yale UP, 1990.

Dickens, Charles. *The Annotated Christmas Carol: A Christmas Carol in Prose*. Ed. Michael Patrick Hearn. New York: W. W. Norton, 2004.

———. *A Christmas Carol*. 1843. New York: Barnes and Noble, 2004.

Guida, Fred. *A Christmas Carol and Its Adaptations: Dickens's Story on Screen and Television*. Jefferson: McFarland & Co., 2000.

Karson, Jill, ed. *Readings on A Christmas Carol*. Greenhaven Press Literary Companion to British Literature. San Diego, CA: Greenhaven P, 2000.

Thesing, William B. *A Companion to the Victorian Novel*. Malden, Mass.: Blackwell, 2002.

University of California. The Dickens Project. Available online. URL: http://www.dickens.ucsc.edu/. Retrieved May 10, 2007.

DAVID COPPERFIELD

READING TO WRITE

C HARLES DICKENS claimed to be surprised when a friend pointed out to him that David Copperfield's initials were in fact Charles Dickens's in reverse. Apparently, this is one element of the connection between his real life and the novel *David Copperfield* that he had not consciously thought through. He was probably well aware that *David Copperfield* was the closest he would ever come to writing his own autobiography. He had started writing his life story at one point but ended up burning most of it. Parts of that original autobiography manuscript survive in *David Copperfield*, making for fascinating study of the line between fact and fiction. The novel was published serially between 1849 and 1850.

Regardless of its origins and connections to Dickens's life, *David Copperfield* is a favorite of many Dickens readers and, in fact, was the favorite of Dickens himself. Paradoxically, David himself is often seen as the dullest character in the entire book, overshadowed by the manic Micawbers, the strong Betsey Trotwood, and the conniving Uriah Heep. The book may also stand out from Dickens's other novels because it is in many ways his least provocative novel, containing most of its action in the domestic sphere, rather than directly taking on society and politics the way that most of his other novels do. This does not mean, however, that *David Copperfield* does not have its own driving force, its own message to send to readers. Looking closely at a few related passages from the novel will allow us to uncover just a few of the possibilities for writing about this novel.

Some of the most telling scenes in the novel are early ones between David, his mother, and Peggotty. The contrasts between the scenes when these three people are alone and when the Murdstones are present provide excellent opportunities for studying all of the various characters

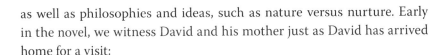

as well as philosophies and ideas, such as nature versus nurture. Early in the novel, we witness David and his mother just as David has arrived home for a visit:

> "Davy, my pretty boy! My poor child!" Then she kissed me more and more, and clasped me round the neck. This she was doing when Peggotty came running in, and bounced down on the ground beside us, and went mad about us both for a quarter of an hour. . . . We dined together by the fireside. Peggotty was in attendance to wait upon us, but my mother wouldn't let her do it, and made her dine with us. I had my own old plate, with a brown view of a man-of-war in full sail upon it, which Peggotty had hoarded somewhere all the time I had been away, and would not have had broken, she said, for a hundred pounds. I had my own old mug with David on it, and my own old little knife and fork that wouldn't cut. (102)

This passage shows us the general atmosphere of the home when Clara Copperfield, Peggotty, and David are left to their own devices. There is a lot of physical and verbal affection and a considerable amount of mutual respect for one another, regardless of age or position in the household. We see that Clara Copperfield regards Peggotty as a friend rather than a servant when she will not allow Peggotty to wait on them and instead insists that the three of them all eat together. There is no hierarchy in Clara's household, and she considers herself no better than the woman who technically works for her. This is clearly an admirable quality of Clara's, as are most of the qualities she demonstrates before the Murdstones infiltrate her home and try to change her. All of the hugs and joy at David's return from school clearly show that separation has been difficult for all of them, and that all three are more joyful when together.

All of this is not only David's nature, we can assume, as he would have inherited some of these traits from his mother; this scene also demonstrates the nurturing atmosphere in which David spent his earliest years. Peggotty treasures not only the boy but his possessions as well, making sure that his special dishes and utensils are preserved safely for him and that he has a chance to use them whenever possible. As an adult looking back on this time of his life, David remembers being perfectly happy and content. He continues remembering his feeling of contentment while learning letters with his mother. This stands in great contrast to the learning methods he experiences under the Murdstones:

Shall I ever forget those lessons! They were presided over nominally by my mother, but really by Mr. Murdstone and his sister, who were always present, and found them a favourable occasion for giving my mother lessons in that miscalled firmness, which was the bane of both of our lives. I believe I was kept at home, for that purpose. I had been apt enough to learn, and willing enough, when my mother and I had lived alone together. I can faintly remember learning the alphabet at her knee. To this day, when I look upon the fat black letters in the primer, the puzzling novelty of their shapes, and the easy good nature of O and Q and S, seem to present themselves again before me as they used to do. But they recall no feeling of disgust or reluctance. On the contrary, I seemed to have walked along a path of flowers as far as the crocodile-book, and to have been cheered by the gentleness of my mother's voice and manner all the way. But these solemn lessons which succeeded those, I remember as the death-blow at my peace, and a grievous daily drudgery and misery. They were very long, very numerous, very hard—perfectly unintelligible, some of them, to me—and I was generally as much bewildered by them as I believe my poor mother was herself. (55–56)

The Murdstones consider David (and, evidently, young boys in general) inherently unlikable and set about to correct the flaws in his demeanor that lead him to cling to his mother and Peggotty and become unable to learn his lessons under the extreme pressure and threat of cruelty with which the Murdstones surround him. There are very interesting questions to ask about these scenes that might lead to worthy paper topics. To what extent does the Murdstones' treatment of David have an effect that is the opposite of what they intend? They want David to learn his school lessons and be seen rather than heard, though his fear of them leads him to wish more fervently than ever for the kind touches and words from his mother and Peggotty and, of course, also leads him to forget all of his lessons and appear unable to learn at all. All of this brings up issues having to do with history and context as well. What is Dickens's message about teaching methods? What were the common teaching methods and theories of the time, and how successful or ridiculous does Dickens make such methods and theories look in this novel?

One more brief scene can help demonstrate paper topic possibilities. Young David reflects on daily life after the Murdstones move into the once cheerful house:

I felt that I made them as uncomfortable as they made me. If I came into the room where they were, and they were talking together and my mother seemed cheerful, an anxious cloud would steal over her face from the moment of my entrance. If Mr. Murdstone were in his best humour, I checked him. If Miss Murdstone were in her worst, I intensified it. I had perception enough to know that my mother was the victim always; that she was afraid to speak to me, or be kind to me, lest she should give them some offence by her manner of doing so, and receive a lecture afterwards; that she was not only ceaselessly afraid of her own offending, but of my offending, and uneasily watched their looks if I only moved. (109)

The main thing that we see in this paragraph is David's perspective. Even though he is writing his story as an older man, some of his memories of this time come through in the voice and thoughts of a young boy. Which words and phrases does Dickens use to demonstrate that the older David writing the story possesses insight that the young David did not? Which words seem to be coming directly from young David himself, rather than through the filter of a much older and presumably wiser man? Which words and phrases in this passage best reflect the tone, or mood, of the situation? How does Dickens continue to make readers sympathize with David rather than with the Murdstones? Some readers even go so far as to be angry with David's mother for allowing these things to happen. Do you think that is Dickens's intention? Why or why not?

David Copperfield is full of scenes and passages that provide a wealth of ideas for paper topics. As you read and reflect on what you have read, pinpoint the characters and scenes that you find most interesting or that you have the most questions about, and use the prompts in this chapter to help you brainstorm ideas for writing.

TOPICS AND STRATEGIES

This section of the chapter addresses various possible topics for writing about *David Copperfield* as well as general methods for approaching these topics. These lists are in no way exhaustive and are meant to provide a jumping-off point rather than an answer key. Use these suggestions to find your own ideas and form your own analyses. All topics discussed in this chapter could potentially turn into very good papers.

Themes

There are any number of themes, ideas, or concepts in *David Copperfield* that help to inform the plot. To write about a theme in a particular work, you must start by identifying words, phrases, chapter titles, and ideas that recur throughout the work. Some of the themes in *David Copperfield* include growing up, loss, respect, love, family, and finding a place to belong. If you choose to write about love, for example, you can start by identifying the ways in which various characters express their love for others. It is important to note that the sheer number of characters in the novel makes it nearly impossible to cover every one of them accurately and in depth, so you may need to narrow it down right away. You can look at the free expressions of love shown by David, his mother, and Peggotty before the Murdstones arrive. This may lead to a larger discussion about why these seemingly natural and healthy expressions of love are prohibited by the Murdstones. Or, you can ask who brings love back into David's life after his mother dies. A very interesting character to investigate along these lines is Uriah Heep. Does he show love? He expresses love for Agnes and for his mother, but do you believe that his words are sincere? Why or why not? Does anyone appear to genuinely love Uriah? Why or why not? You might want to look at the text in a broader sense and determine the types of words, phrases, and gestures Dickens implements to make characters demonstrate love for one another. Or, you could look for reasons why a particular theme is so strong in the novel. This will require some research into Dickens's life and/or the 19th-century context. What were the ways in which people generally expressed love for one another (keep in mind that one's financial status or class might play a significant role in what is allowed and what is not)? Does Dickens's use of love as a theme seem to be attempting to convey a message to society in general?

Sample Topics:

1. **Love:** How do various characters in the book show love, and what does this reveal about them?

   Some of the loving characters in the book play very minor roles (Mr. Mell, for example). Why does Dickens even bother to include such characters? Do you think that the harsh treatment David suffers under the Murdstones and Mr. Creakle is just their way of expressing love for him? Is there anyone who seems to express too much love? David, for example, should probably be a bit more intimidated and hardened by the life he has led, but he lavishes love on Dora, Aunt Betsey, and the Micawbers. Why? What is Dickens conveying about love?

2. **Respect:** Uriah Heep, the Micawbers, Mr. Wickfield, David, Dora, and many other characters are all looking for respect from someone for something. Which characters deserve it? Who already has it? How closely is respect tied to one's finances?

David is shown considerable respect by the Micawbers and the Peggottys, for example. Is there evidence in the text that David has earned that respect, or does he receive it because of social class or the generally respectful nature of these people? What qualities does a person need to possess in order to earn respect in this novel? Choose a character that you feel both Dickens and David respect, and investigate the aspects of this character's personality and life that most clearly earn them such respect. Which qualities in a character seem to earn the most vehement disrespect? What does this reveal about Dickens's attitude?

3. **Family:** David creates his own family in a sense. In what ways are his nonrelatives more important to him than his blood relatives? What is it that bonds all of these people together? Freak circumstance? Genuine affection? Obligation?

Begin by looking at David's actual family—his mother and his aunt. What roles do they play in the story (that is, in David's life)? Which relationships of David's seem stronger than those with blood ties? Why? You might also choose to look at another family—the Peggottys or the Wickfields, for example—to examine how much value is placed on family and who is accepted as family, as well as who is rejected, and why.

Characters

Papers focusing on characters often look at the ways in which a character develops (or does not) in terms of what distinguishes one character from another, ways in which the author characterizes the people (through word choice, tone, etc.), and interpretations of changes made either to or by a character over time. *David Copperfield* gives you a lot to work with in all of these areas.

One of the main complications surrounding any writing about characters in *David Copperfield* is that the work is partly autobiographical. David and Dickens are, in some senses and at some times, interchangeable. It is important to consider David's character through this lens of reality, but it is equally important that not everything in the story be presumed to come from Dickens's life. This crossover between fact and fiction can make fascinating writing topics, especially if you are interested in Dickens's life and would like to determine which parts of David's personality and life actually come from Dickens's personality and life. This research, coupled with careful readings of the novel, can lead to important theses speculating as to why Dickens made such choices.

This doubling of author and character also creates an interesting way of looking at other characters in the book. We see everything from David's perspective, after all, so we really only get his side of the story. What kinds of possibilities does that open up? How would this story be different if told from Uriah Heep's perspective, or Mr. Micawber's?

When writing about characters you always want to keep the author's techniques in mind. What kinds of words, phrases, settings, and moods generally surround a particular character? How does Dickens lead readers to feel that things surrounding Mr. Dick, for example, are light-hearted and sweet, while things surrounding Uriah are bleak and sinister? Understanding the ways in which Dickens manipulates the text can help you focus your writing on the results of such manipulation, or maybe even the reasons behind it.

Sample Topics:

1. **Uriah Heep:** Is he purely evil? What are his motivations? Do readers ever feel sorry for him? How can we tell when (and if) he is sincere?

Dickens uses very subtle foreshadowing and hints to reveal Uriah's true character to readers before the characters understand him fully. How do these techniques keep us from being surprised when Uriah is found to be sinister? Looking at the details surrounding Uriah will help you generate a thesis about why Uriah is or is not the true villain of the story. Maybe you sympathize with Uriah and feel that another character such as Murdstone or Creakle deserves more credit as a true villain. Use precise words from the text to support this argument.

2. **David Copperfield:** What does he learn? What, if anything, does his story teach readers?

David is often viewed as the flattest, least interesting character in *David Copperfield.* Do you think this was Dickens's choice, to make David simply a background on which to display the more fascinating characters? Why or why not? Is David too good to be true? Does he become unrealistic? What kinds of words does Dickens use to describe David (which is also David describing himself)? Since David writes the story as a reflection on his life so far, what perspective (if any) does he seem to have gained through the years? These observations and careful readings can lead you to a thesis about the nature of David's character or the complications for Dickens (and for David) in writing semiautobiographically.

3. **Mr. Micawber:** How closely does he resemble Dickens's father (the model for this character)? Why do you think Dickens portrays his father in this way?

It seems that Dickens wants readers to feel a variety of emotions about Micawber: frustration, bewilderment, love, respect. Which feeling is most associated with Micawber's character? What textual evidence demonstrates this? Why do you feel that this is what Dickens/David wants us to feel about Micawber? Does Micawber change over time, or does the world around him change?

4. **Dora Spenlow:** She is immature and at times dumb as a post. How (and why) does Dickens make readers like her, nonetheless?

Some readers will love Dora, while others will be continually frustrated by her and by David for loving her. Are these contrasting characterizations a reflection of David's feelings for Dora? What seems to be Dora's role in the story and/or in David's life? Delving into Dora's character may help you draw conclusions about such topics as social class and true love.

History and Context

Studying the history and context of a work allows you to address the background of either (or both) the story and the author. Dickens always set his novels at some point in 19th-century England, making investigations into the Victorian period extremely useful.

David Copperfield is understood to be Dickens's least social text, meaning that most of the book takes place in the domestic sphere of home and family, leaving work, politics, and economics on the periphery. Even so, Dickens does ground this novel in the events and attitudes of the day, making a study of history and context very revealing.

Learning about the background of even the smallest detail mentioned in a novel can provide greater insight into characters, plot, and, of course, setting. For a paper focusing on history and context, you might look at general attitudes and behaviors that characters share. It seems to be understood, for example, that women are not supposed to run their own households, as demonstrated by David's mother and her reliance on the Murdstones. Betsey Trotwood, on the other hand, is clearly in charge of her own life and home. Study the details of her character and then research those details to learn whether her status as a (technically) married woman changes society's perceptions of her. Perhaps her social class is a factor. Is her personality strong enough to overcome society's strictures? This type of background information will help you form a thesis about a particular character's actions (or nonactions), about the accuracy of Dickens's settings, and even sometimes about Dickens's opinions of the events and ideologies of his time.

Sample Topics:
1. **Dickens's life:** It is the backbone or at least the jumping-off
   point for David's story.

   Which details of Dickens's life find their way into *David Copperfield*? Do there appear to be specific reasons why Dickens
   would write about these particular details of his life? Which
   elements of Dickens's life are left out of *David Copperfield*?
   Can you speculate as to why? Given its autobiographical
   context, can we safely say that *David Copperfield* represents
   Dickens's truest account of life in general or the world as he
   knows it? What does this book reveal about Dickens's place in
   Victorian England? Remember that *David Copperfield* is still
   in many ways a fictional story. Why did Dickens not write a
   straightforward autobiography?

2. **Education for boys in the 19th century:** How would David's
   education have been different if he had been the girl that Aunt
   Betsey so desperately wanted? How would it have been different
   if he had been from another social class?

   Many young boys in 19th-century England (including David
   and Dickens) had to work in factories rather than attend
   school. Education became compulsory under the Education
   Act of 1870. Look at the history surrounding this law to determine the reasons behind the change. In what ways is this both
   a good and a bad thing? Dickens and David both would have
   been very different people writing about very different things
   if their educations had not been interrupted.

3. **Australia:** Why do the Micawbers and Dan and Em'ly Peggotty
   go to Australia rather than the United States? What is the history of Australia as a colony of Britain?

   Why is it easier for the Peggottys and Micawbers to be successful in Australia rather than in England? What does this
   reveal about England, its laws, and its society? Australia was

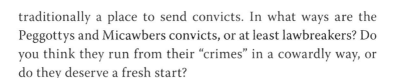

traditionally a place to send convicts. In what ways are the Peggottys and Micawbers convicts, or at least lawbreakers? Do you think they run from their "crimes" in a cowardly way, or do they deserve a fresh start?

Philosophy and Ideas

Writing about the philosophy and ideas found in a text is similar to writing about the text's theme, except that philosophy and ideas are applied more generally and live in some sense outside the text as well. So, when writing about a book's philosophy and ideas, you are looking for the ways in which the work comments on general ideas. Much has been made of *David Copperfield* as a coming-of-age story, for example. Is there a specific point in the story when David loses his innocence? If so, what happens after that? It is important to look not only at David but also at other characters. Are the coming-of-age experiences similar enough for us to make generalizations about Dickens's outlook? Compare the experiences of Steerforth, David, Em'ly, Dora, and Agnes. Even some of the older characters seem to fall from innocence into experience at some point. What does it take to become an experienced, mature individual in this book? What kinds of knowledge and experience are most valuable? How did the country of England in the 19th century move from innocence to experience? All of these questions can be speculated upon by studying Dickens's treatment of coming-of-age stories.

Sample Topics:

1. **A better life in Australia:** Why are some characters' problems resolved by emigrating? What is the nature of these characters' problems, and why can they not be resolved in England?

   Even in Dickens's lifetime, Australia was a place for England's convicts. What were 19th-century English attitudes toward Australia? When did it change from an isolated punishment for lawbreakers into a promising new world? Why does Australia seem to be the only option for Em'ly and the Micawbers? Can these characters be equated with convicts on some level? What does the necessity of emigration reveal about England and the impossibility of success there?

2. **Tabula rasa:** Tabula rasa is John Locke's 18th-century idea that people are born as blank slates, and there is nothing inherently on them. Are people born blank slates? To what extent do we become whatever people tell us that we are?

   David's first lessons come from his mother and Peggotty, and he is able to hold on to them through his difficulties. How is David educated (formally and informally) by others, and to what extent does he teach or create himself? He definitely learns through trial and error—often his own, but sometimes of others. Is David predisposed to the heroism mentioned in the novel's first sentence, or is he just lucky? Does David always become what people say of him (the Murdstones, Peggotty, Micawber, etc.)?

3. **Coming of age:** In what ways is David individualized, and in what ways does he come to represent more people than just himself?

   How does Dickens illustrate David's growth? Do the people around him help him or does he come of age in spite of his surroundings? How much of David's knowledge comes from his own experiences, and how much does he glean from the experiences of others?

Form and Genre

Form and genre provide ways of classifying works that usually allow us to study them more fully. Form is defined as the style and structure of a work, whereas genre is the type, or classification, of a work. Both form and genre are usually distinct from a work's content, though writers use each of them quite specifically to convey a particular message, reach a certain audience, or simply strengthen the impact of their work.

The form and genre of *David Copperfield* distinguish it from all of Dickens's other works. While it is technically classified as fiction, readers understand that *David Copperfield* is at least partly Dickens's autobiography. He structures the story as David's memoir for any number of reasons. Possibly he knew that this was the closest he would ever come to writing his own story; perhaps he needed David to stand in for himself in order to feel that he was not relating too much of his own life. Regardless, this work gives us great insight into Dickens's life as well as his choices for writing. It is not enough, however, to study Dickens's life alongside the novel and simply match up the similarities. Writing about form and genre requires you to push further and ask why Dickens might have used particular techniques.

Sample Topics:

1. **Autobiography/memoir:** How does this form and style of writing affect the story? Is David a reliable narrator?

The full serial title of the novel—*The Personal History, Adventures, Experience and Observation of David Copperfield the Younger of Blunderstone Rookery (Which He Never Meant to Be Published on Any Account)*—tells us that David had no intention of publishing his story, just as Dickens presumably had no intention of publishing a straightforward autobiography (though he did begin writing one and used part of that material in *David Copperfield*). David looks back over a number of years, and, of course, we only get his perspective. This form of writing keeps the novel very personal. Readers never feel like the book is taking on the world to write about large issues outside of David's immediate memories, thoughts, and perceptions. Why would Dickens make these choices, especially since it creates a novel so very different from his other works?

2. **Bildungsroman:** How do David's struggles shape and change his character or personality?

A bildungsroman is a novel about a young person's journey through struggles to reach maturity. How does Dickens appear to define "maturity" in *David Copperfield*? It does not seem to have much to do with age, as characters such as Micawber and Mr. Dick have a particular naïveté and immaturity about them. How does David define maturity? What is it that he strives for above all else? What do these goals say about David's character?

Language, Symbols, and Imagery

Novels (especially those by someone as talented as Dickens) deserve to be studied not only for their content but also for their style. This requires you to avoid summarizing the text unnecessarily and focus instead on the ways in which the work is written. It no longer concerns what the novel is about but rather how it is written. Studying the language of a text allows you to look carefully at syntax, word choice, and general diction. You might, for example, study the various accents and colloquialisms expressed by characters in *David Copperfield* to help you delve more deeply into Dickens's characterizations. What does a character's use of language reveal about him or her? Language might also mean a search into the words most commonly used to describe a character, a setting, or an activity. Look at the tone (mood) surrounding the Micawbers, for example, and pinpoint elements of language that help create that tone. Then take it a step further by discussing why it is significant that such a mood is connected with these particular characters. (And always remember that this mood comes from David's perspective.)

Symbols in a literary work are things that stand for something else. Is it possible that Dan Peggotty's household set up in an old boat symbolizes a certain wanderlust or rejection of society? What was the seafaring life like in 19th-century England? How would Peggotty's lifestyle have been regarded by more traditional society? What kinds of words and phrases does Dickens use to describe Peggotty's home and way of life?

Imagery includes the details in a story that can be perceived by one or more of the five senses. Certainly this is where Peggotty's life by the sea once again becomes significant. You could also look at Betsey Trotwood's home in Dover and the vivid images of her and Janet chasing donkeys off the property. Another example is the meal that David and Dora serve to the Micawbers. How is this meal described in a way that makes us feel that we can see, smell, and even taste its failure?

Sample Topics:

1. **Foreshadowing:** Why are readers suspicious of Steerforth well before we learn of his plans for Em'ly?

Since the action in the book is conveyed by David in retrospect, why does he not just come out and tell readers what will happen? He does, in a sense, when Em'ly (as a child) is on the dock, and he wishes that she would have disappeared into the sea. Yet Dickens more often uses foreshadowing, surrounding a character like Uriah with such a mood that we feel his true character before we know it for sure. Sometimes, given that the book is written as David's memoir, this foreshadowing reveals more about David's character and the nature of his naïveté.

2. **Literary allusion:** When Dickens includes literary allusions, what is he revealing? His own or David's intelligence/knowledge? Someone else's?

Dickens periodically includes references to other works of literature in *David Copperfield*. What do these allusions signify? David survives, on some level, because of books, both at home with the Murdstones and again at Salem House, so we know that the importance of books in his life cannot be overestimated. Can David's life be compared in any way with that of any of the characters in the books he reads? Any time you find an allusion to another work of literature in Dickens, look closely at both Dickens's text and the work mentioned in order to make deeper connections between them.

Compare and Contrast Essays

Comparing and contrasting elements in a story is a very useful way of finding similarities and differences on which you can then comment. Do not simply make a list of similarities and/or differences and assume that you are finished. The purpose of comparisons and contrasts is to invoke the larger issues in the story, and in order to do that effectively, the similarities and differences must be not only found but analyzed.

One of the most obvious elements of a text to compare and contrast is character. This is why the analysis is so important. Of course, you will find similarities and differences between two characters in a novel, just as you would find similarities and differences between any two people you know. So what? You must draw conclusions from those similarities and/or differences. Often, you will find that the most interesting analyses stem from the most unlikely comparisons. In what ways, for example, are David and Uriah similar, and what do these similarities reveal about each character and their relationship to each other?

David Copperfield's status as partial autobiography allows some unique comparisons and contrasts. We know that Mr. Micawber, for example, is modeled after Dickens's own father. What exactly are the similarities and differences between Dickens's father and Wilkins Micawber? What does this seem to reveal about Dickens's feelings toward his father? What are the most striking differences between Dickens's father and Micawber? Why are these differences important for Dickens's storytelling and our understanding of his relationship with his father, and possibly his relationship with his writing and characters?

Sample Topics:

1. **David as narrator and David as character:** Which is more trustworthy? Is it possible to be a completely reliable narrator while you are telling the story of your own life?

   David as narrator is older than David the character and generally seems to be confident, at ease, and at times even omniscient. David the character, on the other hand, is young and very often fumbling and naive. Are there points of the text when the two versions of David seem to overlap? Do Dickens's word choices or descriptions lead us to trust one David more than the other?

2. **Agnes, Dora, and Em'ly:** David loves each of these women at one point in his life. Does he love them all for the same reasons and in the same way? Why or why not?

   The similarities and differences between these three women seem more deliberate than those between other characters. They are each from a different social class with different upbringings, so many of their differences can be attributed to these factors. Does Dickens seem to be using these three women to make points about social class, education, usefulness, intelligence, or other factors? Despite their differences, there are key similarities among these women as well. Each was raised by an unmarried or widowed man. How has that circumstance shaped each of them?

Bibliography and Online Resources for *David Copperfield*

Chesterton, G. K. "David Copperfield." *Appreciations and Criticisms of the Works of Charles Dickens.* 1911. New York: Haskell House, 1970. 129–139.

Dickens, Charles. "Autobiographical Fragment." *The Life of Charles Dickens.* Vol. 1. John Forster. London: Chapman & Hall, 1872. 47–70.

———. *David Copperfield.* 1848. New York: Barnes & Noble, 2003.

House, Humphrey. *The Dickens World.* Oxford: Oxford UP, 1941.

Matsuoka, Mitsu. The Victorian Literary Studies Archive. Available online. URL: http://www.lang.nagoya-u.ac.jp/~matsuoka/Victorian.html. Retrieved January 18, 2007; July 23, 2007.

BLEAK HOUSE

READING TO WRITE

BLEAK HOUSE tells the stories of a number of people from various walks of life, but if we had to narrow it down to only one character, certainly the main story here is Esther's. It is through Esther that most of the connections between characters are finally made, and in following her actions and the circumstances of her life, readers come to understand other characters' backgrounds and motivations.

This central female character is rather unusual for Dickens, whose best known works tend to center on young males, as some of their titles indicate: *Oliver Twist, David Copperfield,* and *Nicholas Nickleby.* Esther Summerson does not perhaps have the physical hardships that many of Dickens's leading male characters do, but she does have troubles that are very difficult indeed, leading readers to wonder about how her life might have been different had she been male instead of female. David Copperfield wonders if he will be "the hero of [his] own life" (15). Esther would never take credit for being the hero of her own life, but perhaps her meekness in that area can be traced back to the way in which she was raised. Looking at an early passage in the novel when young Esther asks her aunt to explain her mysterious birth and parentage can reveal much about the Esther we come to know through the rest of the book:

> "Your mother, Esther, is your disgrace, and you were hers. The time will come—and soon enough—when you will understand this better, and will feel it too, as no one save a woman can. I have forgiven her"; but her face did not relent; "the wrong she did to me, and I say no more of it, though

it was greater than you will ever know—than any one will ever know, but I, the sufferer. For yourself, unfortunate girl, orphaned and degraded from the first of these evil anniversaries, pray daily that the sins of others be not visited upon your head, according to what is written. Forget your mother, and leave all other people to forget her who will do her unhappy child that greatest kindness. Now, go!"

She checked me, however, as I was about to depart from her—so frozen as I was!—and added this:

"Submission, self-denial, diligent work, are the preparations for a life begun with such a shadow on it. You are different from other children, Esther, because you were not born, like them, in common sinfulness and wrath. You are set apart." (32)

Naturally, all of this foreshadows what we later learn about Lady Dedlock and Captain Hawdon. We also find out that Esther's aunt was, in fact hurt by the circumstances of Esther's birth, though perhaps not as badly as she likes to believe. In what ways does this passage also foreshadow Esther's behavior as an adult? Can you pinpoint times in her later life when she follows her aunt's stern advice and practices "submission, self-denial, and diligent work"? Are there times when Esther appears to willfully disregard such advice? What do these situations reveal about Esther's character? Esther is in some ways similar to the male heroes of Dickens's other works. All of them are told by someone else that they are somehow unworthy or stupid or inherently evil, and all of them prove otherwise through the ways in which they live their lives. What message do you think Dickens is trying to send through Esther's character?

There are dozens of questions to ask about Esther, each of which might make an intriguing paper topic. What choices does Esther make in her life? Which choices are made for her? Which circumstances of her life come about because of her gender (what is acceptable for a woman and what is not), and which come about because of her particular circumstance of not knowing her parents? For example, does she feel obliged to marry John Jarndyce because she is a woman with no way of making money on her own, or because her family circumstances have left her with no one else who will care for or about her? Perhaps both elements of Esther's situation play a role in her decisions.

Does Esther's occasional lack of ability or permission to make her own choices make her a victim, a martyr, or a heroine? At what times and for what reasons does she occasionally choose to disobey etiquette or loyalty or common sense? What do these times reveal about her character?

TOPICS AND STRATEGIES

This section of the chapter addresses various possible topics for writing about *Bleak House* as well as general methods for approaching these topics. These lists are in no way exhaustive and are meant to provide a jumping-off point rather than an answer key. Use these suggestions to find your own ideas and form your own analyses. All topics discussed in this chapter could potentially turn into very good papers.

Themes

Readers can often find many of themes in a novel, especially one as long as *Bleak House.* A theme can be defined as an idea or concept that helps to inform the plot and is often found by looking carefully at words, phrases, and chapter titles in the novel. When more than one character experiences the same or similar things or when there is notable repetition of an action or idea, you can bet that you have identified a theme. The next step is to ask what the book is saying about the theme. Do characters have differing opinions on it? Does the author seem to want readers to learn a particular lesson about this theme? In other words, your work is not done once you have identified a theme. The real heart of your paper lies in your analysis and interpretation of a theme.

Just a few of the themes in *Bleak House* are health and sanitation, appearance versus reality, family, love, duty, and secrets. Secrets are pervasive in the novel and play a large role in moving the plot forward. Esther knows that her life is built on secrets held by her aunt and her parents, Lady Dedlock keeps many important secrets that cause her to display coldness to nearly everyone around her, Hawdon keeps his identity a secret, Skimpole keeps his manipulations a secret, Smallweed tries to make money from other people's secrets, and Inspector Bucket's job is to uncover everyone's secrets. Does secret keeping ever turn out to be a wise thing to do in this novel? Would all of the characters have been better off if the secrets had been immediately revealed or never kept in the first place? Is there a character in the novel who does not keep an important secret? Does Dickens seem to want us to value that character more than the others? Esther and Ada periodically swear to remain always honest with each other, yet each ends up keeping at least one secret from the other. Are there degrees of secret keeping, some that are actually beneficial and some that are downright evil?

Of course, all of these secrets help to create the mystery within *Bleak House*. Perhaps the ways in which the secrets are revealed are an even more important aspect of the novel's theme. Readers learn that all of these characters are linked in several ways. Do characters get what they deserve? In other words, does the revelation of secrets equal some form of justice (either legal, psychological, or social)?

Sample Topics:

1. **Health and sanitation:** What message does Dickens send in this book about the importance of health and sanitation? How is a character's health and sanitation related to his or her economic class?

   The characters who seem most clearly affected by poor health and/or sanitation are Jo, Captain Hawdon, Krook, Smallweed, and Esther. Sanitation and health directly affect characters' length of life, appearance, acceptance, judgment, and future prospects. Why does Esther survive the smallpox, and Jo does not? Might Jo have survived if he had stayed at Bleak House? How are daily lives and sanitation practices different for Jenny and her family compared to Lady Dedlock or those of higher classes? Does Dickens support the characters who want to improve sanitation for the lower classes?

2. **Appearance versus reality:** How are various characters' appearances in this novel different from the reality of their lives? How and why does Dickens seem to punish characters who rely mainly on appearances?

Esther's smallpox scars are a clear example of appearance versus reality. She is shunned in some circles for her physical appearance, while in reality she should be accepted by or even in a higher class than those who reject her. It appears to Richard that he will be wealthy eventually, so he lives according to that rather than the reality of his current financial state, as Jarndyce begs him to do. Mr. George appears to have killed Tulkinghorn, and Lady Dedlock appears to be a sophisticated and virtuous woman. Is reality usually worse than appearance in this novel?

3. **Family:** Can a family be created, or are these characters stuck with the one they are born into?

Family situations can be quite burdensome in *Bleak House.* The current Jarndyce generations are left with the legal mess of sorting through wills and waiting for inheritances, yet many characters yearn for some sort of family connection. Caddy Jellyby, Esther, Ada, Richard, and Jarndyce end up forming their own little families after they have been rejected or orphaned by the families they were born into. Yet, Turveydrop, so clearly a burden for Caddy and Prince, is valued because he is family. Richard is ultimately killed by his family's situation (and his interpretations of it), while Esther is eventually informed of her true family connections, which may or may not change her life. What does Dickens seem to be telling readers about families?

Characters

In his lifetime, Dickens created more than 2,000 characters, and at times it seems that most of them are in *Bleak House.* His characterizations in this novel are complex and subtle, making a second reading of the novel even more entertaining and full of discovery.

When studying characters, there are several angles to take. You might look at character development, or what distinguishes one character from another. Esther and Ada, for example, are similar in many ways. How does Dickens differentiate between the two? You might also investigate change in a character, noting when a character seems to evolve (or devolve) in some way. How, for instance, does Miss Flite change over the course of the novel? Does her general personality change, or does the world around her change? Or both? Along the same lines, you can choose to study a character who perhaps should change but does not. Richard, for example, seems to remain a naive child in many ways. How does this explain his actions, and in what ways do readers (and some of the characters) wish he would change? Why?

It is always fascinating to study the ways in which a character is created. This requires you to look at specific words, phrases, settings, or moods that surround and help describe a character in order to see how Dickens helps readers form appropriate opinions of his characters.

Again, there is certainly no shortage of characters in *Bleak House*, and all of them are worth studying in some detail. There are many questions to ask that will get you started on a paper topic. What is Krook's role in the plot, and why is his death so unusual? Guppy reappears throughout the novel, fluctuating between being endearing and being manipulative. How does Dickens help signal readers as to when they should like him (or feel sorry for him) and when they should distrust him? What is the irony of some of the most cheerful characters in the novel living in a place called Bleak House? Why is Krook always surrounded by darkness and filth? How is it that we learn more of the truth about Skimpole from a visit to his home than we learn through his own words? Is it significant that Lady Dedlock is so often gazing away from the activity in the room? Dickens does not skimp on the details surrounding his characters, making them rich topics for papers.

Sample Topics:

1. **Esther:** Is she a martyr? A victim? A heroine? Does she have any flaws?

   It is unusual for Dickens to center a novel on a woman, yet in *Bleak House* he creates a woman who is quite strong and very believable. Esther seems to have become a good person in spite of her life rather than because of it. She is kind and loving in spite of her harsh upbringing by her aunt. She is open and honest in spite of the secrets surrounding her birth. She is outgoing and (eventually) confident in spite of the scars on her face. Is her character developed entirely through adversity? Does she get any lucky breaks, or does she seem to work hard for everything good in her life? What is her role in this book and in the lives of the other characters?

2. **Bucket:** Is he a good guy or a bad guy?

Inspector Bucket is one of the earliest detectives to appear in a novel. What qualities does he exhibit that seem to have become the basis for other detectives in literature? Is Bucket a fair man actually seeking truth and justice, or does he have other motives for learning information from these people? Why is his character so important to the novel? What would the plot be like without him?

3. **Lady Dedlock:** Do we feel sorry for her? Why or why not? Do you think Dickens wants us to feel sorry for her? Why or why not?

Lady Dedlock appears to be in a position of power, yet in many ways she is quite weak. Dickens provides Lady Dedlock with body language and thoughts that often contradict her words and actions. How do we know when she's being herself versus when she's going through the motions? Does Lady Dedlock make a series of poor choices in her life, or is her problem the fact that she has such limited choices in her life? To what degree is she responsible for the problems that result from her secrets, and to what degree did she not have any choice in these matters? What do you think Lady Dedlock would have done if she had been allowed to live life as she wanted to? Would that have been better for everyone?

4. **Jo:** What is Jo's role in this novel?

Dickens seems to have a larger point (about the poor, class differences, how to treat other people) to make through Jo's

character. Jo is not so much a unique character as he is a representative of many others (real people) like him, and his surroundings say as much about him as his dialogue does. Why
do you think Dickens created Jo as a child rather than as an
adult? In some ways, Jo becomes an emblem, a symbol representing the average poor person. He is very proud, and he did
not choose his living situation, even though many people in
the 19th century (and even today) like to believe that the poor
somehow choose to be destitute. What do various characters'
reactions to and treatment of Jo reveal about those characters'
true personalities and goals?

History and Context

A large part of the Victorian world that we now take for granted comes
from Dickens's novels. He described and commented on the world
around him in such detailed and mesmerizing ways that the world of
his novels is now a part of our history. While certainly his works are still
largely fictional, they are grounded in some of the complexities of real
life in Victorian England.

Bleak House stems from Dickens's work as a shorthand reporter of
debates in Parliament, drawing readers into the hierarchical, corrupt,
slow-moving world of the legal system as Dickens viewed it. The simplicity of one little piece of paper resolving generations of legal proceedings
demonstrates Dickens's view of Chancery, the court that determined
cases according to equity or fairness rather than law, as often overrated,
to say the least.

Certainly, *Bleak House* also explores some of the realities of family
life and focuses on women in particular. If the social mores of Victorian
England would have permitted more kindness toward women having
babies out of wedlock and less condescension toward and judgment of
those who really only needed jobs and a bit of encouragement, things
would have been very different for Lady Dedlock, Esther, Jo, and Jenny.
Jo's is a particularly compelling storyline, illustrating the mere happenstance that sometimes brings good people to extreme poverty. Showing
readers a child alone in such dire circumstances allows Dickens to point
out that poverty is often not a lifestyle choice or a condition that only
sinful people acquire. And Jo's death is riveting and pathetic because of

the sheer needlessness of it. Under different circumstances, with minimal help from someone (like the tiny bit of encouragement and money he received from Hawdon before his death), Jo might have survived, prospered, and helped improve the world somehow.

Studying history and context always involves research, and you can begin by choosing a character, a scene, a theme, or a setting from the novel and inquiring as to whether that is what things were really like. Be aware that sometimes the time period in which the action of the book takes place can be different from the time in which the book was written and published, and even a few years can make a big difference. Once you have determined the similarities and differences between the real world and the Dickensian one, you can begin to speculate about what Dickens is trying to convey through his portrayal.

History and context might also pertain to the author's biography. Dickens's background in the court system contributed to *Bleak House.* Are there other details about Dickens's life or beliefs that add depth and understanding to our reading of this novel?

Sample Topics:

1. **Chancery:** Was the 19th-century legal process in England fair? Reasonable? Ridiculous?

Clearly, the legal system in *Bleak House* is incredibly slow and monotonous, to the point where nothing ever seems to get done, while citizens continue to pay money to the courts. The legal and penal systems underwent many changes in the 19th century, and, according to Dickens, such changes were sorely needed. What changes took place in England's legal system in the 19th century? Why? Did Dickens support such changes? What would Dickens's ideal legal system be? What were his personal experiences with courts and the law? How do you think those experiences influenced this book? What does he seem to want readers to understand about the legal system? Tulkinghorn benefits from such a system, but Miss Flite and the wards of Jarndyce are just a few of the people who are somehow punished by the system.

2. **Births out of wedlock:** What was generally done when a baby was born out of wedlock?

The Victorian period is generally known as a very chaste, even stuffy time. The rules of society and sometimes even the laws were quite strict, but remember that rules and laws often reflect ideals that the average individual might be unable to attain. How rare was it in 19th-century England for a baby to be born out of wedlock?

Often a person's treatment after something like a baby born out of wedlock depended on their social and economic class. Would things have been different for Lady Dedlock if she had had more or less money when Esther was born? Why was being born out of wedlock such a shameful thing for the child involved?

3. **Marriage:** To what extent was marriage in 19th-century England an obligation, especially for women?

There seems to have been a double standard in the 19th-century (some would say it still exists) regarding marriage in terms of what is expected of men and what is expected of women. Why was this so? How does Dickens write about marriage in *Bleak House*? Does Esther feel obligated to marry Jarndyce because of her love for him, her gratitude to him, or her vulnerable position as a woman with no evident family? What constitutes a successful marriage in this novel? Why does Esther immediately refuse to marry Guppy?

Philosophy and Ideas

Writing about the philosophy and ideas found in a text is similar to writing about the text's theme, except that philosophy and ideas are applied more generally and live in some sense outside the text as well. So, when writing about a book's philosophy and ideas, you are looking for the ways in which the work comments on general ideas. Murder, for example, is a strong element in this novel, begging readers to pursue the ethics and myriad questions behind the action. Is there such a thing as a "philosophy of murder" or a rationale behind murder? Certainly, if you check legal records, you will find that a number of trials are conducted on the basis of these types of things. Was this true in the 19th century? Could people avoid conviction, for example, by pleading manslaughter instead of murder? Were there "degrees" of murder then as there are now (first-degree murder versus second-degree murder, etc.)? How are such degrees and decisions wrapped up in philosophy rather than simply innate parts of our understanding?

Sample Topics:

1. **Missionary zeal:** How did the English view Africa and India in the 19th century? Why?

   Many English people believed that their country's empire should spread in order to bring civilization to the rest of the world. What did it mean for an English person to "civilize" another country (in terms of religion, dress, government, etc.)? Mrs. Jellyby is certainly the clearest example of missionary zeal in this novel. Why is she so impassioned about it, and how (and why) does Dickens turn her into a caricature, or a cartoonlike character? How does this characterization reveal Dickens's feelings on the subject of missionary zeal? What effects might it have on English people to feel superior to people on other continents? How does this superiority affect one's worldview and treatment of the people in one's immediate surroundings?

2. **Sin:** Are there degrees of sin? If so, what are they? If not, why not?

   Is it worse for Lady Dedlock to have a baby out of wedlock or for her to lie about it? Is Lady Dedlock the biggest sinner in this book? Use evidence from the text to support your answer. Do societies adapt the religious concept of sin in order to use it for their own purposes? In other words, are there social faux pas that people make that are somehow worse in many ways than actual religious sins?

3. **Formation of identity:** How does nature compare with nurture in this book?

In *Bleak House,* do the characters' personalities seem to be formed through biology (nature) or through the ways in which they are raised (nurture)? How is Esther shaped by her upbringing? In what ways is she nevertheless very similar to Lady Dedlock?

4. **Ethics of murder:** Is killing someone ever justified?

Hortense kills Tulkinghorn for what seem to be frivolous reasons compared to the reasons George and Lady Dedlock would have had for killing him. Would the murder seem justified, even satisfactory, if George or Lady Dedlock had done it? What about Jo's death? In some form, is he indirectly murdered by Bucket and Skimpole?

Form and Genre

A book as formidable in length as *Bleak House* holds within it many opportunities for the study of form and genre. Form and genre provide ways of classifying works that usually allow us to study them more fully. Form is defined as the style and structure of a work, whereas genre is the type, or classification, of a work. Both form and genre are usually distinct from a work's content, though writers use each of them quite specifically in order to convey a particular message, reach a certain audience, or simply strengthen the impact of their work.

Inspector Bucket is one of the first detectives to appear in a novel. How does his mere presence influence the form and/or genre of the novel? How do the element of mystery and the large scope of the novel work together in intricate ways?

Sample Topics:

1. **Detective novel:** In what ways does *Bleak House* resemble a modern detective novel?

How and why have detective novels changed over the years? Which elements of today's detective novel are present in *Bleak*

House? Some scholars say that people who read detective novels enjoy being lied to (in that context). Does Dickens lie to his readers? Why or why not? If so, why might the lie be necessary? If not, how does he maintain the mysterious tone while revealing everything to his readers?

2. **Mystery:** How is the mystery of *Bleak House* sustained throughout the book?

This novel can be frustrating to read at first because the mystery is so strong, and readers do not immediately learn all of the connections between characters. Which characters or plot elements lie at the heart of the mystery in this book? How would this book be different if (like many other Dickens novels) it did not contain mystery?

3. **Satire:** Which characters and situations does Dickens seem to be making fun of?

Writing about satire requires an understanding of the history and context of the work. What would 19th-century readers have recognized as satirical? Mr. Turveydrop and Mrs. Jellyby do not play crucial parts in the plot of *Bleak House,* yet they are an essential part of the satire Dickens writes here. How does Dickens use his characters and situations to make fun of them or to make fun of the people they represent?

4. **Scope:** How does Dickens manage to hold our attention throughout this very long novel?

The scope of *Bleak House* is very Victorian in that it covers a wide range of characters and several different plot lines that eventually intersect. George Eliot's *Middlemarch* is another good example of extensive scope in Victorian fiction. *Bleak House* could have simply focused on Esther's story, or Lady Dedlock's, but instead it involves all of these other characters. How does Dickens take on so much and still manage to provide enough detail to make us care about what happens to each and every character? To write this paper, you will want to look at the web of characters and storylines that Dickens creates and decide if there is anything superfluous in the novel. Should Dickens have written a less-involved novel? Think about how this novel might be similar to today's soap operas (especially when in installments) or even blogs. What keeps readers interested?

Language, Symbols, and Imagery

Writing about the language, symbols, and imagery within a novel requires you to look specifically at how the work is constructed, as opposed to just studying the content of the work. Pay particular attention to words, phrases, and their repetition, as well as repetition of ideas, in order to begin to see how Dickens uses language, symbols, and imagery. Summarizing the content may be necessary for illustrating particular points, but it is not the end product of this type of paper. You will want to look at syntax, word choice, and general diction. Do some characters speak differently from others? If so, why? Speech can be tied to all kinds of issues like economic class, education, geography, and stress, just to name a few. Discovering that two characters have distinct ways of speaking might lead you to research on economic classes and their respective educations, requiring some background in the historical context. Ultimately, you are looking at Dickens's choices as a writer and the possible reasons behind such choices.

Finding symbolism in a work involves looking for something that stands for something else. Is a letter just a letter in *Bleak House,* or might a letter stand for a character's honor or the machinations of society or the bureaucracy of the legal system? What kinds of things seem to be important to the novel and its characters? These things might be tangible objects such as letters or particular foods, but they might also be something like a particular color associated with similar things throughout the book.

Imagery encapsulates things that can be perceived with our five senses: sight, sound, taste, smell, and touch. Dickens was a master of imagery, which partially explains why his books are so often made into plays, movies, and television series. Are there elements of imagery that recur throughout the novel, perhaps associated with specific characters, places, or activities? For example, is it always dark and dreary around a certain character, offering a clue to this character's disposition or lifestyle or the ways in which Dickens is asking us to perceive this character?

Sample Topics:

1. **Imagery of Bleak House:** Is it actually bleak? Is the house name actually ironic?

   John Jarndyce has remade Bleak House into a rather cheerful place after Tom Jarndyce killed himself. The Growlery remains, of course, but the rest of the house seems untainted by bleakness. Why do you think Dickens titled the book *Bleak House,* when so much of the action in the novel takes place elsewhere? Some readers find it perplexing that Esther ends up living in yet another home called Bleak House, while other readers find this very appropriate. How are these house names ironic? Is the book as a whole ironic (cheery overall, despite its title)?

2. **Names:** Is Krook really a crook? Is Miss Flite flighty? Is Lady Dedlock locked into something or doomed somehow to be dead?

   Names in Dickens's earlier novels carry great significance, and clearly, that tendency survives in *Bleak House.* Sometimes a character's name is a very thinly disguised description of the person or his or her situation. Sometimes a character's name is ironic, suggesting one thing when the opposite is actually true. How does Dickens use names in this novel? Be aware that some names might require you to learn what various words meant in Dickens's time, as the word's meaning might have changed since then. How do Dickens's characters' names contribute to the imagery and setting of the book?

Compare and Contrast Essays

Writing a paper that compares and/or contrasts elements of the novel involves much more than simply listing similarities and differences between two or more things. These lists might help you early in the drafting process, but your paper eventually needs to go beyond this point to discuss why these similarities and/or differences are notable and important to the novel. You would do well to ask questions such as: Does Dickens intentionally set up some comparisons in order to show different points of view or circumstances? Do we notice particular comparisons and contrasts simply because of the time in which we live and our perceptions of the 19th century?

One of the most interesting things you can do with this type of paper is to make a comparison between two or more things or characters that on the surface seem very dissimilar. The more surprising your comparison or contrast is, the more engaging your paper could be to your readers (provided you back yourself up with sufficient evidence from the text). You cannot make a comparison or contrast statement based solely on your own perceptions and "feelings" about the work. Whatever claim you decide to make must be supportable through the text itself.

Sample Topics:

1. **Esther and Ada:** What circumstances of their lives make Esther and Ada so different from each other? What circumstances of their lives make them so much alike?

   At first, these two young girls appear strikingly similar, and yet we learn throughout the novel that they are different in many ways. Ada is evidently a remarkable beauty, yet Esther seems to get most of the attention. Why is this? What choices does Ada make that Esther definitely would not? Find textual evidence to support your claim. Do you think that Esther and Ada are too competitive (perhaps too much alike) to be the true friends they profess to be?

2. **Lady Dedlock before and after:** What advice do you think Lady Dedlock would give to herself as a young woman?

   We are given only glimpses of Lady Dedlock during her life with Captain Hawdon, but piecing together these details from the text allows us to construct an image of her as a young woman. How does this young woman compare to the Lady Dedlock we meet after all her trials and sorrow? This kind of paper topic might lead to yet another one comparing young Lady Dedlock to Esther. Is young Lady Dedlock carefree or already burdened? Did people find her as cold and beautiful as they do later in her life?

3. **The world during Jarndyce and Jarndyce versus the world after:** It seems that a heavy weight is lifted from many people's shoulders once the Jarndyce and Jarndyce case is resolved. Is there anyone who is not affected by the resolution of this case?

The characters in this novel meet largely because of their associations with Jarndyce and Jarndyce. How do their worlds change once the legal proceedings are over? How does the end of the case reveal the true roles of lesser characters such as Miss Flite and Smallweed? Why is the ongoing court situation so burdensome to so many people, even those who are not directly involved?

Bibliography and Online Resources for *Bleak House*

Bloom, Harold, ed. *Charles Dickens's Bleak House.* Modern Critical Interpretations. New York: Chelsea House, 1987.

Chesterton, G. K. "Bleak House." *Appreciations and Criticisms of the Works of Charles Dickens.* 1911. New York: Haskell House, 1970. 148–59.

Dickens, Charles. *Bleak House.* 1853. New York: Barnes & Noble, 2005.

———. *David Copperfield.* 1849–50. New York: Barnes & Noble, 2005.

Gilbert, Elliot L. *Critical Essays on Charles Dickens's Bleak House.* Critical Essays on British Literature. Gen. ed. Zack Bowen. Boston: G. K. Hall, 1989.

Hawthorn, Jeremy. *Bleak House.* The Critic Debate Series. Gen. ed. Michael Scott. Atlantic Highlands: Humanties P International, 1987.

Kennedy, Valerie. "*Bleak House*: More Trouble with Esther?" *Women's Studies in Literature* 1.4 (1979): 330–347.

Matsuoka, Mitsu. The Victorian Literary Studies Archive. Available online. URL: http://www.lang.nagoya-u.ac.jp/~matsuoka/Victorian.html. Retrieved January 18, 2007; July 23, 2007.

Page, Norman. *Bleak House: A Novel of Connections.* Boston: Twayne Publishers, 1990.

Tambling, Jeremy, ed. *Bleak House: Contemporary Critical Essays.* New Casebooks Series. New York: St. Martin's P, 1998.

HARD TIMES

READING TO WRITE

THE FULL title of this book is *Hard Times, for These Times*, emphasizing the book's place in 1854 England. Dickens does not move the setting of the novel to even a slightly different time from the one in which he is writing, even though he often uses this technique in other novels. The highly contemporary nature of his writing in *Hard Times* is indicative of Dickens's concern with many of the human rights issues of his day, and interestingly, the novel's themes and arguments, although placed in a particular place and time period, remain amazingly relevant today.

When Dickens was about to start writing *Hard Times* as a serialized story in the weekly journal *Household Words*, he contacted his friend and adviser John Forster with a list of possible titles and asked Forster to choose the three he liked best. The list of possible titles offers some insight into Dickens's thoughts about framing the story. A few of the titles Dickens came up with include *According to Cocker, Prove It, Stubborn Things, Mr. Gradgrind's Facts, The Grindstone, Hard Times, Two and Two Are Four, Something Tangible, Our Hard-headed Friend, Rust and Dust, Simple Arithmetic, A Matter of Calculation, A Mere Question of Figures*, and *The Gradgrind Philosophy*. Forster and Dickens each chose their three favorites, and the only one that they both chose was *Hard Times*, which, of course, became the title of the story.

It is important, first of all, to note that Dickens brainstormed these titles before he began writing the book. This fact helps us see what his ideas were for the book before he began it, and we can make note of which ideas ended up in the book and which were not developed in this story. How do some of these title choices emphasize themes, characters, and philosophies in the novel? Was *Hard Times* really the best choice from this list? Why or why not? Looking at these title possibilities allows us to glimpse Dickens's thought process before writing the installments of *Hard Times*. Of course, we know that the end product was likely not exactly what Dickens had in mind when he started, as the natural processes of writing and revision tend to bring writers to places they had not expected to go. Yet, we can see, for example, that Dickens expected to emphasize mathematics or calculations and numbers to a large degree. Does he accomplish this with *Hard Times*? How does the title *Hard Times* encompass more (or less) of the book than some of the other choices?

The characters, events, and setting details that Dickens ended up including in the book are also crucial points for discussion and interpretation. Particularly interesting is the way in which Dickens ends the book, with Louisa once again staring into a fire and wondering:

> Here was Louisa on the night of the same day, watching the fire as in days of yore, though with a gentler and a humbler face. How much of the future might arise before *her* vision? . . .
>
> A working woman, christened Rachael, after a long illness once again appearing at the ringing of the Factory bell, and passing to and fro at the set hours, among the Coketown hands; a woman of pensive beauty, always dressed in black, but sweet-tempered and serene, and even cheerful; who, of all the people in the place, alone appeared to have compassion on a degraded, drunken wretch of her own sex, who was sometimes seen in the town secretly begging of her, and crying to her; a woman working, ever working, but content to do it, and preferring to do it as her natural lot, until she should be too old to labor any more? Did Louisa see this? Such a thing was to be.
>
> A lonely brother, many thousands of miles away, writing, on paper blotted with tears, that her words had too soon come true, and that all the treasures in the world would be cheaply bartered for a sight of her dear face? At length this brother coming nearer home, with hope of seeing her, and being delayed by illness; and then a letter in a strange hand, saying "he died in hospital, of fever, such a day, and died in penitence and love of you: his last words being your name"? Did Louisa see these things? Such things were to be.
>
> Herself again a wife—a mother—lovingly watchful of her children, ever careful that they should have a childhood of the mind no less than a childhood of the body, as knowing it to be even a more beautiful thing,

and a possession, any hoarded scrap of which, is a blessing and happiness to the wisest? Did Louisa see this? Such a thing was never to be.

But, happy Sissy's happy children loving her; all children loving her; she, grown learned in childish lore; thinking no innocent and pretty fancy ever to be despised; trying hard to know her humbler fellow-creatures, and to beautify their lives of machinery and reality with those imaginative graces and delights, without which the heart of infancy will wither up, the sturdiest physical manhood will be morally stark death, and the plainest national prosperity figures can show, will be the Writing on the Wall,—she holding this course as part of no fantastic vow, or bond, or brotherhood, or sisterhood, or pledge, or covenant, or fancy dress, or fancy fair; but simply as a duty to be done,—did Louisa see these things of herself? These things were to be.

Dear reader! It rests with you and me, whether, in our two fields of action, similar things shall be or not. Let them be! We shall sit with lighter bosoms on the hearth, to see the ashes of our fires turn gray and cold. (189–190)

There is a certain omniscience to the voice in this excerpt when the narrator tells us, "Such things were to be" and "Such a thing was never to be." The tone offers a finality, almost a sense of foreboding, to the novel's conclusion. Louisa "sees" correctly into the futures of everyone except herself, speaking perhaps to the inability of humans to predict accurately their own futures or even to see themselves fully. Sissy appears as the shining example of success. Rachael is described as "cheerful" when doing her duty, but Sissy is downright "happy" about her life. Does this happiness stem from a general disposition learned from her time with her father as part of Sleary's circus? Does it come from Sissy's inability (frustrating though it was when she was in school) to learn only facts and not see the joys and pains of humanity? She has, in other words, been unable to internalize Gradgrind's lessons on facts and has instead developed the ability to see people as they really are and empathize with them.

Perhaps the most interesting part of this excerpt is the second to last paragraph, when Sissy's and Louisa's characters become conflated, indistinguishable from each other. Why would Dickens choose to do this? Are the two children (women by the end of the book) interchangeable? Are they more alike than they are different, regardless of their vastly different upbringings? Or, since the "setting" for all of this thought is Louisa's mind, maybe Louisa simply wishes to be more like Sissy so badly that she begins a thought that concerns Sissy and ends with the same thought concerning herself, in hopes that they are basically alike. Then we have to ask, if Sissy is the example Louisa chooses or longs to follow, is Sissy set up as an example for readers as well? What is it about Sissy that makes her a character to emulate above the others?

Finally, we might ask what these final paragraphs in the book are meant to say to readers. Dickens directly addresses readers in the last paragraph, but what is he asking of them? When he writes, "Let them be!" does he simply want readers not to mourn or complain about the fates of these characters? If the "two fields of action" include the world of the book and the "real world" of the book's readers, then in addressing the idea of "similar things," maybe Dickens is commenting on the verisimilitude of the book and wanting readers to note that, for better or worse, they might endure the same fate as some of these characters. The last sentence puts readers into Louisa's traditional place, staring into the fire. Has Louisa been the voice of "everyman" all along? Does she come to represent the general population in some way? Does Dickens want or expect readers to feel most strongly connected to Louisa, thus making it natural for them to put themselves in her place?

Even though it is one of Dickens's shortest novels, *Hard Times* contains a wealth of varying interpretations and ideas for paper topics. As you read through the book for the first or subsequent time, take careful notes about not only plot points but the ways in which Dickens colors them for us through his writing strategies. Think about what interests you most about the book, the characters, the time period, the writing, etc., and try to construct a paper topic that truly interests you and affects you.

TOPICS AND STRATEGIES

This section of the chapter addresses various possible topics for writing about *Hard Times* as well as general methods for approaching these topics. These lists are in no way exhaustive and are meant to provide a jumping-off point rather than an answer key. Use these suggestions to find your own ideas and form your own analyses. All topics discussed in this chapter could potentially turn into very good papers.

Themes

A theme in a literary work is an idea, an action, an occurrence, or a system that in some way threads itself throughout the book. Themes are often identifiable through a close reading of words, phrases, ideas, and even chapter titles, and they are recognizable as something about which the character(s) and/or author appear to have much to say. In other words, if a book's action and/or characters continually return to a similar idea, you have probably identified a theme of the book.

The themes in *Hard Times* are delivered with a heavier hand than those of Dickens's other novels, perhaps because Dickens wrote the book in shorter, weekly installments rather than his usual monthly installments, giving him less time for nuance. *Hard Times* is often regarded by scholars as a kind of skeletal novel, providing the bare bones of a semifictional world without Dickens's usually extensive detail. Nevertheless, there are a number of themes present in *Hard Times* that in some ways express Dickens's worldview more clearly than his lengthier novels.

Dickens alludes to the Bible a number of times in the novel; indeed, he does it in the very first chapter title, "The One Thing Needful," which alludes to verses in Luke. It is a remarkably short chapter, yet such a title directs us to look for what is missing in addition to what is immediately presented to us. Looking closely at the biblical passage from which this phrase is taken could lend insight into Dickens's themes as well. We can see that these four simple words quickly begin to describe people, events, and situations throughout the entire book. Everyone seems to be in need of something. Some, like Stephen Blackpool, need many things, but perhaps there is one thing in particular that would help to satisfy everyone. So, we are left with the question of what that "one thing needful" might be. It is not enough, in this case, to point out that Dickens feels there is something needful in Coketown. Identifying what you think "the one thing needful" is (and why) will lead you to a true investigation of this theme. Will the same "one thing" satisfy everyone, or does the phrase refer to the idea that each person needs only one thing, even if each person's need is different from another's?

Sample Topics:

1. **"The one thing needful":** What is it that so many characters seem to need? Will "one thing" satisfy everyone?

The specific reference for this phrase is in the book of Luke 10:40–42. The idea that something is missing pervades the novel and the lives of all characters from the first chapter, which carries this telling title. The word *needful* means necessary, but it also brings up images of people and places that are "full of need." Both interpretations work in *Hard Times*. Are any of the characters able to figure out what it is that they need? It seems that characters who believe they know what others need are always wrong and end up harming people. Those (such as Stephen Blackpool) who know what is actually needed (mercy, love, kindness) have no power to get or give it in large amounts. An important element in any study of "the one thing needful" is the title of the first chapter in the novel's third book: "Another Thing Needful." How does this (the title and the chapter content itself) address or possibly answer the questions already posed?

2. **"Key-note"**: To what does Dickens refer when he repeats the metaphor of the keynote? How do the themes of the keynote itself as well as the things to which it refers pervade the novel?

Like a song we have heard before and cannot resist, Dickens keeps striking the same notes. In chapter 5 (titled "The Keynote"), he writes, "Let us strike the key-note, Coketown, before pursuing our tune" (18), before asking, "Is it possible, I wonder, that there was any analogy between the case of the Coketown population and the case of the little Gradgrinds?"(18). In chapter 8, titled "Never Wonder," he writes, "Let us strike the key-note again, before pursuing the tune"(20). In this same chapter, Louisa and Tom have a conversation, while Louisa stares into the fire and wonders about many things. Dickens has made the connection for us; now we must speculate on the precise similarities between the "key-note" of Coketown and the "key-note" (perhaps particularly the conversation in chapter 8) of the Gradgrind children. Why does Dickens keep bringing readers back to Coketown and the Gradgrinds?

3. **Fear of change:** How does each character in *Hard Times* demonstrate a fear of change?

The rigid, unchanging world preferred by Gradgrind seems less admirably portrayed in some ways than the ever-shifting ground of Sleary's circus. Louisa wants change but can't get it (so do Stephen, Rachael, and Sissy). Gradgrind perhaps changes the most. Does he become a sort of hero in this book? Or, does he at least become important proof that change can be very healthy? Which characters long for change, and which characters fear change? Some characters do both. Stephen, for example, fears the changes associated with unions but longs to change his home life. How does Dickens portray each situation? Are characters punished for not moving forward with societal or familial changes? Consider that the 19th-century world was changing faster than ever before, due in large part to the Industrial Revolution. How might this situation influence Dickens's use of fear of change as a theme?

4. **Victorian values:** Is this Dickens's most "Victorian" work? Does the book stand somehow outside of Victorian ideologies to become Dickens's most scathing critique of the society in which he lived?

Some well-known Victorian values include morality, duty, public service, respectability, earnestness, industriousness, piety, conventionality, and domestic propriety. Reading a list like that can seem stifling, even from the distance of nearly 200 years, but it is important to remember that many of these values were Victorian ideals, meaning that people aspired to but did not necessarily reach such lofty goals. Dickens delivers some crushing blows to these commonly held Victorian values. We see how difficult it is for characters such as Stephen to practice domestic propriety and even morality in the face of his wife's troubles and his extreme poverty. Dickens seems to indicate that Victorian priorities are out of line and that perhaps Stephen and Rachael are the most admirable characters in the book. What values do they uphold? While Dickens attacks aspects of Victorian culture in *Hard Times*, he also lives and writes in the midst of it and surely cannot help adhering to some. Which Victorian values does the book seem to promote? Do you think Dickens does this on purpose, or is it just because he cannot help being a product of his culture?

Characters

On June 12, 1870, a writer for the *Sunday Observer* noted: "There have been within our day writers of fiction with subtler insight into the working of human passions, with more varied knowledge of society, with greater constructive faculty, with higher faculty of diction, but there is none who, like [Dickens], could make his characters live, move, and be." This is true of all of Dickens's writing, but is particularly notable concerning *Hard Times,* his shortest novel. It is common in a Dickens novel to encounter more than 80 named characters, but in *Hard Times* there are only 25, providing an excellent opportunity for studying these characters in some depth.

First you will want to ask yourself which characters are able to "live, move, and be" to the greatest degree. Which characters strike you as the most "real"? In answering this question, you will also want to define what you mean by "real" (not necessarily the dictionary definition, but what the word in this context means to you). Who do you think are the heroes and heroines of this story? Why? How does Dickens use a single character to represent an entire population of people? For example, the character of Stephen Blackpool comes to represent factory workers in general, making readers feel sorry for such men and inducing (perhaps) a call for factory reform. Does Dickens use his characters effectively to represent larger groups and get his overall points across, or does he create or perpetuate stereotypes?

Another unusual aspect of *Hard Times* is the degree to which the city of Coketown becomes a character in the novel. When writing about characters you always want to keep the author's techniques in mind. What kinds of words, phrases, settings, and moods generally surround a particular character? If you want to study Coketown as a character, look carefully at some of Dickens's descriptive passages:

It was a town of red brick, or of brick that would have been red if the smoke and ashes had allowed it; but, as matters stood it was a town of unnatural red and black like the painted face of a savage. It was a town of machinery and tall chimneys, out of which interminable serpents of smoke trailed themselves for ever and ever, and never got uncoiled. It had a black canal in it, and a river that ran purple with ill-smelling dye, and vast piles of building full of windows where there was a rattling and a trembling all day long, and where the piston of the steam-engine worked monotonously up and down, like the head of an elephant in a state of melancholy madness. It contained several large streets all very like one another, and many small streets still more like one another, inhabited by people equally like one another, who all went in and out at the same hours, with the same sound upon the same pavements, to do the same work, and to whom every day was the same as yesterday and to-morrow, and every year the counterpart of the last and the next. (18)

What strikes you about this description? If repetition signifies an important point, what is the important point being made in this paragraph? Notice the words that Dickens uses to describe Coketown: *unnatural, savage, serpents, black, ill-smelling*, etc. One of the first things he does is to give Coketown a face and then make that face menacing. There are certainly animalistic qualities listed here, too. What do they mean? What would they have meant to Dickens? Coketown is a very particular world, certainly not unique in England at this time, but still distinct from many other areas of the country. What qualities does Coketown have that make it into a setting so notable that we can call it a character? Why is it so important for Dickens to emphasize Coketown in this novel?

Papers focusing on character often look at the ways in which a character develops (or does not) in terms of what distinguishes one character from another, ways in which the author characterizes the people (through word choice, tone, etc.), and interpretations of changes made either to or by a character over time. Even the relatively few characters in *Hard Times* provide a wealth of material for character studies.

Sample Topics:

1. **Coketown:** What action(s) does Coketown take to help develop the plot of *Hard Times*?

In many ways, it is the lack of action surrounding Coketown that helps to move the plot along. Unions are forming, but in general there are no big strikes, movements, or catastrophes in town to move the plot along. What characterizes Coketown is its stubborn stability. There does not seem to be hope for change in this place. Why does Coketown need to remain somewhat static in order to propel the plot? Interestingly, *Hard Times* is the only Dickens novel set entirely in a factory/industrial town. Coketown as a character adds a layer of bleakness to the novel that lies in perfect contrast to the energy and fruitfulness of the circus.

2. **Mr. Bounderby:** Why is he so careful to disguise his past? Does he end up gaining anything from his deception?

Do readers ever feel sorry for him? Should they? Does Dickens treat Bounderby like a cad or a villain, or does he seem to want us to sympathize (or empathize) with this character? What is the significance of some of the words associated with Bounderby, such as *wind, explosive,* and *maggot?* Bounderby does not demonstrate the fluidity of class system or the "pull yourself up by your bootstraps" mentality, as he professes to. Rather, his character reinforces the difficulty of moving from low or working class up to middle class. Learning of Bounderby's deception helps readers to feel the despair of Stephen Blackpool and the lack of hope for a better life, since class systems are so frighteningly rigid.

3. **Stephen Blackpool:** Is he the true hero of the story? A martyr?

Late Victorian novelist George Gissing wrote that Stephen Blackpool "represents nothing at all; he is a mere model of meekness, and his great misfortune is such as might befall any man anywhere, the curse of a drunken wife" (201). Yet, many readers feel tremendously empathetic toward him. How does Dickens make readers feel such compassion for Stephen? Why does his fate seem both appropriate and inevitable? Dickens uses characters like Stephen to raise the awareness and indignation of readers. Dickens does not provide solutions for characters like Stephen but rather appears to be trying to anger readers into taking some sort of action on behalf of people like Stephen. He is the voice of reason. He is used by factories, by Bounderby, and by Tom. He is defeated by his own wife while tragically in love with her sister. Is he the only truly good person in this story?

History and Context

Hard Times is so deeply embedded in the history and context of the mid-19th century that at times it might be more revealing to study what Dickens left out rather than all the things he includes. We know that Coketown is modeled partly after a town Dickens visited called Preston. At the time of his visit, however, Preston was in the middle of a textile-workers' strike. Why, then, does Dickens not show Coketown workers on strike? This would not have been an uncommon occurrence for the time, and there were certainly other writers (Elizabeth Gaskell, for instance) including such detail in their novels. Does the exclusion of a strike make Coketown's factory workers seem more helpless or just better organized and cared for?

During Queen Victoria's reign, England became the Workshop of the World, producing 30 percent of global industrial output by 1870. *Hard Times* gives us a taste of the Industrial Revolution as it affected people from various classes of factory town society. It is clear in the novel that the Industrial Revolution affected people's attitudes and education just as it affected the nuts and bolts of industry and economy. How does Dickens incorporate both the factual aspects of 19th-century industry and the more "humanitarian" aspects (such as the Poor Law Amendment Act) into this novel?

In a letter to a friend, dated April 1855, Dickens writes:

> There is nothing in the present age at once so galling and so alarming to me as the alienation of the people from their own public affairs. . . . They have had so little to do with the game through all these years of Parliamentary Reform, that they have sullenly laid down their cards, and taken to looking on. . . . [Y]ou can no more help a people who do not help

themselves than you can help a man who does not help himself. . . . I know of nothing that can be done beyond keeping their wrongs continually before them. (*Letters*, 458–460)

Many books of these times attempted to influence thoughts and attitudes about the Industrial Revolution, especially as it concerned the troubles of working people and their lack of governmental representation. So many novels focused on this area that in the 1840s there developed a group of novels known as "industrial novels." These books included Charlotte Brontë's *Shirley*, Frances Trollope's *Michael Armstrong* and *The Factory Boy*, Benjamin Disraeli's *Sybil*, and Gaskell's *Mary Barton*. *Hard Times* was published slightly after this period, in 1854, showing (along with books such as Gaskell's *North and South*) that in the 1850s, writers were still concerned with working conditions and disenfranchised populations.

When studying history and context, you might also look into the life of Dickens himself. Did he have particular reasons for being concerned about education in his time? What did he think of the circus? There are a number of troubled marriages in this book. What were attitudes toward marriage at this time? What was happening in Dickens's own marriage that might lend itself to a better understanding of the personal context of the work?

Writing about the history and context of a novel always involves outside research. It is important to allow your paper topic to remain somewhat flexible, as the information you find through research might require a topic change. It is also important that you remain selective when writing. Do not include all of the history you find about the 19th century and/or Charles Dickens. Choose only the most relevant details from your research to include in your paper, and support them with your ideas and evidence from Dickens's novel.

Sample Topics:

1. **Industrial Revolution:** Where in the book do we see Dickens's attitudes toward the Industrial Revolution?

In the 19th century, when progress in many areas was being made more quickly than ever before, people began to move from the country into the cities. Many people (like Stephen and Rachael) worked in factories and came to be regarded in terms of what they could do rather than just who they were. In other words, a person's personality was not as important as the quantity and quality of their output—how much money they could bring in for factory owners (therein lies the reason for the nickname *hand*). They were not regarded as entire people—they were only useful for the work they did with their hands. Some scholars say that the railway opening in 1830 at which a man was killed by a steam engine foretold the destruction about to be brought on by advances in technology and industry. The focus during the Industrial Revolution moved away from nature and away from science of discovery. People focused instead on manmade objects and science of productivity.

2. **Poor Law Amendment Act:** In what ways does *Hard Times* read as a critique of legal policy and societal norms?

The Poor Law Amendment Act of 1834 stated that no able-bodied person could receive money or other help from Poor Law authorities except in a workhouse. Workhouse conditions were kept harsh in order to discourage people from wanting help and enforce the popular belief that "God helps those who help themselves." Why would Dickens and others view this amendment and general belief as backward?

3. **Elementary education:** Given the experiences of Sissy, Louisa, Tom, and Bitzer, which of the competing theories of education does Dickens appear to subscribe to?

In the 1850s, England was struggling to establish comprehensive elementary education. Up until this point, private schools (like Gradgrind's) were prevalent and practiced different theories of education. There were certainly schools very much like Gradgrind's, but there were also schools that emphasized play and fun for the children. In 1846, Sir James Kay-Shuttleworth became the director of a utilitarian educational program that emphasized facts and strict discipline. The utilitarian school of thought, as well as other educational precepts of the time, came largely from Scotland, which might explain the Scottish origins (as well as the menacing connotation) of the teacher at Gradgrind's school, Mr. M'Choakumchild. To determine Dickens's attitude toward modes of education in the book, look at the characterizations of Gradgrind and Bounderby. Do they really want "the facts" from everyone? How does Dickens weave tales of or references to fancy into the story to emphasize his point?

Philosophy and Ideas

Clearly the fact-based philosophies and ideas of Gradgrind and Bounderby nearly overwhelm the book, ultimately demonstrating the fruitlessness and ridiculousness of teaching and living only in facts. How does Dickens's emphasis on this utilitarian philosophy actually highlight his own belief in the importance of imagination (or what he often called "fancy")?

Hard Times is centered on Gradgrind's fact-based life and educational system, which is based on utilitarianism, a popular idea in the 19th century purporting that people focus on actions that provide the greatest good for the greatest number. Utilitarian thinkers measure the value of lives and actions according to their usefulness. We see the price that Louisa, Tom, Sissy, Stephen, and eventually even Gradgrind and Bounderby pay for the exclusion of human feeling, wonder, and compassion from their lives. Does Dickens believe that life should be dominated by fancy? Or, does he aim for some sort of middle ground? Which character(s) in the book (if any) seems to embody most closely Dickens's ideal for how life should be lived (philosophy of life)?

In 1939, George Orwell wrote:

The truth is that Dickens's criticism of society is almost exclusively moral. Hence the utter lack of any constructive suggestion anywhere in his work. He attacks the law, parliamentary government, the educational system and so forth, without ever clearly suggesting what he would put in their places. Of course it is not necessarily the business of a novelist, or a satirist, to make constructive suggestions, but the point is that Dickens's attitude is at bottom not even DEstructive. There is no clear sign that he wants the existing order to be overthrown, or that he believes it would make very much difference if it WERE overthrown. For in reality his target is not so much society as "human nature." ("Charles")

Do you think that Dickens criticizes philosophies and fails to submit a better idea? If so, why? Is there simply no better way of thinking about the world? If you think that Dickens does encourage his own philosophy (or at least another philosophy, if not necessarily his own), what is it? How does he demonstrate the benefits of this alternative philosophy?

Sample Topics:

1. **Utilitarianism:** How does Dickens demonstrate his belief that utilitarianism does not work?

Utilitarianism, led most famously by Jeremy Bentham (1748–1832), was a school of thought dedicated to empiricism (reliance on fact and experiment). Scholars sometimes claim that Dickens misinterprets utilitarianism in this novel, but all agree that in Mr. Gradgrind he captures the essence of Bentham. John Stuart Mill, the son of a famous utilitarian, has done some significant writing on *Hard Times.* Utilitarian thinkers concerned themselves with "the greatest good for the greatest number," deciding that even major sacrifices by some people are probably worth it if society in general will benefit. Dickens applies utilitarianism to the context of schools, using Gradgrind and Bounderby as the mouthpieces. We see utilitarianism propounded upon the children in the form of intense focus on facts. Sissy and Louisa are the only children who begin (inadvertently at first) to poke holes in this theory, and we see them strengthen and grow because of their senses of wonder and imagination. We also see the two girls punished for these senses. We know that Dickens was concerned with loss of "fancy," or imagination, and it is easy to see why this would concern a fiction writer. Is Dickens denouncing utilitarianism specifically, or is he saying that too strictly following only one philosophy is never a good idea, no matter which philosophy it is?

2. **"God helps those who help themselves"**: In what ways does *Hard Times* refute or support this philosophy?

Stephen would like to help himself, but laws and finances prevent him. It seems important that he is at least trying to be proactive. His wife clearly gave up long ago and is not a respectable person. The children at school cannot help themselves in terms of finances or educational decisions. Most of them would not even know what their options are. Does Dickens appear to subscribe to the notion that it can become impossible for a person to help him- or herself? In what ways is he also critical of this idea, hinting that people cannot simply sit back and wait for fortune to fall on them?

Form and Genre

Form and genre provide ways of classifying works that usually allow us to study them more fully. Form is defined as the style and structure of a work, whereas genre is the type, or classification, of a work. Both form and genre are usually distinct from a work's content, though writers use each of them quite specifically in order to convey a particular message, reach a certain audience, or simply strengthen the impact of their work.

The most recognized feature of Dickens's form and genre is the serial novel. Dickens wrote most of his novels as monthly installments to be published in a magazine. *Hard Times,* however, was written in weekly installments over a four-month period, which perhaps accounts for the lack of description and detail compared to Dickens's longer works. The weekly installment schedule may also account for the brevity of *Hard Times;* it is the shortest of Dickens's novels.

Hard Times is nevertheless packed with insight and information, shining through Dickens's use of the novel as a vehicle for social criticism. The very act of writing this novel seems one of defiance, railing against a popular frame of mind and an even more popular emphasis on industry (and away from family, empathy, and imagination). Perhaps the true genius of Dickens is his ability to disguise his social analysis and criticism enough to keep the novel readable and entertaining. He could have simply written his views in pamphlet form but instead chose throughout his life to open discussion of social issues by embedding them deep in the world of fiction, fancy, and imagination. That *Hard Times* exists as a novel and not a tract shows the extent to which Dickens practiced what he preached.

Sample Topics:

1. **Social criticism:** Is Dickens criticizing specific groups of people in this novel? If so, whom? If not, is he indicting the entire population somehow?

Certainly, *Hard Times* is an examination of educational practices and philosophies in mid-19th-century England. The book takes us beyond arguments and issues surrounding education and addresses a number of other important issues in society as well: laws, social norms, factories, marriage practices, gender expectations, and strict class distinctions. Dickens is famous for his activism through writing, campaigning in his novels for societal change of one kind or another. How does his use of social criticism affect the form and genre of the novel? In what ways is he able to meld the social criticism and the fiction together to create an enjoyable and informative read, and in what ways are these two forms necessarily distinct from each other?

2. **Moral fable:** What is it that we learn from *Hard Times*? What does Dickens expect readers to learn?

A number of elements in *Hard Times* can, for better or worse, be attributed to the serialization of the original story, particularly in this case because the story appeared in weekly rather than Dickens's usual monthly installments, making the plot move more quickly. Literary critic F. R. Leavis calls *Hard Times* a moral fable in which, "The intention is peculiarly insistent, so that the representative significance of everything in the fable— character, episode, and so on—is immediately apparent as we read" (188). Technically the term *parable* might more accurately describe the novel. *Hard Times* works as a moral fable or parable and does not simply read as a book in which Dickens did not have time to develop the characters. Clearly, there is a message in the book, even though lessons learned from it today may vary widely from those learned by its first readers.

3. **Weekly installments:** How might digesting this book in short installments affect one's reading of it? How might the short installments have affected Dickens's writing?

Hard Times appeared in *Household Words* once a week between April 1 and August 12, 1854. It is Dickens's shortest novel, with only 25 named characters, compared to his usual average of 80 characters per novel. The book contains less detail than his usual work and less emphasis on the psychology of characters. Some characters appear as types or ideas rather than fully dimensional people. *Hard Times* is Dickens's 10th novel, so his readers were accustomed to the serialized form and presumably held particular expectations for a Dickens novel by the time this publication began. How could these briefer, more frequent installments, combined with changes in characterizations and detail, have affected Dickens's contemporary readers? How do these things affect us now?

Language, Symbols, and Imagery

Dickens has been described as a very cinematic writer, ready for movies long before movies were ready for him. This explains, to some degree, the level of popularity that Dickens's novels have achieved in the areas of film and television. This ability to frame a scene, to show the setting, action, and characters to readers rather than simply telling them about it, involves Dickens's use of imagery and language. Studying the language of a text allows you to look carefully at syntax, word choice, and general diction, while imagery includes the details in a story that can be perceived by one or more of the five senses. From the very first chapter of *Hard Times*, readers get an overview of the world in which some of these characters live:

The scene was a plain, bare monotonous vault of a schoolroom, and the speaker's square forefinger emphasized his observations by underscoring every sentence with a line on the schoolmaster's sleeve. The emphasis was helped by the speaker's square wall of a forehead, which had his eyebrows for its base, while his eyes found commodious cellarage in two dark caves, overshadowed by the wall. The emphasis was helped by the speaker's mouth, which was wide, thin, and hard set. The emphasis was helped by the speaker's voice, which was inflexible, dry, and dictatorial. The emphasis was helped by the speaker's hair, which bristled on the skirts of his bald head, a plantation of firs to keep the wind from its shining surface, all covered with knobs, like the crust of a plum pie, as if the head had scarcely warehouse-room for the hard facts stored inside. The speaker's obstinate carriage, square coat, square legs, square shoulders,—nay, his very neckcloth, trained to take him by the throat with an unaccommodating grasp, like a stubborn fact, as it was,—all helped the emphasis. (5)

How does Dickens use physical features of a character's body and environment to help characterize that person? In other words, how do a character's physical attributes and surroundings help to demonstrate that character's temperament and philosophy? We have a very detailed physical description of Gradgrind before we even learn his name. Phrenology, a theory stating that one's character can be determined by studying the shape of one's head, was widely popular in 19th-century Europe. Dickens repeatedly refers to Gradgrind's physical appearance (particularly concerning the head) as "square." What qualities can be attributed to the term *square*? What qualities did 19th-century English people associate with the word? Why is it so important that Gradgrind be imagined in a square or squares? This kind of attention to physical detail shows why Dickens is often regarded as a cinematic writer.

Dickens also uses symbolism to lend deeper meaning to *Hard Times*. Symbols in a literary work are things that stand for something else. Louisa is often either near a fire or described in terms of fire. Sometimes she even does it herself: "I was encouraged by nothing, mother, but by looking at the red sparks dropping out of the fire, and whitening and dying. It made me think, after all, how short my life would be, and how little I could hope to do in it" (Dickens 39).

Sample Topics:

1. **Fire:** Why is fire such a prominent symbol for Louisa's character?

   Take note of all the time that Louisa spends staring into the fire. What does this tell us about her personality? How do the Gradgrinds feel about the time she spends staring at the fire? What descriptors or traits are often associated with fire? How do they surface through Louisa? One example would be Louisa's observation that people usually see smoke most of the time, and very few see the fire burst from the chimneys at night. The sparks from these chimney bursts remind her how short life is, and she feels she will not accomplish much. What do you think she would like to accomplish if she could choose?

2. **Physicality:** What do we come to understand about characters based solely on Dickens's descriptions of their physical characteristics?

   Dickens's use of phrenology (a theory that the shape of one's head determines personality traits) and his general descriptions of a character's physical presence offer great insight into various characters. In the second paragraph of the book, Dickens uses the word *square* repeatedly in his description of Gradgrind's physical presence. Looking at such passages and then asking yourself what the connotations (then and now) for a word such as *square* might be can lead to tremendous insight into not only the character but Dickens's attitude toward him or her.

3. **Character and place-names:** What is the added significance of names such as Gradgrind, Bounderby, Old Hell Shaft, and Blackpool?

   Dickens often gives characters names that already have a meaning. What connotations do names like Gradgrind and

Bounderby hold? Gradgrind, for example, calls to mind grinding gears or things being ground up, both of which might be elements of factory jobs and neither of which sounds particularly lovely or serene. How does Bounderby "bound" through life, rather than walking or strolling? Remember to put words in 19th-century context—they might mean something different now. How does a character's name reveal something about that character before we are fully introduced to him or her? Have any names from *Hard Times* acquired a life of their own and come into common usage? Has the meaning of any character's name changed over time, making the word either more or less significant to readers' understanding of the character? Keep in mind that names such as Stephen and Rachael may be biblical allusions as well.

Compare and Contrast Essays

In *Hard Times*, Dickens creates a world that readers hope lies in stark contrast to the one in which they live. Even if 19th- or 21st-century readers do not live in factory towns, however, the comparisons are set up in order to help them, we assume, appreciate not being in circumstances like those of Stephen Blackpool. The contrast with many readers' lives might also help to generate empathy for the characters in the book and people like them who are in similar or maybe even worse situations.

Comparing and contrasting elements in a story is a very useful way of finding similarities and differences on which you can then comment. Do not simply make a list of similarities and/or differences and assume that you are finished. The purpose of comparisons and contrasts is to invoke the larger issues in the story, and in order to do that effectively, the similarities and differences must be not only found but also analyzed.

One of the most obvious elements of a text to compare and contrast is character. This is why the analysis is so important. Of course, you will find similarities and differences between two characters in a novel just as you would find similarities and differences between any two people you know. You must draw conclusions from those similarities and/or differences. Often, you will find that the most interesting analyses stem from the most unlikely comparisons. In what ways, for example, are Louisa and Tom similar, and what do these similarities reveal about each character and their relationship to each other?

Sample Topics:

1. **Louisa and Tom:** Which of these two characters does Dickens assume readers will sympathize with more readily?

Contrary to gender stereotypes, Louisa always seems to be stronger than Tom. She leads him to the circus, where they are caught by their father. She sacrifices her happiness (if there was potential for any happiness in her life) in order to benefit Tom. Essentially, Louisa learns how to play the system as she understands it, whereas Tom seems to be simply trying to survive (and often failing at that). How do we see the differences and similarities between Tom and Louisa even when they are first introduced? Does Tom (with help from their father) drag Louisa into an unhappy life, or is she responsible for her own decisions? Whom or what do Tom and Louisa represent? Is Dickens setting readers up to have to choose between them? If so, why, and which character does he push readers to support?

2. **Gradgrind and Bounderby:** How does Gradgrind redeem himself, while Bounderby only becomes more pathetic and ridiculous?

Gradgrind and Bounderby are very similar men in the beginning of the novel, but the gulf between them widens when Gradgrind begins to sympathize (or maybe, more important, empathize) with Louisa. Why is Gradgrind the one who changes, even though Bounderby is the one whose life (as he constructed it) has been revealed as a sham? If there were a sequel to *Hard Times*, what would happen to each of these two characters?

3. **Louisa and Sissy:** Are they more alike than they are different?

Society says that Sissy must try to be like Louisa, but in reality Louisa wants to be more like Sissy. What is Louisa's advice for Sissy? Will Sissy succeed where Louisa failed? What are our hopes for each girl/woman? The second to last paragraph of the book begins by discussing Sissy and ends by discussing Louisa, conflating these two characters and making it even harder to distinguish one from the other. Could Sissy and Louisa have survived (even excelled) in each other's worlds? Would Louisa have been happy as a part of the circus? Could Sissy have loved Bounderby?

4. **Circus society versus Coketown-Gradgrind society:** Are there any similarities between these two societies?

Read the description of the circus people carefully. They sound loving, much like an extended family. Their entire living is made by defying the type of logic on which Gradgrind and others have built their world. Yet, there is still a system, even a hierarchy, to each society. Why might Dickens have chosen to pair these particular groups of people?

Bibliography and Online Resources for *Hard Times*

Birchenough, C. *History of Elementary Education in England and Wales from 1800 to the Present Day.* London: W. B. Clive U Tutorial P, 1914.

Bloom, Harold, ed. *Charles Dickens's Hard Times. Modern Critical Interpretations.* New York: Chelsea House, 1987.

Chesterton, G. K. *"Hard Times." Appreciations and Criticisms of the Works of Charles Dickens.* 1911. New York: Haskell House, 1970. 169–177.

Dickens, Charles. *Hard Times.* 1854. New York: W. W. Norton, 2001.

———. *The Letters of Charles Dickens.* Eds. Mamie Dickens & Georgina Hogarth. Volume 1. 1833–1856. New York: Charles Scribner's Sons, 1879.

Discovering Dickens: A Community Writing Project. Stanford University. Available online. URL: http://dickens.stanford.edu/hard/times.html. Retrieved September 11, 2007.

Gissing, George. *Charles Dickens: A Critical Study.* London: Blackie & Son, 1898.

Gray, Paul Edward, ed. *Twentieth-Century Interpretations of Hard Times.* Englewood Cliffs, NJ: Prentice-Hall, 1969.

Leavis, F. R. *The Great Tradition.* London: Chatto & Windus, 1948.

Orwell, George. "Charles Dickens: Essay I." *The Complete Works of George Orwell.* Available online. URL: www.george-orwell.org/Charles_Dickens/O.html. Retrieved April 2007.

————. *"Hard Times."* David Perdue's Charles Dickens Page. Available online. URL: http://charlesdickenspage.com/hardtimes.html. Retrieved September 11, 2007.

Simpson, Margaret. *The Companion to Hard Times.* Robertsbridge, UK: Helm Information, 1997.

"Some Discussions of Dickens's *Hard Times.*" The Victorian Web. Retrieved 11 September 2007. <http://www.victorianweb.org/authors/dickens/hard timesov.html>.

A TALE OF TWO CITIES

READING TO WRITE

I N *A Tale of Two Cities*, it is specifically the character Dr. Manette who is "RECALLED TO LIFE" (15). This theme of being "recalled to life" occurs throughout the novel, however. Readers might feel that Charles, Lucie, and even Sydney are "recalled to life" in some way by the end of the novel. Dickens himself "recalled to life" the French Revolution, as well as English perceptions of this time in history.

A Tale of Two Cities, published in 1859, begins with one of the most famous passages in literature:

> It was the best of times, it was the worst of times, it was the age of wisdom, it was the age of foolishness, it was the epoch of belief, it was the epoch of incredulity, it was the season of Light, it was the season of Darkness, it was the spring of hope, it was the winter of despair, we had everything before us, we had nothing before us, we were all going direct to Heaven, we were all going direct the other way—in short, the period was so far like the present period, that some of its noisiest authorities insisted on its being received, for good or for evil, in the superlative degree of comparison only. (7)

How well does this opening serve the book? Does it encapsulate the themes, plot, characters? Is it too broad or vague? Does it add elements of universality? Does it distance the reader? Does it reflect Victorian England? What tone does this paragraph set for the book? If you back up just one more step and think carefully about the title, even more questions arise. Why is it a tale of two cities when it is basically about the French Revolution? What does London have to do with it, and why is it important enough for Dickens to highlight in the title?

Return to this opening paragraph after finishing the book. Which events in the book does this paragraph foreshadow or illuminate? Why does Dickens write it as one long sentence? Each *it was* statement is a sentence of its own, yet he separates them with commas. What effect does this punctuation have on the message, its pacing, and/or the melding together of these ideas and impressions? Who is the *we* Dickens refers to in this paragraph? Why does he capitalize *Light* and *Darkness*? (There might be many ways to answer this question, though it can be helpful to note that the late 18th century is often referred to as the Age of Enlightenment. You will want to start with a book such as *The Encyclopedia of the Enlightenment*, edited by Alan Charles Kors, to learn why the 18th century came to have such a name. How are/were light and darkness used in that context? What does the conclusion of the sentence address? Is Dickens saying that the mid-19th century is similar to or different from the late 18th century? Why and how? Why is he careful to make this distinction, to separate the days of the French Revolution from the time period in which he is writing, right at the beginning of the novel? Why would this historical perspective be important to convey? Did Dickens and his contemporaries view the French Revolution in the same ways that people view it now, or do we gain or lose perspective as more time passes?

This book is atypical for Dickens. He viewed it as a sort of experiment in including historical detail, mostly to tighten the story and tell about events rather than characters. Any footnoted edition of the book will tell you that many characters seem to be modeled after actual people, and it seems that all of the characters are stand-ins for a type of person, a historical figure, or a conglomeration of people or types of people. Why do the most devoted characters, in terms of patriotism and cause (Miss Pross, the Vengeance, etc.), seem almost ridiculous? How did Dickens use these character stand-ins or types to express his views on the French Revolution and/or European history in general?

Since this book is so different from Dickens's more character-driven novels, it is important to investigate the book as a whole as well. Why, for example, is this one of Dickens's most widely taught and most widely read books? What insight does this book provide into Dickens's world and his opinions?

TOPICS AND STRATEGIES

This section of the chapter addresses various possible topics for writing about *A Tale of Two Cities* as well as general methods for approaching these topics. These lists are in no way exhaustive and are meant to provide a jumping-off point rather than an answer key. Use these suggestions to find your own ideas and form your own analyses. All topics discussed in this chapter could potentially turn into very good papers.

Themes

As with almost any novel, there are a number of themes present in *A Tale of Two Cities*. Themes are often identifiable because an author returns to or utilizes the same idea in various plotlines or character details. Since *A Tale of Two Cities* is partly a story of doubles, parallels, and connections, the themes become very clear as more than one character or storyline deals with similar ideas and issues.

Freedom and sacrifice are universally understood as important ideas in times of war or great strife, and it is certainly no surprise to find Dickens using them as themes for this work. In what ways do issues of freedom and sacrifice pertain not only to the large-scale issues concerning France and England but also to the personal lives of each character? How does Dickens thread those themes throughout the entire work? To find this information, you might look closely at word choices (particularly when words and ideas are repeated), syntax, and chapter titles.

Sample Topics:
   1. **Madness:** Which characters succeed in staving off madness? Who fails?

   Are there characters generally regarded (by readers and/or other characters) as sane who may really be mad, and vice versa? How much does madness depend on perspective? The Marquis thinks the commoners are crazy for mourning their children; they think he is insane for disregarding them. Do the English characters think the French (revolutionaries, at least) are insane? Why or why not?

2. **Freedom:** Is freedom always a good thing in this novel?

The French Revolution was all about freedom: to earn, to keep, to educate, to hope. Other freedoms are addressed in *A Tale of Two Cities* as well: Manette's freedom from prison (and from madness), Charles's freedom from his family name, and Sydney's freedom from his love for Lucie, among other examples. Who takes freedom for granted? Why? Are there degrees of freedom, depending on nationality, economic status, gender, influence, education, etc.?

3. **Citizenship:** What does it mean, in this novel, to be a citizen?

Revolutionaries refer to each other (and eventually everyone) as "citizen." The word becomes a sort of title, bestowed upon everyone. Why? What sorts of rights and obligations does the title of citizen entail?

4. **Sacrifice:** Which characters make sacrifices willingly, and which characters are forced?

Why do revolutionaries claim that all must be sacrificed for the good of the republic, including family, possessions, even (or especially) life? Loyalists to the monarchy claimed that all must be sacrificed for the king. Is Sydney's final decision truly a sacrifice for Lucie? Or, does he value his own life so little that he would have simply killed himself anyway? Think of the different meanings and uses of the word: A person can sacrifice something, and a person can also be sacrificed. How are both of these uses applicable to *A Tale of Two Cities*?

Characters

Dickens spends less time on characterizations in *A Tale of Two Cities* than in some of his earlier novels. The book as a whole contains less general material than Dickens's usual work, eliminating some of the excess melodrama and description that he often used and boiling it down to what amounts to a very simple story.

That story, without any extensive background or complicated sub-plots to guide it or distract from it, is told through and by the characters in *A Tale of Two Cities*. In many ways, the simplicity and immediacy of Dickens's characterizations reflect the overall mood of the book and possibly its historical context. The French Revolution was a time of such great upheaval for countries as well as individuals that one's lengthy background ceased to matter. What did matter (and does in the story) was who you are now and where you stand on issues fanning the revolution. And yet, after moments of great crisis, people begin to ask why, and that is when background details are revealed. Thus, with *A Tale of Two Cities*, we are plunged into the lives of these characters with little more than the most immediately relevant knowledge about them, and only after the crises have come do we begin to learn why each character has played his or her particular role in the plot. In some ways, this is closer to real life than novels with extensive background, which give readers an omniscience that the characters cannot possibly share. In other words, it is the characterizations (or lack thereof) in this novel that place it most firmly and urgently within its chosen historical moment—the passion and panic of the French Revolution.

In 1859, Dickens wrote about *A Tale of Two Cities* in a letter to his friend John Forster: "I set myself . . . the little task of making a *picturesque* story, rising in every chapter with characters true to nature, but whom the story itself should express, more than they should express themselves, by dialogue" (*Letters*, 115). Characters are individuals, providing a small glimpse of particular lives, but they are also symbols and types, providing views (however brief) of the variations of lives at this time in history and adding an element of universality to the novel. Are the characters in this book able to stand outside of the story, or do they require the specific context in order to seem real? Which characters represent or display what seems to have been the true spirit of the French Revolution? How are various characters defined by their Englishness or Frenchness? Why? Which characters seem the most realistic? Most unrealistic? Why? Do you think Dickens intended them to appear as such?

Sample Topics:

1. **Marquis St. Evrémonde:** Does Dickens characterize him as strong and ruthless or ignorant and pathetic?

Dickens compares Marquis St. Evrémonde, part of the old regime toppled by the revolution, to the gargoyles on his home. How does such a comparison help to characterize the Marquis? Look particularly at the scenes through which the Marquis is introduced. Why does Dickens want these to be the first things we learn about the Marquis? How do descriptions and characterizations of the Marquis compare to descriptions and characterizations of Charles Darnay? Why would Dickens draw similarities or distinctions between the two men? What effect does this have on the text and our impressions of the characters?

2. **Sydney Carton and Charles Darnay:** How does Dickens both differentiate and fuse these men?

It seems that together Sydney and Charles make an entire hero. Scholars say that Sydney in particular is modeled after Dickens himself, although Charles is the one who shares his first name and initials. Is it Dickens's dark side (Sydney the jackal) that must die? Is the life of one man worth more than the other? It is interesting to note that on stage these two characters were often played by the same actor.

3. **Stryver:** What is his role in the book?

Stryver seems to be a minor character, yet Dickens devotes quite a lot of time to him. In what ways does Dickens reveal his feelings toward Stryver? How do other characters feel about him? Note the small details, such as the fact that Stryver is always "shouldering" his way into and out of things.

4. **Madame Defarge:** Do we feel pity for her? Does Dickens want us to? How can you tell?

Does her family history excuse her attitude and behavior? How do readers feel about her before and then after learning about her connections to Evrémonde? Why does her husband seem to be more sympathetic?

5. **The Vengeance:** What specific population of people does she represent?

She is a particular individual with limited knowledge and interactions, yet she represents (as her moniker reveals) not only a larger group of people but the spirit of the Terror. Why is it significant that she is a woman and that she is connected to the Defarges? Does she have a counterpart? Lucie? The apathetic? The English?

History and Context

Clearly, history plays an enormous role in *A Tale of Two Cities*. Dickens is careful to place his characters in actual events and situations surrounding the French Revolution, or at least in situations that would have been plausible or likely at this point in history. Despite various anachronisms (intentional or not), the world portrayed in *A Tale of Two Cities* is quite accurately the world of late 18th-century France and England.

One of the pitfalls of historical fiction is the ability the genre gives readers to dissociate with the text. In other words, it is easy to read such novels and assume that their themes and philosophies only applied to the time in which the book is set. It becomes important to ask why a writer such as Dickens would take on the French Revolution as a setting. What interested him? How did the English world of 1859 compare to that of 1785? Why would Dickens and his readers take a particular interest in this period of history?

It is crucial when writing about the history and context of a historical fiction work that you do more than simply point out places at which historical events or people appear. Your paper must explore possible reasons why these historical events and/or people appear. How does Dickens seem to feel about these tidbits of history? Why does he involve certain fictional characters? How does Dickens want readers to feel about these historical events and/or figures?

Sample Topics:

1. **Thomas Carlyle's *The French Revolution:*** In what ways is Carlyle's influence felt in this novel?

Dickens was an admirer of Carlyle and even dedicated *A Tale of Two Cities* to him. Carlyle's work as a historian was very popular and remains worth the challenge of reading it. He did not think it was right for historians or others to judge historical people or events based on their own standards, morals, and beliefs rather than those belonging to the historical event or person being studied. Does Dickens seem to be judging characters with Victorian ideals, or is he able to contextualize the judgment in the 18th century? Carlyle also sought out the fissures between appearances and reality, which is a recurring theme in much of Dickens's writings as well. Does Dickens's use of anachronistic detail successfully demonstrate that the reality is not as important as the appearances? As long as the details appear to be accurate, readers will not question the book's historical import. On the other hand, these anachronistic details in *A Tale of Two Cities* might demonstrate just the opposite. It does not matter, Dickens might be saying, if the history is completely accurate in a novel, because reality is more important, and readers should use the book only as a reflection of their worlds so as to prevent similar occurrences in real life. Which interpretation do you feel is best supported by *A Tale of Two Cities*?

2. **The Reign of Terror:** How does Dickens seem to regard the Reign of Terror?

The Reign of Terror, September 1793–July 1794, was led largely by Georges Danton and Maximilien Robespierre, who was rather ironically guillotined himself. During the Terror were mass executions, more than 1,000 of which took place in July alone! Interpretations of the influence and effects of the Reign of Terror vary from the belief that it gave birth to tyrannical governments that followed to an understanding that it was a radical example of the growing pains of democracy. Look at the chapter called "The Grindstone" to see if you can pinpoint a tone in Dickens's writing that might reveal his point of view. Why would Dickens center so much of his book on such an ugly, bloody, violent 10 months?

3. **La Guillotine:** What is the significance in *A Tale of Two Cities* of the guillotine as a female entity?

Dickens writes of "the sharp female called La Guillotine" (272). The guillotine was invented, in some form, long before the 18th century, but the French Revolution, and particularly the Reign of Terror, made it famous. It now stands as the main symbol for the French Revolution. At the time of the revolution (indeed until the late 20th century) the guillotine was the only legal means of execution in France. Further research on the guillotine can help you answer important questions. Why did executions during the revolution attract such mobs of spectators? Why is the guillotine in *A Tale of Two Cities* referred to as female? Was this Dickens's invention or a common connection of the time?

Philosophy and Ideas

Just as with other novels, finding philosophies and ideas in *A Tale of Two Cities* involves looking for general concepts that apply to the wider world—our world, Dickens's world, or in this case, the world of revolutionary France and England. You might, for example, investigate the differences and similarities between the philosophies of France and England at this time. It seems clear in the novel that many French people (particularly the villainous ones) are easily caught up in (or in charge of creating) a mob mentality. They think and act as a group, exemplifying the "fraternity" part of their revolutionary motto, "Liberty, Fraternity, Equality." Several of the English characters in the book, however, accomplish their most important tasks completely alone. Miss Pross and Sydney Carton are two apparent heroes in the novel, and they both act independently.

Sample Topics:
1. **Individualism versus collective:** What is Dickens's tone when he writes about the mob?

Often in this book, individual acts (for example, Sydney's sacrifice) win out over mob mentality. Victorian England favored the distinct individual. Mob mentality does not permit people to heed the needs or safety of individuals, yet the book as a whole focuses on the individuals and the drama of one family for whom one another's needs and safety are paramount. Look at the first scene of mob mentality, in the chapter titled "The Wine-shop," when a cask of wine breaks in the street and Dickens shows startling images of want and bloodthirst to foreshadow revolutionary activities.

2. **Utilitarians:** How does Dickens try to promote individual fancy over utilitarianism?

Utilitarians viewed religion as outdated and unnecessary, a point of view similar to that of French revolutionaries who used or changed Christian symbols to achieve their own ends. In utilitarianism, and perhaps in the revolution as well, the individual loses to the common good, and Dickens does not seem to like it. This ties in with the idea of sacrifice, that one must give one's life if it can help the cause in some way. Which characters embody the utilitarian ideal? Which characters oppose it? With which characters does Dickens want readers to sympathize?

3. **Revolutionary idealism:** How does Dickens's writing about revolutionaries such as the Defarges, about the Vengeance, and about the mobs reveal his attitude toward their actions?

Dickens seemed to think that this kind of violent revolution only makes things worse. He believed in reform from within. Dickens also knew that the legal process could be long and fruitless and that many people had no way to make themselves heard in any influential context. So, he may not be arguing that change should not occur—just the opposite in fact—but he seems to have specific opinions about the ways in which such changes should be carried out.

Form and Genre

Form and genre provide ways of classifying works that usually allow us to study them more fully. Form is defined as the style and structure of a work, whereas genre is the type, or classification, of a work. For example,

A Tale of Two Cities is a historical novel. Clearly, the work would be dramatically different if it were simply a novel without the historical elements. Both form and genre are usually distinct from a work's content, though writers use each of them quite specifically in order to convey a particular message, reach a certain audience, or simply strengthen the impact of their work.

To effectively study form and/or genre, ask questions about the book as a whole and its place in popular and/or literary culture. This may be particularly interesting in this case, as *A Tale of Two Cities* was a departure for Dickens, who did not ordinarily write historical novels. How was *A Tale of Two Cities* received by readers and critics in Dickens's time? Did readers seem to like it more than Dickens's other novels? Do readers now seem to prefer it to Dickens's other novels? How much do readers' likes and dislikes about this book stem from the fact that it is a historical novel?

Sample Topics:

1. **Historical novel:** How does such a popular novel influence our understanding and perceptions of the French Revolution?

   Dickens does not use real people in the fore- or background of this book; instead, he places fictional people against a backdrop of real events. Of course, this genre is a crucial element of the book and adds much resonance to the characters' stories. What does *A Tale of Two Cities* reveal about Victorian attitudes toward the revolution? How does it influence your reading of the book to learn that some of the historical details are anachronistic or inaccurate? How does it influence your reading to learn that some of the characters are based on real revolutionary figures and perhaps even Dickens himself?

2. **Story within a story:** How does Dickens give the impression that the storytelling in this novel is not always completely within his authorial control?

   This structure allows Dickens to keep readers in suspense about Manette's past, the wedding day promise between Manette and

Darnay, the role of Sydney Carton, and the connections between the Manettes, Darnay, and the Defarges. Placing Manette as the writer of this story within a story also reveals the ugly irony faced by Manette upon learning that divulging his story will condemn his son-in-law. This technique also demonstrates the power of stories. What is powerful about *A Tale of Two Cities*? What does Dickens's work "call up" in its readers?

Language, Symbols, and Imagery

As with any Dickens novel, there is no shortage of language, symbols, and imagery in place to convey particular points. Language, of course, is used creatively in *A Tale of Two Cities* to emphasize barriers between people. Look at the scene between Miss Pross and Madame Defarge. They cannot understand a word the other is saying, yet they carry on a conversation resulting in extraordinary actions. Does Dickens's emphasis on language differences unveil his bias toward English, or is he able to be impartial?

Symbols are elements in literature that stand for something else, and *A Tale of Two Cities* is full of them. Look for items or actions or abstract concepts that are often associated with a particular setting or character. Study the context of the item, and find out what associations people made with it not only in Dickens's time but also during the French Revolution. What, for example, were some common symbols of the French Revolution? Do they appear in this book? Where and why?

Imagery provides readers with something they can perceive with one or more of their five senses. Think about scenes such as the broken wine cask and the mayhem that ensues. Study how and why Dickens makes readers see, hear, smell, touch, and even taste elements of that scene. What effects does such imagery have on readers, then and now?

Sample Topics:

1. **Knitting:** Why is it so chilling to see women knitting under such extraordinary circumstances?

   People often knit items that provide warmth and comfort. How does knitting enemies' names into her work give Madame Defarge warmth and comfort? The most extreme example is of the women knitting while watching guillotine executions. Knitting is often used as a metaphor for or a description of people who are connected or bound together—a close-knit group, for example. Knitting implements take on particular significance as well. Madame Defarge stands "Pointing her knitting-needle at little Lucie as if it were the finger of Fate" (Dickens 266). Knitting in this book is also an exclusively female activity. Why, in such a male-centered work, does knitting become such an integral activity? How does knitting affect the lives of all the characters in the novel?

2. **Echoes and mirrors:** How do the effects of echoes and mirrors pervade this book?

The Manettes' home on the corner is "a wonderful corner for echoes" (Dickens 100). Lucie tells Darnay that she sits and listens "until [she has] made the echoes out to be the echoes of all the footsteps that are coming by-and-by into [their] lives" (Dickens 104). Echoes generally imply the past—something that has already occurred but reverberates into the present again and again. In this conversation, however, Lucie indicates that she hears echoes of the future—of action yet to come. Certainly, readers later learn how Manette's actions in the past will affect Darnay's (and indeed the entire family's) future. Dickens uses mirrors in similar ways, in that their effects seem to continue and even gain importance over time.

3. **Prison:** How does Dickens demonstrate prison as the great equalizer?

Nearly everyone in the book is imprisoned somehow. Are death and insanity the only means of escape? Lucie is imprisoned by her frailty and innocence; the Marquis, by his lifestyle (and acceptance of it); Sydney, by his despair and loneliness; Manette, first literally and then by his past and also loneliness; and Madame Defarge, by her past and desire for revenge.

4. **Color and light/dark:** How do associations with light and/or dark enhance characterizations?

It is no accident that Lucie is consistently associated with light and luminescence, while Madame Defarge seems to exist largely in the dark. Are there other characters associated with lightness, darkness, and/or color in some way? What associations do we make with light, dark, or a particular color? What associations would Dickens or people of the late 18th century have made?

5. **Animals:** Are associations with animals positive or negative?

Most characters in the novel are associated with at least one animal. Madame Defarge is a tigress; poor people are dogs, wild animals, and rats. Stryver is a lion, Sydney Carton is a jackal, and Lucie is a bird. This kind of symbolism and imagery makes it easy to classify the action in the book as that of a circus or zoo. Might there be something else that Dickens is saying through his use of animals? Keep in mind that some of these animals used as characterizations are unique to Dickens (Sydney as a jackal), and some were in regular use in Dickens's time and before (poor people as dogs). Do characters generally live up to their animalistic descriptions? Why or why not?

Compare and Contrast Essays

Writing a paper that compares and/or contrasts elements of the novel involves much more than simply listing similarities and differences between two or more things. These lists might help you early in the drafting process, but your paper eventually needs to go beyond this point to discuss why these similarities and/or differences are notable and important to the novel. You would do well to ask questions such as: Does Dickens intentionally set up some comparisons to show different points of view or circumstances? Do we notice particular comparisons and contrasts simply because of the time in which we live and our perceptions of the 19th century?

The most obvious comparison and contrast topic from this book would be about the two cities or countries in question. How do French characters compare to English? Do such comparisons and contrasts reveal Dickens's biases?

One of the most interesting things you can do with this type of paper is to make a comparison between two or more things/characters that on the surface seem very different. The more surprising your comparison or contrast is, the more engaging your paper could be to your readers (provided you back yourself up with sufficient evidence from the text). You cannot make a comparison or contrast statement based solely on your own perceptions and "feelings" about the work. Whatever claim you decide to make must be supportable through the text itself.

Sample Topics:
1. **England versus France:** To what degree are readers expected to side with one country over the other?

   Miss Pross says to Madame Defarge: "You might, from your appearance, be the wife of Lucifer. . . . Nevertheless, you shall not get the better of me. I am an Englishwoman" (Dickens 363). They have a rather epic battle, first with their words (even though neither can understand the other's language) and then with their bodies. Do they represent a struggle (physical or otherwise) between France and England? It might be interesting to consider that at the time of the French Revolution, Britain had recently lost a war with the thirteen colonies and their ally, France, in the American Revolution. Then, in the first decade of the 19th century, France and Britain battled again during the Napoleonic Wars. By the time Dickens wrote *A Tale of Two Cities,* Britain and France had recently joined forces to fight imperial Russia in the Crimean War of the 1850s. What impact might this history of battle have had on French-British relations at the time of the French Revolution and/or the time in which Dickens is writing? What reasons would Dickens have had, for example, for making the (arguably) most English character in the novel murder the (arguably) most French character?

2. **Madame Defarge, Miss Pross, and Lucie Manette Darnay:** Are any of them heroines? True villains?

There are very few women in the book, and these three give us distinct personalities and activities. How are their motivations actually very similar? *A Tale of Two Cities* has very masculine overtones and subject matter, in terms of war and gore, yet in many ways the book is dominated by the lives and personalities of its female characters. How do similarities and differences between these three women help to establish the book's plot and overall characterizations?

Bibliography and Online Resources for *A Tale of Two Cities*

Beckwith, Charles E., ed. *Twentieth-Century Interpretations of A Tale of Two Cities.* Englewood Cliffs, NJ: Prentice-Hall, 1972.

Bloom, Harold, ed. *Charles Dickens's A Tale of Two Cities.* Modern Critical Interpretations. New York: Chelsea House, 1987.

Carlyle, Thomas. *The French Revolution: A History.* Eds. K. J. Fielding & David Sorenson. Oxford: Oxford UP, 1989.

Dickens, Charles. *The Letters of Charles Dickens.* Vol. II. 1857–1870. Eds. Mamie Dickens & Georgina Hogarth. New York: Charles Scribner's Sons, 1879.

———. *A Tale of Two Cities.* 1859. New York: Barnes & Noble, 2004.

Glancy, Ruth. *A Tale of Two Cities: Dickens's Revolutionary Novel.* Twayne Masterwork Studies No. 89. Ed. Robert Lecker. Boston: G. K. Hall, 1991.

———, ed. *Charles Dickens's A Tale of Two Cities: A Sourcebook.* London: Routledge, 2006.

Kors, Alan Charles, ed. *The Encyclopedia of the Enlightenment.* Oxford: Oxford UP, 2003.

Nardo, Don, ed. *Readings on A Tale of Two Cities.* Greenhaven Press Literary Companion to British Literature. San Diego, CA: Greenhaven, 1997.

"A Tale of Two Cities." David Perdue's Charles Dickens Page. Available online. URL: http://www.charlesdickenspage.com/cities.html. Retrieved November 27, 2007.

GREAT EXPECTATIONS

READING TO WRITE

IN ITS intense focus on Pip's expectations, *Great Expectations* paradoxically becomes about everybody else, including the reader: Magwitch expects Pip to become a gentleman, Miss Havisham expects Estella to exact revenge on men, and the reader (coming from a history of marriage plots) expects Pip and Estella (or maybe Pip and Biddy) to end up married happily ever after. These expectations wind everyone around until they are more or less back where they started: Miss Havisham is dead (she was dead, to some extent, all along), Estella is disappointed with her life and accountable to others, and Pip is back in the blacksmith's forge. In some sense, this puts Joe at the center of the novel—the one constant around which the action and characters revolve. Pip's life begins again with Joe and Biddy's son, also named Pip, and characters and readers alike are left with great expectations for him.

But where does this leave the reader? Disappointed, maybe, because Pip does not end up married at the end. Frustrated, perhaps, because neither Pip nor Estella has ended up completely happy with their lives as we leave them. Confused, most possibly, because Dickens in fact wrote two endings to *Great Expectations*, published serially in 1860–61.

These endings are fascinating to study not only because Dickens wrote two but because both endings are very different from the conclusions of most other Dickens novels. The conclusion most commonly printed now has Estella and Pip meeting again on the grounds of Satis House just before it is demolished. In this version, readers hear Estella's regret: "There was a long hard time when I kept far from me, the remembrance of what I had thrown away when I was quite ignorant of its worth. But, since my duty has not been incompatible with the admission of that remembrance, I have given it a place in my heart" (Dickens 538). We know that Estella's husband is dead at this point, and we assume that the "remembrance" of which she speaks is in fact her relationship with Pip. It seems that Estella has finally come around to see that her cruelty toward men (but toward Pip in particular) was hurting her as much as it was hurting them and would never lead to a happy life. We know that Pip forgives Estella and still loves her when he answers, "You have always held a place in *my* heart" (Dickens 538). After this, the rest of the ending continues as follows:

> "But you said to me," returned Estella, very earnestly, "'God bless you, God forgive you!' And if you could say that to me then, you will not hesitate to say that to me now—now, when suffering has been stronger than all other teaching, and has taught me to understand what your heart used to be. I have been bent and broken, but—I hope—into a better shape. Be as considerate and good to me as you were, and tell me we are friends."
>
> "We are friends," said I, rising and bending over her, as she rose from the bench.
>
> "And will continue friends apart," said Estella.
>
> I took her hand in mine, and we went out of the ruined place; and, as the morning mists had risen long ago when I first left the forge, so, the evening mists were rising now, and in all the broad expanse of tranquil light they showed to me, I saw no shadow of another parting from her. (538–539)

As with any passage you choose to write about, this one should leave you with many questions. The main question we are left with here is whether Pip and Estella will stay together and possibly marry or go their separate ways once again. Estella says they will "continue friends apart," indicating an intention or assumption of them going separate ways. But Pip takes note of the rising mists and falls back into his first memories and impressions of Satis House and Estella, noting that he "saw no shadow of another parting from her." Does this seem realistic? Is there textual evidence to support their staying together? Or, is this Pip deluding himself about Estella as he has done so many times through his life?

Other questions we might ask about this ending involve the ways in which Pip and Estella were raised and particularly the way in which they were introduced and expected to treat each other. Does Estella's regret show that Miss Havisham was evil? She says that "suffering has been stronger than all other teaching," indicating that she, like most people, had to learn for herself what to do rather than simply being instructed by someone. Can we find redeeming qualities in Miss Havisham in general and her treatment of Estella and/or Pip in particular? Did she do anything good for either Pip or Estella?

The original ending was evidently too depressing to keep, and Dickens was advised by friends to change it. In the original ending, Pip knows that Drummle is dead and Estella is remarried. This ending is seen almost entirely through Pip's thoughts:

> I was in England again—in London, and walking along Piccadilly with little Pip—when a servant came running after me to ask would I step back to a lady in a carriage who wished to speak to me. It was a little pony carriage, which the lady was driving; and the lady and I looked sadly enough on one another.
>
> "I am greatly changed, I know; but I thought you would like to shake hands with Estella too, Pip. Lift up that pretty child and let me kiss it!" (She supposed the child, I think, to be my child.)
>
> I was very glad afterwards to have had the interview; for in her face and in her voice, and in her touch, she gave me the assurance, that suffering had been stronger than Miss Havisham's teaching, and had given her a heart to understand what my heart used to be. (541)

As nearly as the last line comes to being poetry, this original ending is very somber and final. There is no hope for Estella and Pip to be together, as she is already married. Perhaps the thin thread of hope is what readers take from the new ending, and that is why it works better, according to most.

It is interesting that nearly the same words are used in one part of both endings, yet the tone of each is so different. The last line of the original ending is spoken by Estella near the end of the ending more commonly published: "Suffering has been stronger . . . your heart used to be." The tone of the new ending fills these words with more hope than they initially possessed, likely because Estella goes on to say that she hopes she has learned and become a better person from all this suffering. She also says it as a part of asking Pip's forgiveness, which redeems her in the eyes of many readers who may still be hesitant to trust or to like her. In a few changed paragraphs, Dickens revises Estella into a chastened girl who may finally be worthy of Pip's love, and he also gives readers the smallest hope that Pip may end up happy after all.

In what ways is this ending more or less fulfilling to readers than the revised ending? In what ways do both endings leave readers with even more great expectations for Pip and Estella? What do you think Dickens's intentions were for each of these endings? Do any of the characters truly have a happy ending? Does this reflect life in more realistic ways than the average novel?

TOPICS AND STRATEGIES

This section of the chapter addresses various possible topics for writing about *Great Expectations* as well as general methods for approaching these topics. These lists are in no way exhaustive and are meant to provide a jumping-off point rather than an answer key. Use these suggestions to find your own ideas and form your own analyses. All topics discussed in this chapter could potentially turn into very good papers.

Themes

There are a number of Dickens scholars who believe that repetition in Dickens's work is always significant. One thing that repetition might signify in a work is a theme. You might take particular note of words, phrases, and ideas that recur. Then you need to read the text closely enough to speculate about what the work says about the theme you have identified. This might require outside research as well, and you will likely find that the theme intersects with the author's biography or history and context of the novel, or other facets of the work.

Some of the themes present in *Great Expectations* are rehabilitation, crime, ambition, prodigal son and father, loyalty, and regret. If you have noted that a number of characters, for example, seem unhappy (or unworthy) in their current state, you can study the theme of rehabilitation. Who needs to be rehabilitated in order to meet society's standards? Who fits into society quite well but may need to make personal changes in order to be happy? Think of how many characters can be used to answer one or both of these questions: Pip, Magwitch, Miss Havisham, and Estella, to name a few. Certainly, making changes (or longing to make changes) to oneself or one's life is a pervasive theme in this book. You will want to narrow your focus rather than attempting to discuss too many characters, scenes, or ideas. Spreading the theme too thinly will make your writing underdeveloped and your argument weaker. Choose one character, or one instance (scene) in which the theme is emphasized, or one element of the theme that repeats or that several characters experience, and write about it using detailed examples from the text. In some cases, it might be more interesting to write about the elements or scenes or characters that do not fit in with the theme. Joe, for example, may well be the only character in *Great Expectations* who does not appear to require rehabilitation, though he certainly undergoes some changes throughout the novel. What are the admirable qualities that Joe possesses? Is he held up as a good example in the book? Is Dickens trying to say that all of the other characters should be more like Joe? Why?

Sample Topics:

1. **Rehabilitation:** Do people really change?

   Magwitch "beats the system" partly because of belief in rehabilitation. He earns money from a farmer (probably a former convict) who has land in Australia. Magwitch appears to have changed through the course of the novel, but he always seems to have ulterior motives (revenge on society by making Pip into a gentleman, etc.). What would Magwitch have been like if he had not died or if the penal system in England had been different? Pip, too, is not entirely innocent. In what ways is Pip also rehabilitated in the novel? Is anyone in the book innocent, or could they all stand some changing? What do these examples taken together reveal about Dickens's feelings toward rehabilitation?

2. **Ambition:** How do Pip's "great expectations" take over his life? Are the most ambitious people in the book the true villains?

Does Dickens portray that some people ought to just be satisfied with their lot in life?

Joe has no notable ambitions. Does he live the best and fullest life of any of the characters? Is the problem ambition in general, or is it the vague notion of ambition—getting a leg up however you can, taking help from anyone, and/or assuming that you know what you are doing?

3. **Prodigal:** Several characters return to their roots, or to themselves, in *Great Expectations*. Are they accepted, or even welcomed, back?

Would Estella have opened her arms to Magwitch, her "prodigal father," had she known about him? The circularity of people's lives and the need for acceptance are pervasive in this book and worth looking at from several angles. How does Dickens portray the theme of being true to the good in oneself and in one's past by bringing his characters home again?

Characters

Great Expectations is a fascinating book for character study because most everyone in it is seriously flawed. As the main character, Pip is probably the richest character description given, but there are many ways of looking at Pip. You might look at the methods Dickens uses for distinguishing Pip from other characters, particularly those he could otherwise be very similar to, such as Herbert Pocket. How does Dickens develop the differences and similarities between Pip and Herbert? Do these differences and similarities bode well for Pip? Why or why not? Herbert educates Pip on how to conduct himself in society, but Herbert needs Pip's help in order to fulfill his own dreams.

You can also study the ways in which a character changes throughout the book. Pip is again the clearest example, since he quite literally grows up over the course of the novel. You may decide, however, to look at a character whose changes are much more subtle—Estella, for instance. Does she meet Miss Havisham's expectations? How is she affected by her encounters with Pip? You will need to not only make note of any changes in character that you find significant but also provide your interpretation of these changes.

Dickens's writing techniques are another compelling aspect of character. Which words, phrases, or settings are typically associated with a particular character? Is Magwitch, for example, often described with words indicating darkness? Is there a character who is particularly associated with water, and if so, what might that association indicate about that character? In other words, you are looking at not only what Dickens writes about a character but how he writes it. How does he create the menacing mood that surrounds Orlick? What does a character's vocabulary or manner of speaking reveal? Any number of questions can be asked and answered about Dickens's characters.

Sample Topics:

1. **Abel Magwitch:** He is more complicated than we might expect an escaped convict to be. How does Dickens help us to like him?

   How is Magwitch punished and manipulated by the penal system, and what does this treatment lead him to do? How does Magwitch manipulate his own life and those of others? Is he always in control? Is he at heart a good man? Is Dickens's point that people are more complicated than their actions and subsequent labels?

2. **Estella:** How does her relationship with Pip parallel that of Miss Havisham and Compeyson?

   What does Estella really seem to want? Does she fully understand her life? Her role in Miss Havisham's (and Pip's) life? Do you want Pip to marry her? Why or why not? Do you think Dickens wants/intends readers to like her? Why or why not?

3. **Miss Havisham:** In what ways does Miss Havisham represent a large number of women?

   In some ways she is the scariest character in a book filled with terrifying characters and situations. How does her treatment of Estella affect readers' impressions of her? Does she redeem herself through her affection for Pip? What are her great expectations for herself? For Estella? Do you think that we are supposed to feel sorry for her?

History and Context

Studying history and context compels you to research the actual circumstances surrounding the action in the book and/or the process of writing the book. In *Great Expectations*, the action begins in the earlier part of the 19th century, even though Dickens published it in 1860–61. Why would Dickens choose a setting for this book that is decades earlier than the time in which he and his readers live?

Great Expectations takes place largely before the Industrial Revolution; in fact, it takes place (or at least begins) even before Queen Victoria takes the throne. How and why might the people of the early 19th century have had a much different outlook compared to people of the mid-19th century? What changes had already taken place when the book was published, making the earlier setting of the novel even more distinct from its first readers' lives?

Studying history and context allows you to look not only at the background of the story and/or its setting but at the author's background as well. *Great Expectations* is sometimes considered Dickens's darkest work, the one on which he refused to attach a traditionally happy ending. Were there events or circumstances in Dickens's own life that might have caused him to change his writing for this novel? *Great Expectations* is also considered somewhat self-reflective for Dickens. It is not semi-autobiographical the way that *David Copperfield* is, but it does include some associations with Dickens's own life and world. What are those associations, and what do they bring to the story or your reading of it?

Sample Topics:

1. **Justice system:** What are the various characters' attitudes toward crime, punishment, criminals, and convicts? How do these attitudes reflect actual beliefs in 19th-century England?

    Transportation of convicts to Australia had nearly ended by the time Dickens wrote *Great Expectations*, but in the first decades of the century, in which this part of the book is set, it was still common practice. George Newline's *Understanding Great Expectations* contains historical documents helpful for understanding Australia as a part of England's penal system. The 19th century saw great changes in the penal system so that by the time Dickens died, it was quite similar to today's system. What message is Dickens trying to send about crime or about punishments for crime or about the criminals themselves? What kinds of reform took place in the 19th century? What kinds of reform would have satisfied Dickens?

2. **Class system:** Why is it so important to Pip to be disassociated from Joe? What would likely have happened to Miss Havisham if she had not been a very rich woman?

   Why is it so important to Magwitch that Pip become a gentleman? Pip does become a gentleman, though he seems to be the only one in the book. How do these situations illustrate the changing class system of 19th-century England?

3. **Marriage:** Miss Havisham clearly exaggerates the situation, but what was it like for jilted and/or unmarried women in the early 19th century?

   Like so many issues, social and legal aspects of marriage often depend on one's social class. In the original ending of *Great Expectations*, Estella has married twice. Does this reflect on Estella's character and Miss Havisham's expectations for her, or does it reflect on the dire situations of many unmarried women of the time? There are many circumstances surrounding marriage in the book to study: Miss Skiffins and Wemmick, Clara and Herbert, Joe and Biddy, Joe and Mrs. Joe. If Pip had been female, his "great expectations" would very likely have included marriage.

4. **Work:** How are Pip's great expectations counterintuitive to the world of work that surrounds him?

Pip is trained for nothing, while Joe is a blacksmith, Wemmick a clerk, Jaggers a lawyer, and Herbert a businessman. England in the mid- to late 19th century was known as the Workshop of the World, seemingly displacing or reducing the number of gentlemen in the country. Even Magwitch takes on several working roles to give Pip what seems to be an outdated liberty; a man trained for nothing is relatively useless in industrial society. How does *Great Expectations* reflect the ways in which jobs and money and lifestyles were redistributed during the Industrial Revolution?

Philosophy and Ideas

Philosophy and ideas in a novel are similar to the theme, but they are more general or more universal. Writing about the philosophy and ideas in a book means that you identify broad philosophical ideas and investigate the ways in which the book comments on them. Some examples of philosophy and ideas from *Great Expectations* are lost childhood, self-realization, love, desire, and survival of the fittest. Clearly, the philosophy behind survival of the fittest stems from Charles Darwin and is therefore connected to the history and context of the book as well. Outside research may come in handy in this case, but a close reading of Dickens's novel should be your focus.

Great Expectations, in many ways, reads like a story of several characters, all pushing and shoving each other in order to make their own progress. Is there any character in this work who does not seem wholly concerned with his or her own survival? Are there characters who consistently sacrifice themselves for others? Are there characters who consistently crush others on their way to the top? In what ways do characters in *Great Expectations* defy laws of state, rules of society, and norms of etiquette in order to ensure their own survival? Orlick may do this in particularly nasty ways, but remember that even Pip is not immune to the fight for survival, turning his back on Joe several times in order to maintain the illusion of high class and keep up with his great expectations. Does Dickens punish characters who behave in particular ways, or is he advocating a level of selfishness that is necessary for survival?

Sample Topics:

1. **Lost childhood:** Which characters in the novel seem to have lost their childhood too early, and which characters seem to have never had a childhood at all?

   Pip retains aspects of his childhood, partly through the mandated retention of his nickname, but Herbert makes him grow up through his use of a new nickname. Miss Havisham demonstrates the impossibility (though in some ways the remarkable possibility) of freezing time. There is a certain irony in Pip needing to return to his childhood setting in order to grow up, and we can see that the "great expectations" for Joe's new son, Pip, will certainly be very different. What seems to be the book's message about childhood and time's influence on people?

2. **Self-realization:** Where do personalities come from? Are they based on what people do, their class, their gender, their self-perception, their public perception, coincidence, luck, or fate?

   The plot of *Great Expectations* centers on Pip's search for himself and his place in the world. How does his character come to realize his true self? Estella is shaped largely by the world around her (that is, Miss Havisham), yet her sadness indicates her knowledge that her true self is someone other than the woman she has been forced to become. Pip always seems uncomfortable, unsure of where he fits in or who he really is, as well as to whom he owes credit or allegiance. Wemmick lives two fairly separate lives, yet he seems to know exactly who he really is.

3. **Survival of the fittest:** What does it take to be considered the "fittest" in the society of *Great Expectations*? Are those who appear to survive somewhat ruthless, or do the polite, kind people come out on top?

   Unlike some other Dickens characters, Pip is not immune or oblivious to evil in the world. He is confronted by evil directly through his initial encounters with Magwitch and his later run-in with Orlick. Pip feels that he must take part in law-breaking in order to survive (and help his friends survive). His first test is to steal for Magwitch. Did he have other viable options? When does one's survival outweigh the law, religion, morality, or the general good?

Form and Genre

The way in which a book is written and presented can have an enormous impact on readers' reception and interpretations. The form that a work takes involves its shape and stucture, including chapter length, format, and so on. A work's genre is its classification. *Great Expectations* is classified as a novel. More specifically, it is a bildungsroman, or coming-of-age story.

Form in Dickens is intriguing partly because it has changed over time. *Great Expectations* was originally published in weekly installments, so readers had to wait to learn what became of Pip, Magwitch, Estella, and Miss Havisham. Dickens had intended to publish *Great Expectations* in monthly installments, which would have likely made it a longer work. Studying the history of Dickens's form might give you insight into his intentions, readers' reception, and the state of the work itself. In some ways, Dickens's serial novels were similar to today's blogs or Internet texts. Readers wait for the next installment from their favorite writer and in the intervening time, will speculate among themselves about what might come next.

The bildungsroman was a fairly popular form in the Victorian period, and the novel itself was rapidly becoming the most popular and increasingly well-respected literary genre. In what ways does Dickens's work contribute to both of these trends?

Sample Topics:

1. **Bildungsroman:** How do we know when Pip has finally grown up? What are the signs that he is no longer childlike?

   A bildungsroman is a story that centers on a young person's journey and struggle to reach maturity. What qualities are valued (by Dickens, by the society in the novel) in children? In adults? Are there any characters in *Great Expectations* who are able to maintain their valuable childlike qualities as they become adults? What effect does our knowledge of Pip's childhood (or Estella's) have on our perceptions of the rest of the story? What, ultimately, does Pip learn? Is his story unique? In what sense is this the story of Estella's coming of age as well?

2. **Retrospective:** Pip looks back on his life, so we are able to get glimpses of where he came from and what he has learned. Are we able to completely trust his perspective?

By the time he is grown, Pip is able to look more lightheartedly at events from earlier years. We see Pip's acknowledgment of some of his mistakes. It is important to understand that we are getting Pip's perspective of himself. He relates events and then interprets them through hindsight, but we are left to determine whether we can always trust his interpretations.

3. **Tragicomedy:** How (and why) is it that a novel so filled with terrifying events can be so funny at the same time?

The humor found in young Pip's terror over stealing from his sister's larder is partly due to the perspective of older Pip telling the story. Pip is almost more afraid of his sister's wrath than he is of the escaped convict who has threatened him. The tragicomic elements of *Great Expectations* help us to see the difference between what seems scary (darkness, fog, cemeteries, convicts) and what is really scary (betrayal, the unknown, being poor and unloved).

Language, Symbols, and Imagery

Dickens's novels are filled with language, symbols, and imagery that enrich the story and give us the Dickensian worlds that generations of readers have loved. To effectively study language, symbols, and imagery, you must move beyond unnecessary summary to investigate how the book is written, and then make speculations about how these methods of writing and literary elements affect the content of the novel.

Studying language gives you an opportunity to look closely at syntax, word choice, and diction, among other things. Dickens gives his characters particular ways of speaking depending on geography, education, gender, social class, and background, so dialogue in his novels is rife with material for the study of language. The contrasts between Magwitch's manner of speaking and Herbert's can reveal much about each character. Language might also mean a search into the words most commonly used to describe a character, a setting, or an activity. Look at the tone (or mood) surrounding Joe's forge, for example, and pinpoint the elements of language that help to create that tone. Then, take it a step further by discussing why it is significant that such a tone is connected with Joe's forge. Always remember whose perspective this mood comes from. Certainly Pip's point of view is much different from his sister's, and both might be quite different from Joe's.

Symbols can be found when something comes to represent something else. We know that Miss Havisham wears white because time stopped for her on her wedding day. What does white symbolize for a bride in early 19th-century England? What is the significance of the once-white clothing and décor yellowing, fading, and decaying?

Imagery in literature includes the details that can be perceived using one or more of the five senses. Certainly, Miss Havisham in particular and Satis House in general provide rich imagery, which is partly why Miss Havisham is one of the most widely known of Dickens's characters. Pip travels among very different environments, however, so readers get the imagery of the countryside or marshlands, as well as that of Satis House, London, Newgate Prison, a bit of the seafaring life, and imagery of the working as well as upper classes. How does Dickens describe each new environment? Which seems to be best for a particular character, and how can we tell? How is Dickens's imagery a significant part of his theme, philosophy, and ideas? How much of the imagery is grounded in historical context, and which parts appear to be purely fanciful? As always, you must not only answer the question that guides your focus; you also need to explain why the question, issue, or argument is significant.

Sample Topics:

1. **Miss Havisham all in white:** What is the significance of Miss Havisham languishing in her wedding clothes? What can we

make of the fact that these symbolically white clothes are now yellowing with age?

Miss Havisham certainly demonstrates the inability to stop the progress of time. Her world may be stopped, but everything around her continues to move and grow and live or decay. If white at first represented innocence and purity (the great significance of a wedding dress), what has its yellowing come to represent, besides simple age or wear and tear? Does the yellowing show the decay of innocence and purity? Miss Havisham's cynicism? Vindictiveness?

2. **Satis House:** What does this house symbolize for Estella? For Pip?

Time for Miss Havisham has literally stopped in many ways; meanwhile, Satis House and the genteel class it represents and contains have become outdated, overrun by industry and people moving into towns for gainful employment. The house is demolished at the end of the novel, and new buildings will be erected on the same ground. Will the new buildings also become overgrown with the new sprouts of ivy that Pip sees? Why might Estella and Pip be glad to see this house gone and yet still feel sentimental about it?

3. **Mist:** What hides in the fog?

The mist and fog are most associated with the graveyard and Satis House. Both places are shrouded, and both play fateful roles in Pip's great expectations. Fog was common in Dickens's London, yet in this book, the city seems clear, as if things can be more clearly seen there.

4. **Doubles/symmetry:** Which characters seem to have a double, or counterpart (Mrs. Joe and Miss Havisham, Estella and Biddy, Magwitch and Compeyson, Pip and Bentley, etc.)?

Some scholars argue that Dickens could not write plausible situations and that his plots always involve unrealistic coincidence. This does not happen so much in *Great Expectations*, but the connections between characters (however unlikely it is that Magwitch would end up being Estella's father) demonstrate the circular nature of the plot: family at the center, connected with outside characters who eventually become equally central. Many characters have a counterpart, someone who mirrors them or provides an antithesis for them in some way. Investigating the character, personality, and/or actions of one will often lead to insight into another.

Compare and Contrast Essays

Dickens's tendency in *Great Expectations* to pair up his characters (each one seems to have his or her own equal or opposite character somewhere in the text) can lead to very interesting studies in comparisons and contrasts. It is important that you do not simply point out similarities and differences between characters, settings, actions, or other elements of the text. The purpose of comparison and contrast writing is to invoke larger issues from the novel, making your analysis and interpretation of similarities and differences a crucial part of your writing.

One of many potential topics for a comparison and contrast paper is the study of Mrs. Joe and Miss Havisham. It is unlikely that the two women would ever have traveled in the same circles or even have known of each other had it not been for Miss Havisham's desire to see Pip, and yet there are important connections between them. Mrs. Joe, in some ways, has what Miss Havisham does not: marriage. Yet this is nearly the only thing that Mrs. Joe has, while Miss Havisham has money and status at her disposal, precisely the things that Mrs. Joe longs for. Would Miss Havisham have valued her own marriage more than Mrs. Joe values her life with Joe Gargery? These women envy each other both directly and indirectly, consciously and unconsciously. How is this envy significant to the theme of *Great Expectations*? How is Mrs. Joe's catatonic state similar to Miss Havisham's self-induced time warp?

Sample Topics:

1. **City versus country:** Is corruption everywhere?

Typically, the country represents purity and resilience, whereas the city exemplifies grime and greed. The roles seem to go back and forth in *Great Expectations.* Pip's encounter with Magwitch occurs in the country, as do Orlick's crimes. Crime is ostensibly contained in the city, as the visits to Newgate show. Is that just a facade? Good characters such as Herbert are found in the city, yet Pip returns to the countryside for his ultimate and inevitable fulfillment. Is the point that corruption is everywhere? That one should not necessarily have to leave where they came from to find themselves?

2. **Original versus current ending:** Which ending to the novel is best? Why?

The two endings that Dickens wrote for *Great Expectations* are fairly different. Can either one be considered a happy ending? Why or why not? How and why might readers react differently to each conclusion?

Bibliography and Online resources for *Great Expectations*

"Charles Dickens's *Great Expectations*: Literary Relations: Sources, Analogues, Influences." The Victorian Web. Available online. URL: http://www.victorianweb.org/authors/dickens/ge/litrel.html. Retrieved July 23, 2007.

Chesterton, G. K. "Great Expectations." *Appreciations and Criticisms of the Works of Charles Dickens.* New York: Haskell House, 1970. 197–206.

Cotsell, Michael, ed. *Critical Essays on Charles Dickens's Great Expectations.* Boston: G. K. Hall, 1990.

Dickens, Charles. *Great Expectations.* 1860. New York: Barnes & Noble, 2003.

"*Great Expectations* Page." The Victorian Web. Available online. URL: http://www.victorianweb.org/authors/dickens/ge/geov.html. Retrieved July 23, 2007.

Hornback, Bert G. *Great Expectations: A Novel of Friendship.* Twayne's Masterwork Studies No. 6. Boston: Twayne Publishers, 1987.

Leavis, Q. D. "How We Must Read *Great Expectations.*" *Dickens the Novelist.* F. R. and Q. D. Leavis. London: Chatto & Windus, 1970. 277–331.

Matsuoka, Mitsu. The Victorian Literary Studies Archive. Available online. URL: http://www.lang.nagoya-u.ac.jp/~matsuoka/Victorian.html. Retrieved January 15, 2007; July 23, 2007.

Newlin, George. *Understanding Great Expectations.* Westport, CT: Greenwood Press, 2000.

Sadrin, Anny. *Great Expectations.* London: Allen & Unwin, 1988.

OUR MUTUAL FRIEND

READING TO WRITE

OUR MUTUAL *Friend*, published from 1864 to 1865 in serial form, is
Dickens's last completed novel. In many ways, it is the pinnacle of
his career—a culmination of his talents and the issues he emphasized in
most of his earlier writing. We are lucky enough to have Dickens's own
words regarding his thought process while conceiving ideas that were to
become this novel:

> I think a man, young and perhaps eccentric, feigning to be dead, and
> *being* dead to all intents and purposes external to himself, and for years
> retaining the singular view of life and character so imparted, would be
> a good leading incident for a story. . . . A poor imposter of a man mar-
> rying a woman for her money; she marrying *him* for *his* money; after
> a marriage both finding out their mistake, and entering into a league
> and covenant against folks in general: with whom I propose to connect
> some Perfectly New people. Everything new about them. (Engel vi)

Clearly, the young man Dickens refers to becomes John Rokesmith/
Harmon in the novel. It seems, however, that he is describing the Lammles's marriage more accurately than the Rokesmiths'. This shows us
that Dickens had a basic premise for the novel, that he had worked
out many plot elements in advance. Still, characters and events probably evolved somewhat differently from his first conceptions of them.
Certainly, he was able to make changes as the reading public began to
respond to the first installments of the book, too.

Together with *Dombey and Son, Little Dorrit,* and *Bleak House, Our Mutual Friend* represents "attempts to convey both extensively and comprehensively a great vision of the wonder and misery of the world" (Engel v). The words *extensively* and *comprehensively* are particularly appropriate here, as Dickens used more of an ensemble cast of characters for this novel, as opposed to earlier novels that clearly focus on one person (*David Copperfield*) or a small group of people (*Nicholas Nickleby*). The titles of Dickens's novels are interesting to study in this respect. If the title of the novel is one person's name, that seems to indicate a microscopic focus on an individual life, and others are introduced only in terms of their relationships with that individual. The word *our* in the title of this book, on the other hand, opens up new possibilities for characters, and Dickens follows a number of storylines simultaneously. Does he then tie things up neatly at the end and somehow relate all characters to one another? What is the significance of doing or not doing this? How do relationships between characters in his novels place Dickens in the tradition of the Victorian novel? Did readers' responses to various installments have great effects on the way the book ended? The word *our* in the title also leads us to ask who the word refers to. All readers? One group specifically? Only the characters? Answers to these questions can lead to fascinating paper topics.

Another expansive element of *Our Mutual Friend* that is common to most Dickens novels is his treatment of a wide variety of issues and types of people. This one novel investigates deceitfulness; doubt; appearances different from reality; working people, from river scavengers to landlords; people piecing lives (and, in the case of Mr. Venus, even other people!) back together; investigators solving mysteries; murder; money issues; wooden legs; class issues; and marriage, to name a few.

The topic of class issues is certainly one that stands out in this novel. Even a very early scene at an upper-class dinner party shows readers that in many ways class distinctions lie at the heart of *Our Mutual Friend*:

> In the meantime a stray personage of a meek demeanour, who had wandered to the hearthrug and got among the heads of tribes assembled there in conference with Mr. Podsnap, eliminated Mr. Podsnap's flush

and flourish by a highly unpolite remark; no less than a reference to the circumstance that some half-dozen people had lately died in the streets of starvation. It was clearly ill-timed, after dinner. It was not adapted to the cheek of the young person. It was not in good taste.

"I don't believe it," said Mr. Podsnap, putting it behind him.

The meek man was afraid we must take it as proved, because there were the Inquests and the Registrar's returns.

"Then it was their own fault," said Mr. Podsnap.

Veneering and other elders of tribes commended this way out of it. At once a short cut and a broad road.

The man of meek demeanour intimated that truly it would seem from the facts as if starvation had been forced upon the culprits in question—as if, in their wretched manner, they had made their weak protests against it—as if they would have taken the liberty of staving it off if they could—as if they would rather not have been starved to upon the whole, if perfectly agreeable to all parties.

"There is not," said Mr. Podsnap, flushing angrily, "there is not a country in the world, sir, where so noble a provision is made for the poor as it is in this country."

The meek man was quite willing to concede that, but perhaps it rendered the matter even worse, as showing that there must be something appallingly wrong somewhere. (135–136)

Consider Dickens's use of such words as *meek, noble, culprits, tribes,* and *liberty.* A close consideration of his use of language would make a very compelling paper. What are the literal meanings of the words in Dickens's time? What connotations did the words hold for Dickens's first readers? What do these words reveal about class issues in the novel?

Dickens does not make any attempt to disguise his contempt for the English system of "helping" the poor. How is this scene funny and tragic all at once? Why is the disruptive individual only known as the "meek man"? How widespread was the "it was their own fault" mentality in Dickens's time? Any of these dinner parties in the book offer a window into a world in which Dickens participated but seems to have also reviled in many ways.

When Noddy Boffin asks Silas Wegg to read to him, he says, he wants reading "as'll reach right down your pint of view, and take time to go by you" (49). Boffin might as well have been describing *Our Mutual Friend,* or any other Dickens work. It is important, when studying a writer like Dickens, to take the time to appreciate each word and let the words, ideas, memories, and themes "reach into your point of view."

TOPICS AND STRATEGIES

This section of the chapter addresses various possible topics for writing about *Our Mutual Friend* as well as general methods for approaching these topics. These lists are in no way exhaustive and are meant to provide a jumping-off point rather than an answer key. Use these suggestions to find your own ideas and form your own analyses. All topics discussed in this chapter could potentially turn into very good papers.

Themes

Pay particular attention to names, words, phrases (especially those that are somehow repeated), and chapter titles, and make note of what stands out to you. There is a conglomeration of characters in *Our Mutual Friend* who at first seem unconnected to one another, so try to notice when subjects come up for more than one or two characters. Chances are you have identified one of the themes from *Our Mutual Friend.*

One example of a prevalent theme in *Our Mutual Friend* is the issue of marriage. Certainly, it was not at all uncommon for characters in Victorian novels to marry or discuss marrying. In this book, however, marriage takes on further meaning. It is not just a convention or a method for moving the plot along; it is an issue to be discussed, shunned, desired, and regretted for any number of reasons. The entire novel, in fact, hinges to some extent on the proposed marriage between Bella and John Harmon. Then there is Noddy and Mrs. Boffin, who might be the only example of a healthy marriage in the book, and the Lammles, who become miserable after deceiving each other into marriage. Rather than merely pointing out marriage as a theme of *Our Mutual Friend,* ask questions to help you determine why it is so important here. For example, What connections are made between marriage and money? Which characters reject marriage (either to specific people or as a concept altogether) and why? Which characters are most anxious to marry and why? One important question to include as part of your investigation is why did Dickens make marriage a theme of *Our Mutual Friend*? In some cases, your work might touch on historical context as well, although it is certainly possible, encouraged, and sometimes required, that your argument come from the primary text alone.

Sample Topics:

1. **Education:** Why is Gaffer so against education? How does Headstone represent education and teaching?

   Boffin seeks education immediately after getting money. Lizzie finally finds education with Wrayburn. Charlie is somewhat miseducated by Headstone. Dickens saw "that merely educating the democracy may easily mean setting to work to despoil it of all the democratic virtues. It is better to be Lizzie Hexam and not know how to read and write than to be Charlie Hexam and not know how to appreciate Lizzie Hexam" (Chesterton 217). The notes of the novel reveal that Dickens referred to Headstone's school as a ragged school, run to educate the poorest children with good intentions but not always great results. Why is education so important to everyone in this novel?

2. **Pride:** Is pride a class issue in that only those with "worthy" lives are permitted by society to show pride in themselves, their work, or their families?

   Many characters in *Our Mutual Friend* might be called proud, and each one seems to have his or her own reason for feeling this way. In some cases, it seems to be a "false pride." In others, such as with Lizzie Hexam, pride is tied into self-denial. Pride turns somewhat evil in Headstone and Riderhood in that it proves to be self-destructive and/or hurtful to others.

3. **Marriage:** What does the novel convey overall about marriage?

Why would John Harmon refuse his fortune by not marrying Bella (whom he has never met)? Marriage is a center point for this novel, and there are a number of examples, both good (Noddy and Mrs. Boffin) and bad (the Lammles). For the upper class, marriage equals money (and vice versa). The Lammles deceive each other and end up trapped in their marriage. Those for whom marriage equals love are duly rewarded: Lizzie and Wrayburn, Bella and John.

4. **Deceit and doubt:** Are there any characters who are able fully to trust one another?

The novel is filled with characters who are suspicious of one another. Lizzie wonders about Gaffer's innocence or guilt, and the Lammles constantly distrust each other. Even Mrs. Boffin doubts her husband, if only for a moment. Rokesmith's initial deceit of the Boffins and Bella is of course a pivotal point in the novel. Silas Wegg feels betrayed by Mr. Venus, Headstone tries to deceive Riderhood, and the list goes on. Is all of this doubt and deceit simply a ploy to maintain the sense of mystery in the novel, or are there other reasons for such themes?

Characters

Our Mutual Friend introduces many characters who are some of Dickens's most eccentric and, in some ways, extreme. Think of Silas Wegg and Jenny Wren, for example. Surely they are both unusual, within the context of the book as well as the context of Victorian society. What sets these characters apart? (For your writing you might want to narrow your focus to only one character.) Why would Dickens want and/or need them to be unusual in these particular ways? Do they remain somewhat abnormal throughout the book, or is there a point where true normalcy (you would have to decide what you mean by "normal") lies with them? In what ways does the novel center on the people who live on the fringes, those who are not fully acceptable to society? Why might Dickens make these odd characters into the hero or heroine of his tale?

Bradley Headstone is an unusual character, something that had not been encountered in Victorian novels before: "It was a new notion to add to the villains of fiction, whose thoughts go quickly, this villain whose thoughts go slow but sure; and it was a new notion to combine a deadly criminality not with high life or the slums (the usual haunts for villains) but with the laborious respectability of the lower, middle classes" (Chesterton 217). Is Headstone a villain, a victim, or both? How so? Why is it important for Dickens to portray an outwardly respectable man as depraved in some way?

Since *Our Mutual Friend*'s characters have regularly been viewed by scholars as particularly strange or over the top, you may also choose to ask whether any of these characters are likely to exist in the real world or are simply caricatures or types. Why would Dickens find it more important for a character to embody a frame of mind, a philosophy, or a social class than to appear recognizable as someone you might actually meet on the street?

Sample Topics:

1. **Jenny Wren:** Does the entire book somehow center on her?

> Jenny Wren seems to encapsulate imagination and childhood in its most colorful glory, yet she is beaten down, ignored, and crippled by the world. She plays a role in order to protect herself and even goes so far as to change her name. Why is her name change so significant? She captures reader's imaginations, including famous readers such as Paul McCartney, who wrote a song called "Jenny Wren" and refers to her as the daughter of the person in his earlier song, "Blackbird." Why is she such a fascinating character? In what ways is she the pivotal point around which the others evolve? Does Jenny grow and change at all?

2. **Bella:** Does she change? Is she tested by circumstances and other people, or does she test herself?

> Bella is described as "a *very* nice girl; promising!" (Dickens 41), and she asks, "Am I for ever to be made the property of strang-

ers?" (367). What attempts at social reform seem to be embodied in Bella's character? Why is her plotline so embroiled in questions and problems surrounding marriage?

3. **John Rokesmith:** Is he a genuinely good character, or is he as deceptive as the worst of them?

John Rokesmith is very quickly associated with the title of the work when Mr. Boffin first speaks to Mrs. Wilfer about him: "I may call him Our Mutual Friend. . . . What sort of fellow is Our Mutual Friend, now? Do you like him? . . . you must know that I am not particularly well acquainted with Our Mutual Friend, for I have only seen him once" (Dickens 108). Those few short lines introduce all of the mystery and importance surrounding Rokesmith and give readers a taste of his pivotal role in the novel. Is Rokesmith a hero, a martyr, or a villain? At times, it seems that Dickens wants us to distrust him, though eventually it is clear that we are to like him. Find these instances in the book, and try to determine what Dickens's purposes were for inciting various reader reactions.

4. **Lizzie Hexam:** Are Lizzie's dreams and expectations ever the same? Are either realistic?

Eugene Wrayburn tries to reach Lizzie by offering education, which is at the heart of what Lizzie really wants. She is self-sacrificing, part of a string of martyred sisters in Victorian novels, sacrificing themselves so that their brothers might have wealth and/or education. How is Lizzie's character encapsulated in her own question, "Does a woman's heart . . . seek to gain anything?" (Dickens 514).

History and Context

The reality of Dickens's work is often quite startling, as it was in his time as well. *Our Mutual Friend*, Dickens's final completed novel, has been called "a great artist's ultimate effort to isolate and convey the reality of his experience" (Engel v). To make up a story is difficult enough, but to make up a story and ground it in the world as you

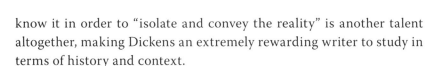

know it in order to "isolate and convey the reality" is another talent altogether, making Dickens an extremely rewarding writer to study in terms of history and context.

There is no doubt that Dickens took certain liberties. He is well known for exaggeration, particularly when it comes to humor. But Dickens is also well known for his portrayals of reality. The world in a Dickens book is often quite literally Dickens's world reflected back at us. This means, of course, that studying *Our Mutual Friend* in terms of history and context requires research outside the book itself. Such research might include books such as Henry Mayhew's *London Labour & the London Poor* or Liza Picard's *Victorian London: The Life of a City 1840–1870*. There are many topics involving history and context to research. You might, for example, look into Silas Wegg's wooden leg and research to learn why it was so important to Silas to find his missing leg before he died. What 19th-century ideology would send a man on such a quest? Did it happen often? Why? What does this search add to Dickens's characterization of Silas?

Writing about history and context also allows you to look into Dickens's own life. Again, Silas Wegg can lead you to a paper topic. Dickens wrote about men with wooden legs more than once in his life. What experiences in Dickens's own life created this fascination with wooden legs? Does he generally treat the matter with seriousness or humor? Why? To which class of people in *Our Mutual Friend* would Dickens have belonged? Was he proud of his class affiliations or ashamed of them? What evidence of those feelings can you find in the novel?

Sample Topics:

1. **River scavengers:** What were general opinions of river scavengers of the time? Thieves? A necessary evil? Helpful citizens?

   River scavengers were common in 19th-century London. They would search for bodies in rivers, almost always finding them with no money on them, because the scavengers stole money and whatever other valuables were on the corpses. There seems to have been a code of ethics among river scavengers, though. Gaffer splits with Riderhood once Riderhood steals from a live man. Stealing from dead people is an accepted way to "earn" money, but stealing from living people is against their ethics. There also seems to be a sense of shame. Lizzie feels she owes people after profiting from bodies. Many people made a living from the river, one way or another. These river scavengers seem to teeter on the edge between life and death. The river was a source of both life (food and water) and death (disease and drowning). Why would Dickens choose to involve so many characters with this particular way of life?

2. **Dustman:** What were people hoping to find in their searches of the dust heaps?

Did people search through them for lost items? Hope? Wealth? Happiness? Dust heaps connect the book with reality but might also be symbols of class, or a search. It was a very profitable business. As Boffin says in the book, items found in the dust heaps could be sold to various parties and recycled into usable goods. The dust heaps in the book may also be a metaphor for hidden treasure (especially considering the fairy-tale way things turn out for the Boffins). Why is the air of filth and grime so important to the overall tone of this book? How important were dust heaps to London culture in 1865? Why would Dickens choose to make them such a focal point here?

3. **Jews:** What attitude toward Jewish people is expressed in *Our Mutual Friend*?

Many scholars say that Dickens writes positively about Jews in this novel to make up for the negative portrayal of Fagin the Jew in *Oliver Twist,* for which he received some criticism. What was the general feeling toward Jewish people in England in 1865? Dickens seems to have a particular message to send, as we can see through the words of the old man Riah: "They take the worst of us as samples of the best; they take the lowest of us as presentations of the highest; and they say, 'All Jews are alike'" (708). Why would Dickens feel the need to express

Riah's thoughts in this way? How does the history of Jewish people in England affect Riah's characterization?

4. **Workhouses:** What kind of ethical considerations went into creating and maintaining workhouses?

By 1865, Dickens had spent decades writing against poor laws and workhouses. Betty Higden tells Mrs. Boffin that she would rather they all die than be taken to the workhouse (193). Betty's fear is very real; children and the elderly were particularly susceptible to death in workhouses. Workhouses condescended to the poor and took their comfort and dignity. Workhouses were ideally a threat, a warning, so that everyone would work and be able to earn a living and not have to go to the workhouse, but they were eventually filled with people who were disabled, old, orphaned, or sick. It is not that they were not willing to work hard but that they were (many of them) unable. Workhouses were established with a kind of "survival-of-the-fittest" mentality. Did it work? Why would it backfire, at least in some circumstances? Why did one's perspective and social class so dramatically affect one's knowledge and opinions of workhouses?

Philosophy and Ideas

Some of the concepts embedded in *Our Mutual Friend* are larger than the book; in other words, these ideas or philosophies can be found at work in Dickens's world or even in ours. Philosophies and ideas help us to move beyond the text itself to make discoveries about the world or human nature in a more general or even universal sense.

Money, for example, is certainly a key theme in *Our Mutual Friend*. The idea that money changes people moves us outside of the book in some way and allows us to see how worldly principles deflate or gain strength when placed inside a particular fictional world.

The extreme contrast between high and low society is evident throughout *Our Mutual Friend*. Party conversation among the Veneerings and their acquaintances strikes us as utterly ridiculous because of the speakers' disdain for people with less money than themselves.

We see that the divisions between upper and lower classes, between someone like Eugene Wrayburn and someone like Lizzie Hexam, are arbitrary and dependent on possession of money. What happens, then, when one of the have-nots, Noddy Boffin, suddenly finds himself quite wealthy? Does money change him? If so, how and why? If not, why not? Scholars sometimes argue that careful reading reveals that the change Noddy Boffin undergoes when he kicks John Rokesmith out was real and that Dickens intended to show that money changed Boffin in drastically negative ways. (He did not, they say, because he simply could not sustain the length such a plot would have taken to unravel.) The nature of the serial novel allowed Dickens to make Boffin's change into a rather darkly comical instance of play acting, but he could not return to the earlier chapters to disguise Mrs. Boffin's very believable disgust and dismay over her husband's transformation. So, did Dickens actually plan to demonstrate that money does change people for the worse?

Sample Topics:

1. **Money changes people:** Why does Dickens allow some characters to change once they acquire money and hold other characters to their original personalities?

   The assumption from all classes speaking in the novel seems to be that money changes people. Rich people assume or require that money makes people better, while many poor people believe the opposite. Do the Boffins outsmart them all?

2. **Better dead than poor:** Are the poor sometimes equated with the dead?

   Betty Higden has taken rather extreme measures to avoid the workhouse, and still she is disregarded by much of society, leaving finally only Lizzie to bury her honorably, without parish involvement. The poor and the dead are both useless, a loss for society, something that remains undiscussed or even ignored, yet part of everyday life. At the same time, society profits quite literally from both the poor and the dead.

3. **Necessity of lying:** Is lying actually viewed as a good thing in this novel?

Gaffer and Riderhood earn a living by taking from bodies and then lying about it (sort of a well-known secret). Rokesmith lies in order to help himself and Bella so that they can grow to love each other rather than it appearing as if he has bought her. The Lammles feel it necessary to lie to each other in order to marry well (though their lies backfire when not told with pure intentions). Lizzie lies to her father about Charlie in order to preserve her relationship with her father.

Form and Genre

Our Mutual Friend seems to house stories within its story. Look for ways in which characters become stories that other characters tell each other. How does such storytelling invigorate the plot while illuminating some of the novel's thematic and philosophical elements? For example, there seems to be a lot of time at the Veneerings' dinners during which Twemlow, the Lammles, and other acquaintances regale each other with stories of those less fortunate. Our introduction to high society in the book, in fact, centers on Mortimer's story of "the man from somewhere." In his telling of the story, Mortimer indicates his awareness of it as a story, possibly even a fiction, rather than the account of an actual life when he receives a message while finishing his speech and remarks, "The story is completer and rather more exciting than I had supposed. Man's drowned!" (Dickens 17). You can investigate Dickens's reasons for using this storytelling element by answering questions such as: How do people react to these stories about other people? Which social class tells more stories about the others? Why? Who is most affected by these stories? Why? How do these stories exacerbate divisions between social classes? Can readers tell the difference between truth and fiction in these stories? Can characters? At what point (and for whom) do these stories start to become real, showing characters' realization of these stories' effects on people?

In what ways does Dickens's writing style indicate how he wants readers to feel about these stories and/or storytellers? How is the larger story of the novel also a tale about real people that is understood as fiction? How does Dickens want readers to apply lessons from *Our Mutual Friend* to real life? How does he want readers to regard him as a storyteller?

Sample Topics:

1. **Poor characters become a story for the rich:** How do the rich characters dismiss poor members of society in every way?

Attendees of the Veneerings' dinner party make Lightwood tell the story of John Harmon as if it is a fable, or a completely fictional tale. They discuss the poor as if they do not actually exist, hence Mr. Podsnap's sense of distaste when the "meek man" has the gall to mention that people really do starve to death. Which rich characters begin to actually see and care about poor people? How does Dickens treat these characters?

2. **Satire:** Where and when do we see characters ridiculing the vices and follies of one another?

One of the great examples of satire in this novel is the Veneering dinner party. Readers see and hear not only from the party guests but also from the servants. In particular, we know some of the thoughts and reactions of a servant cleverly called the Analytical Chemist. As we see him practically rolling his eyes after hearing some of the dinner party conversation, we start to understand that "Nowhere in literature is the truth about servants better told" (Chesterton 213).

Language, Symbols, and Imagery

A close reading of *Our Mutual Friend* makes it apparent that this novel was written late in Dickens's career. His writing here indicates the perfected use of language, symbols, and imagery, often melded together to reveal a unified message, theme, or philosophy.

Birds, names, and money are perhaps the most prevalent examples of symbols and imagery in *Our Mutual Friend*. This is not the first time Dickens has employed these particular symbols and images. Birds, for example, are prevalent in Miss Flite's storyline in *Bleak House*. Here, however, the symbolism and imagery of the birds seems more sophisticated and complex, so much so that when writing a paper you might choose to focus on only one instance of birds as symbols or imagery in the book. The name Jenny Wren, for example, conjures up images, certainly becomes symbolic, and begs a number of questions worth answering at some length. What is the significance of Jenny naming herself after a character in the fairytale of Cock Robin? Wrens are generally small, loud birds, a fact that gives Jenny's self-endowed name even more significance.

Sample Topics:

1. **Birds:** What do all the bird references mean to an individual character and/or to the entire book?

   Mr. Venus buys a parrot from Miss Riderhood and falls in love with her, although the parrot dries up. Riderhood uses the term *poll parrot* more than once. Bella wants an aviary for her baby. Fanny Cleaver changes her own name to Jenny Wren. An establishment near Betty Higden's home is called the Three Magpies. Bella compares herself to a canary and a magpie. Many chapter and book titles refer to birds: "Tracking the Bird of Prey," "Birds of a Feather," and "More Birds of Prey." Riderhood calls Gaffer a vulture. There are many more examples of bird references in the book. What do they mean? Each one might have a particularly loaded meaning and be worth focusing on for an entire paper. On the other hand, the extensive use of bird imagery in this novel as a whole might be worth studying as well. Did Dickens have a particular relationship with or feeling about birds? What associations did 19th-century readers make with these birds?

2. **Names:** Is every name in the book significant for some reason?

   Think about some of the names in this book: Headstone, Noddy Boffin, Sloppy, Silas Wegg, Bella, John Harmon, Veneering, Podsnap, Lightwood. Some names, like Headstone, carry connotative or denotative meaning beyond the name itself. Some names, like Boffin and Podsnap, may have no particular meaning as words but carry a certain tone or impression or sound that leads readers to make associations. Boffin has a bit of a bumbling note to it, while Podsnap sounds a little bit vicious and quick. Not only that, but names carry additional meaning when you consider that John Rokesmith is actually John Harmon, a fact that he cannot reveal until the end. Consider Jenny Wren here, too. She changes her own name, so you may want to research the name Jenny Wren to learn of its context and possible reasons for this particular girl to adapt it. Remember to keep the names within their historical context. Look at possible connotations and denotations in Dickens's time, rather than in ours.

3. **Money is dirty:** Does all of the money in the book eventually point back to the dirty dust heaps?

There is no escaping the dirt in *Our Mutual Friend.* A fine coating of dust seems to cover everything, and it usually comes from the dust heaps. From the dust heaps also comes money. Something about those piles of dirt and garbage symbolizes hope and a brighter future for many people, particularly those digging through the heaps. Yet, the dirtiness remains. Do characters who profit in any way from the dust heaps seem dirtier in some ways than others? How do the higher-class people talk about the dust heaps? Why?

Compare and Contrast Essays

There are several instances of parallel or opposite stories in *Our Mutual Friend,* including the dichotomy between people with money and people without, life and death (and the appeal or disgust of each at various times), the river as active hero or villain in the novel, and Jenny Wren's story next to Bradley Headstone's.

We can often get a clearer idea of what something is by understanding what it is not, and vice versa. Papers that use comparison and contrast methods include not just lists of similarities and differences but theories and interpretations about why such similarities and differences exist, and what effect they have on the novel as a whole.

At first, Jenny Wren and Bradley Headstone seem completely unrelated, and this makes a comparison or contrast paper on the two of them all the more interesting. They both live in imaginary worlds to some degree, though the end result for each is quite different. They both adore Lizzie Hexam, though it is clear that one relationship is healthy and the other is not. In some ways, you could argue that the entire book centers on the stories of Jenny Wren and Bradley Headstone. Does one of them become a hero and the other a villain? How do their similarities and/ or differences illuminate larger issues of social class, gender, disability, imagination, education, power, alcoholism, and childhood? Both possess names with significant symbolism and imagery. How do their names evoke the true character of each?

Sample Topics:

1. **People with and without money:** Does the possession of money require or indicate a strong moral code in the possessors?

   The Lammles become embittered in their quest for more money, while Bella and the Boffins are unchanged by their financial well-being, as is Lizzie (or perhaps they are improved). Are the Boffins the only people with money who also manage to be happy? Wrayburn and Lightwood appear simply to observe (and somewhat reluctantly take part in) high society. They do not seem to take themselves or others (especially of higher classes) very seriously. Did Dickens intend Boffin to descend into miserly crabbiness? The changes in him (for the worse) seem real until we learn it is all an act. The line between the world of money and the world without (the river) is very fine, and both groups are terrified of scandal.

2. **Death and life:** Is anyone in the novel better off dead?

   Are people as affected by death as by life? Mr. Venus, Gaffer, Riderhood, and even Boffin and the dust heaps deal in death everyday to some degree. Is death more pervasive in this novel than life? How are death and life affected or influenced by money and/or class? In some ways, death and life wind around in a cyclical pattern: The river means death for many, which brings money to some, which helps them to continue living.

3. **River as hero versus river as villain:** How is the river personi-fied even to the point of becoming another character in *Our Mutual Friend*?

The river sustains Gaffer even as it destroys Lizzie's hopes for education and a better life. She sends Charlie away so that he can be educated and escape a life on the river. Yet, the river seems merciful when Headstone uses it to kill himself and escape the tortures of his mind. At the exact same time, the river is once again vengeful in killing Riderhood. Is it actually the river, rather than a person, who might be perceived as "our mutual friend"?

4. **Jenny Wren and Bradley Headstone:** Is the entire book some version of their stories?

Jenny Wren and Bradley Headstone exemplify different sides of the uses of imagination. Jenny's imagination usually creates what for her seem idyllic places, while Headstone's imagina-tion leads him to a world where he always gets what he wants, regardless of the desires of others. How do Jenny Wren and Bradley Headstone illustrate the question of appearance (per-ception or misperception) versus reality? Which of the two characters is truer to him- or herself?

Bibliography and Online Resources for *Our Mutual Friend*

Altick, Richard D. "Education, Print and Paper in *Our Mutual Friend.*" *Nine-teenth-Century Literary Perspectives.* Ed. Clyde de L. Ryals. Durham, NC: Duke UP, 1974. 237–254.

Chesterton, G. K. *"Our Mutual Friend." Appreciations and Criticisms of the Works of Charles Dickens.* 1911. New York: Haskell House, 1970. 207–217.

Dickens, Charles. *Our Mutual Friend.* 1865. New York: Modern Library, 2002.

Engel, Monroe. "A Note to *Our Mutual Friend.*" *Our Mutual Friend.* Charles Dickens. New York: Random House, 1960. v–xii.

Mayhew, Henry. *London Labour and the London Poor.* 4 vols. New York: Dover, 1968.

Picard, Liza. *Victorian London: The Life of a City, 1840–1870.* New York: St. Martin's Griffin, 2005.

Varese, John Michael, and David A. Perdue. "*Our Mutual Friend*: The Scholarly Pages." The Dickens Project. Available online. URL: http://dickens.ucsc.edu/dickens/OMF/index.html. Retrieved November 28, 2007.

INDEX

Note: Characters are listed by first names, followed (in parentheses) by the title of the work in which they figure.

Abel Magwitch (*Great Expectations*) 208
accents 140
Ackroyd, Peter 62, 66
Adventures of Huckleberry Finn (Twain) 8
Age of Enlightenment 187
Alfred Jingle (*Pickwick Papers*) 61–62
ambition 206–207
analytical papers 1–2
analytical reading 1
　of *Bleak House* 144–146
　of *Christmas Carol* 110–112
　of *David Copperfield* 127–130
　of *Great Expectations* 202–205
　of *Hard Times* 162–165
　of *Nicholas Nickleby* 92–94
　of *Oliver Twist* 72–73
　of *Our Mutual Friend* 220–223
　of *Pickwick Papers* 55–58
　of *Tale of Two Cities* 186–187
Anderson, Hans Christian 45
animals 199
appearance versus reality 147–148
Arabian Nights, The 45
Artful Dodger (*Oliver Twist*) 90
"August 2026" (Bradbury) 2–3
Australia 136–137, 209–210

author
　background of 100, 209
　as character 133
authorial presence 56
autobiographical elements 133, 136, 138–139, 142, 209, 228
autobiography 139

Bardell-Pickwick case 64
"Bartleby, the Scrivener" (Melville) 3–4
Bella (*Our Mutual Friend*) 227–228
biblical references 166
bildungsroman 52, 67, 139, 213–214
birds 233–234
births, out-of-wedlock 153
Bleak House (Dickens) 47, 47–48, 144–161
　analytical reading of 144–146
　characters in 144–146, 148–151, 159–160
　comparison/contrast studies of 158–160
　context of 151–153
　female characters in 49
　form and genre of 155–157
　language, symbols, and imagery in 157–158
　philosophy and ideas in 153–155
　themes in 146–148
　topic suggestions 146–160
block quotations 31–32
body paragraphs 21–25

Bounderby (*Hard Times*) 183
boyishness 65
boys, education for 136
brackets 32
Bradbury, Ray 2–3
Bradley Headstone (*Our Mutual Friend*) 237
brainstorming 10
Brontë, Charlotte 173
Browning, Robert 3
Bucket (*Bleak House*) 150

Carlyle, Thomas 45, 192–193
chancery 152
change/changes 168, 206
character names 88, 158, 181–182, 234–235
characters
    autobiographical elements of 133
    in *Bleak House* 144–146, 148–151, 159–160
    in *Christmas Carol* 114–116
    comparison/contrast studies of 53, 69, 89–90, 108–109, 124, 141–142, 159, 182–184, 200, 217
    in *David Copperfield* 133–135, 142
    of Dickens 48–50
    female 49–50, 144
    flat 3
    in *Great Expectations* 202–204, 206, 207–209, 211, 217
    in *Hard Times* 169–172, 180, 182–184
    lower class 72
    narrator 115–116, 142
    in *Nicholas Nickleby* 92–93, 96–99, 108
    in *Oliver Twist* 72–73, 76–79
    in *Our Mutual Friend* 225–227, 236, 237
    physical features of 180
    in *Pickwick Papers* 55–56, 60–62
    in poetry 3
    poor 233
    from real life 97
    round 3
    in *Tale of Two Cities* 189–192, 201

title 92, 221
    as types 97
    use of language by 68, 157
    writing about 2–4
charity 79, 81
Charles Darnay (*Tale of Two Cities*) 53, 191
Chesteron, G. K. 55, 58, 61
childhood 45–46, 51, 212
child labor 75
children 116
children's needs 47
Christmas 43
Christmas Carol (Dickens) 47, 110–126
    analytical reading of 110–112
    characters in 114–116
    comparison/contrast studies of 123–125
    context of 116–118
    form and genre of 120–121
    language, symbols, and imagery in 53, 122
    philosophy and ideas in 118–120
    themes in 112–114
    topic suggestions 112–126
Christmas celebrations 117–118
circus society 184
citations 30–38
citizenship 189
city versus country 90–91, 218
class differences 57, 221–222, 230–231
class system 76, 93–94, 96, 101, 116, 117, 210
clustering 10
coherence 22–25
Coketown (*Hard Times*) 169–171, 172, 184
collectivism 194–195
colloquialisms 140
colonization 44
colons, with quotation marks 33–34
color 199
comedy 4, 67, 87–88
coming-of-age stories 137, 138, 213–214
commas, with quotation marks 33
common knowledge 38

compare and contrast essays
  on *Bleak House* 158–160
  on *Christmas Carol* 123–125
  on *David Copperfield* 141–142
  on Dickens 53
  on *Great Expectations* 217–218
  on *Hard Times* 182–184
  on *Nicholas Nickleby* 108–109
  on *Oliver Twist* 89–91
  on *Our Mutual Friend* 235–237
  on *Pickwick Papers* 69–70
  on *Tale of Two Cities* 199–201
  writing 8–9
conclusions 28–30
context
  of *Bleak House* 151–153
  of *Christmas Carol* 116–118
  of *David Copperfield* 135–137
  in Dickens's writing 48–49, 50–51
  of *Great Expectations* 209–211
  of *Hard Times* 172–175
  of *Nicholas Nickleby* 99–102
  of *Oliver Twist* 79–82
  of *Our Mutual Friend* 228–230
  of *Pickwick Papers* 62–64
  of *Tale of Two Cities* 192–194
  writing about 7–8
corruption 75–76
country versus city 90–91, 218
courtship 70
Cratchit (*Christmas Carol*) 124
cultural context 1–2, 7–8

darkness 123, 199
Darwin, Charles 211
David Copperfield (character) 134, 142
David Copperfield (Dickens) 45, 47,
  127–143
  analytical reading of 127–130
  autobiographical elements in 133,
    136, 138–139, 142
  characters in 133–135, 142
  comparison/contrast studies of
    141–142
  context of 135–137
  form and genre of 138–139
  imagery in 140

language and style 139–141
philosophy and ideas in 137–138
symbols in 140
themes in 131–132
topic suggestions 130–142
death 113–114, 125, 236–237
Death of a Salesman (Miller) 4
deceit/deception 47–48, 225
Defoe, Daniel 45
detective novel 155–156
dialect 107–108
Dickens, Charles. *See also specific
  works*
  background of 80, 209
  death of 54
  influences 45–46
  legacy 43–45
  life of 136, 152, 228
Dickens World 44
Dickinson, Emily 5, 9
diction 157
Disraeli, Benjamin 173
Dora Spenlow (*David Copperfield*) 135
doubles/symmetry 216–217
doubt 225
drama 4
dustman 229

echoes 198
education 46, 100–101, 136, 174–175,
  224
1842 Parliamentary Report 116–117, 118
Eliot, T. S. 3
ellipses 32–33
endings, for *Great Expectations* 218
England 200. *See also* Victorian
  England
episodic tales 104, 105
essays 4
Estella (*Great Expectations*) 202–205,
  208
Esther Summerson (*Bleak House*) 144–
  146, 149–150, 159
ethics 119, 155
exaggeration 228
exclamation marks, with quotation
  marks 33–34

Fagin (*Oliver Twist*) 78–79, 79–80
fairy tales 85–86
family 47, 95–96, 112, 113, 132, 148
farce 104–105
Faulkner, William 2
fear of change 168
female characters 49–50, 144
fiction 4
Fielding, Henry 45
fighting 96
figurative language 5
film adaptations 44, 87
fire 180–181
first person 12
flat characters 3
Fleet Prison 63
fog 123
"Fog" (Sandburg) 5–6
foreshadowing 140–141, 145, 164, 187
form
     of *Bleak House* 155–157
     of *Christmas Carol* 120–121
     of *David Copperfield* 138–139
     in Dickens's writing 51–52
     of *Great Expectations* 213–214
     of *Hard Times* 177–179
     of *Nicholas Nickleby* 103–106
     of *Oliver Twist* 84–86
     of *Our Mutual Friend* 232–233
     of *Pickwick Papers* 66–67
     of *Tale of Two Cities* 195–197
     writing about 4–5
Forster, E. M. 3
Forster, John 162, 190
France 200
Frankenstein (Shelley) 8
fraternity 64–65, 194
freedom 70, 189
freewriting 10
French Revolution 64, 187, 192–194, 197
French Revolution, The (Carlyle)
     192–193

Gaskell, Elizabeth 173
genre
     of *Bleak House* 155–157
     of *Christmas Carol* 120–121

     of *David Copperfield* 138–139
     in Dickens's writing 51–52
     of *Great Expectations* 213–214
     of *Hard Times* 177–179
     of *Nicholas Nickleby* 103–106
     of *Oliver Twist* 84–86
     of *Our Mutual Friend* 232–233
     of *Pickwick Papers* 66–67
     of *Tale of Two Cities* 195–197
     writing about 4–5
Gissing, George 52–53, 60–61, 92
Goldsmith, Oliver 45
Gradgrind (*Hard Times*) 183
Great Expectations (Dickens) 48,
     202–219
     analytical reading of 202–205
     characters in 202–204, 206, 207–
          209, 211, 217
     comparison/contrast studies of
          217–218
     context of 209–211
     form and genre of 213–214
     language, symbols, and imagery in
          204–205, 214–217
     philosophy and ideas in 211–213
     themes in 205–207
     topic suggestions 205–218
guillotine 193–194

haiku 4
Hard Times (Dickens) 162–185
     analytical reading of 162–165
     characters in 169–172, 180,
          182–184
     comparison/contrast studies of
          182–184
     context of 172–175
     form and genre of 177–179
     language, symbols, and imagery in
          53, 179–182
     "one thing needful" 166–167
     philosophy and ideas in 175–179
     themes in 8, 166–169
Hawthorne, Nathaniel 6
health and sanitation 147
historical context. *See* context
historical novel 192, 196

historical reality 63
Hobsbaum, Philip 64
holiday spirit 112–113
human rights 47, 114
humor 104–105, 228

idealism 195
ideas 1, 8. *See also* philosophical
  issues
identity formation 155
Ignorance (*Christmas Carol*) 122
imagery 5, 6
  in *Bleak House* 157–158
  in *Christmas Carol* 122–123
  in *David Copperfield* 140
  in Dickens 52–53
  in *Great Expectations* 215–217
  in *Hard Times* 179–182
  in *Oliver Twist* 86–87
  in *Our Mutual Friend* 233–235
  in *Tale of Two Cities* 197–199
imagination 51
individualism 83–84, 102–103,
  194–195
industrial novels 173
Industrial Revolution 44, 172–173,
  173–174, 209
influences 45–46
initial reception 100
innocence 137
Inspector Bucket (*Bleak House*) 155
interpolated tales 66
introductions 25–27
invention 10
irony 69

Jenny Wren (*Our Mutual Friend*) 227,
  237
Jews 79–80, 80–81, 229–230
Jo (*Bleak House*) 150–151
John Rokesmith (*Our Mutual Friend*)
  228
justice system 209–210

Kate Nickleby (*Nicholas Nickleby*)
  97–98, 108–109
keynote metaphor 167

knitting 197–198
Kors, Alan Charles 187

Lady Dedlock (*Bleak House*) 150,
  159–160
language
  in *Bleak House* 157
  in *Christmas Carol* 122
  in *David Copperfield* 139–141
  in Dickens 52–53
  figurative 5
  in *Great Expectations* 204–205,
    214–215
  in *Hard Times* 179–182
  in *Nicholas Nickleby* 106–108
  in *Oliver Twist* 86
  in *Our Mutual Friend* 222–223,
    233–235
  in *Pickwick Papers* 68
  in *Tale of Two Cities* 197
  writing about 5–6
Leavis, F. R. 178
legacy, of Dickens 43–45
legal system 94, 152, 209–210
life of 236–237
light 123, 199
literary allusion 141
literary culture 196
literary devices 106
literary texts
  cultural context of 1–2
  writing about 1–2
literary themes. *See* themes
Lizzie Hexam (*Our Mutual Friend*) 228
Locke, John 8, 138
London Labour & London Poor
  (Mayhew) 228
lost childhood 212
Lost (TV show) 44
Louisa (*Hard Times*) 183–184
love 74–75, 131–132
"Love Song of J. Alfred Prufrock, The"
  (Eliot) 3
lower classes 47, 56, 72
Lucie Manette Darnay (*Tale of Two
  Cities*) 201
lying 232

Madame Defarge (*Tale of Two Cities*) 191, 201
madness 188
mapping 10
Marquis St. Evrémonde (*Tale of Two Cities*) 190–191
marriage 70, 153, 210, 223–224, 225
masculinity 65
Mayhew, Henry 228
McCartney, Paul 44
Melville, Herman 3–4, 6
memoirs 139
men, women and 70
metaphors 5
middle class 47
Miller, Arthur 4
mirrors 198
miscommunication/misunderstanding 59
Miss Havisham (*Great Expectations*) 202, 208–209, 215–216
missionary zeal 154
Miss Pross (*Tale of Two Cities*) 201
mist 216
MLA style 34, 35
Moby Dick 6
Modern Language Association (MLA) 34
money 111, 230, 231, 233, 235, 236
moral fable 178–179
Mr. Bounderby (*Hard Times*) 171
Mr. Micawber (*David Copperfield*) 134
Mr. Pickwick (*Pickwick Papers*) 61
Mrs. Nickleby (*Nicholas Nickleby*) 99, 108
murder, ethics of 155
"My Last Duchess" (Browning) 3
mystery 156

names 88, 158, 181–182, 233, 234–235
Nancy (*Oliver Twist*) 74, 77–78, 90
narrative structures 87
narrator, as character 115–116, 142
nature versus nurture 84
necessity 82–83
needfulness 166–167
Newline, George 210

Newman Nogs (*Nicholas Nickleby*) 99
Nicholas Nickleby (Dickens) 43, 92–109
    analytical reading of 92–94
    characters in 96–99, 108
    comparison/contrast studies of 108–109
    context of 99–102
    form and genre in 103–106
    genre 52
    language use in 106–108
    philosophy and ideas in 102–103
    themes in 94–96
    topic suggestions 94–109
19th-century England. *See* Victorian England

Oliver (*Oliver Twist*) 78, 90
Oliver Twist (Dickens) 47, 72–91
    analytical reading of 72–73
    characters in 72–73, 76–79
    comparison/contrast studies of 89–91
    context of 79–82
    form and genre of 84–86
    language, symbols, and imagery in 86–87
    philosophy and ideas in 82–84
    themes in 74–76
    topic suggestions 74–91
Online Writing Lab (OWL) 34
orphans 79, 81–82
Orwell, George 175–176
Our Mutual Friend (Dickens) 220–238
    analytical reading of 220–223
    characters in 225–227, 236, 237
    comparison/contrast studies of 235–237
    context of 228–230
    form and genre of 232–233
    language, symbols, and imagery in 222–223, 233–235
    philosophy and ideas in 230–232
    themes in 223–225
    topic suggestions 223–237
outlines 13–20
out-of-wedlock births 153

parable 178–179
paragraphs 21–22, 21–25, 22–25
parenthetical citations 34, 35–36
periods, with quotation marks 33
personification 106–107
philosophical issues
 in *Bleak House* 153–155
 in *Christmas Carol* 118–120
 in *David Copperfield* 137–138
 in Dickens's writing 51
 in *Great Expectations* 211–213
 in *Hard Times* 175–179
 in *Nicholas Nickleby* 102–103
 in *Oliver Twist* 82–84
 in *Our Mutual Friend* 230–232
 in *Pickwick Papers* 64–65
 in *Tale of Two Cities* 194–195
 writing about 8
philosophy 1
physicality 181
Picard, Liza 228
Pickwick Papers (Dickens) 43, 55–71
 analytical reading of 55–58
 characters in 55–56, 60–62
 comparison/contrast studies of
  69–70
 context of 62–64
 form and genre of 51, 66–67
 language and style 68
 misogyny in 49–50
 philosophical issues in 64–65
 themes 58–60
Pip (*Great Expectations*) 202–204
place-names 181–182
plagiarism 37–38
plays 121
poetic justice 65
poetry 4, 120–121
 characters in 3
 citations for 34
Poor Law Adjustment Act 172, 174
popular culture 44, 44–45
*Posthumous Papers of the Pickwick
 Club, The* (Dickens). *See Pickwick
 Papers*
poverty 231, 233
pride 224

primary sources 30, 34–35
prison 70, 93–94, 102, 198
prodigal 207
pronouns 23
punctuation, of quotations 33–34

question marks, with quotation marks
 33–34
quotations 30–34

Ralph Nickleby (*Nicholas Nickleby*) 93,
 99
realism 50–51, 79, 112
reality versus appearance 147–148
reform 47, 51, 59–60, 79, 93
rehabilitation 205–206
Reign of Terror 193
religion 83, 119
repetition 23, 157
research 80, 100, 152
respect 132
responsibility 119
retrospective 214
revolutionary idealism 195
river 237
river scavengers 228–229
"Rose for Emily, A" (Faulkner) 2
Rose (*Oliver Twist*) 90
round characters 3
Russo, Richard 70

sacrifice 189
sample essay 38–42
Sam Weller (*Pickwick Papers*) 62
Sandburg, Carl 5–6
sanitation 147
sarcasm 86, 88–89
satire 156, 233
Satis House (*Great Expectations*) 215,
 216
scarlet A 6
Scarlet Letter, The (Hawthorne) 6
schools for boys 100–101
scope 156–157
Scrooge (*Christmas Carol*) 114–115,
 124
secondary sources 35–37

secrets 146–147
self-help 177
self-knowledge 51, 120
self-realization 212
self-reflexive voice 12
semicolons, with quotation marks
  33–34
sensation novel 84, 85
serialization 105–106
serial novel 43, 51, 58, 67, 177, 179, 213
settings 48, 52–53, 90–91, 179
Seymour, Robert 66
Shakespeare, William 45
Shelley, Mary 8
Sikes (*Oliver Twist*) 77
similes 5
sin 154
Sissy (*Hard Times*) 183–184
Smike (*Nicholas Nickleby*) 98
Smollett, Tobias 45
social activism 110–112
social classes 47, 57, 221–222, 230–231,
  232
social criticism 177–178
songs 121
sonnets 4
spirits 125
stage adaptations 87, 121
Stephen Blackpool (*Hard Times*)
  171–172
story within a story 196–197
Stryver (*Tale of Two Cities*) 191
style 68, 112, 139–140. *See also*
  language
survival of the fittest 212–213
Sydney Carton (*Tale of Two Cities*) 53,
  191
symbols/symbolism 6
  in *Bleak House* 157
  in *Christmas Carol* 122
  in *David Copperfield* 140
  in Dickens 52–53
  in Great Expectations 215–217
  in Hard Times 180–181
  in *Oliver Twist* 86
  in *Our Mutual Friend* 233–235
  in Tale of Two Cities 197–199
symmetry 216–217

tabula rasa theory 8, 138
Tale of Two Cities, A (Dickens)
  186–201
  analytical reading of 186–187
  characters in 50, 189–192, 201
  comparison/contrast studies of 53,
    199–201
  context of 192–194
  female characters in 49
  form and genre of 195–197
  introduction about 26–27
  language, symbols, and imagery in
    53, 197–199
  philosophy and ideas in
    194–195
  themes in 188–189
  thesis for 11
  topic suggestions for 188–201
television adaptations 44
Tennyson, Alfred, Lord 45
theater 95
themes
  in *Bleak House* 146–148
  in *Christmas Carol* 112–114
  in *David Copperfield* 131–132
  of Dickens 47–48
  in *Great Expectations* 205–207
  in *Hard Times* 166–169
  in *Nicholas Nickleby* 94–96
  in *Oliver Twist* 74–76
  in *Our Mutual Friend* 223–225
  in *Pickwick Papers* 58–60
  in *Tale of Two Cities* 188–189
  writing about 2
thesis statements 10–13
time 68–69
title characters 92, 221
titles 2, 3–4, 162–163, 221
Tom (*Hard Times*) 183
topic, focus 10
topic suggestions
  for *Bleak House* 146–160
  for *Christmas Carol* 112–126
  for *David Copperfield* 130–142
  for *Great Expectations* 205–218
  for *Hard Times* 165–184
  for *Nicholas Nickleby* 94–109
  for *Oliver Twist* 74–91

for *Our Mutual Friend* 223–237
for *Pickwick Papers* 58–70
for *Tale of Two Cities* 188–201
tragedy 4, 87–88
tragicomedy 214
transitional words and phrases
     23–25
Trollope, Frances 173
truth 59
Twain, Mark 8
type characters 97

upper class 47
Uriah Heep (*David Copperfield*)
     133–134
usefulness 103
utilitarianism 1, 8, 51, 175–176, 195

values, Victorian 168–169
Vengeance (*Tale of Two Cities*) 192
Victorian England 43, 44, 50–51, 151
     class system in 76, 93–94, 96, 101,
          116, 117, 210
     education in 100–101, 136,
          174–175
     social mores of 151–152
     value of money in 111
Victorian London (Picard) 228
Victorian values 168–169

Want (*Christmas Carol*) 122
weather 123
women
     concept of fraternity and 65
     men and 70
     portrayal of 49–50, 144
     in Victorian England 151–152
work 210–211
workhouses 79, 81, 88, 230
works cited page 35, 36–37
writing
     about character 2–4
     about context 7–8
     about form and genre 4–5
     about language 5–6
     about philosophy and ideas 8
     about themes 2
writing context, of Pickwick Papers
     63–64. *See also* context
writing process
     body paragraphs 21–25
     citations and formatting 30–38
     conclusions 28–30
     introductions 25–27
     outlines 13–20
     preparation for 9–10
     thesis statements 10–13

Yorkshire schools 100, 101